Fly-Fishing Secrets of the Ancients

Books on Fly Fishing by Paul Schullery

American Fly Fishing: A History

Shupton's Fancy: A Tale of the Fly-Fishing Obsession

Royal Coachman: The Lore and Legends of Fly Fishing

The Rise: Streamside Observations on Trout, Flies, and Fly Fishing

Cowboy Trout: Western Fly Fishing As If It Matters

If Fish Could Scream: An Angler's Search for the Future of Fly Fishing

Fly-Fishing Secrets of the Ancients: A Celebration of Five Centuries of Lore and Wisdom

Fly-Fishing Secrets of the Ancients

A Celebration of Five Centuries of Lore and Wisdom

PAUL SCHULLERY

University of New Mexico Press
Albuquerque

 Published 2009
Printed in the United States of America

13 12 11 10 09 1 2 3 4 5

Completion of this book has been facilitated by the scholar-in-residence program at the Montana State University Library, Bozeman.

Library of Congress Cataloging-in-Publication Data

Schullery, Paul.

Fly-fishing secrets of the ancients : a celebration of five centuries of lore and wisdom / Paul Schullery.

p. cm.

Includes bibliographical references and index.

ISBN 978-0-8263-4688-9 (cloth : alk. paper)

1. Fly fishing. 2. Fly fishing—History. I. Title.

SH456.S3628 2009

799.12'4—dc22

2009021696

—For Bill Cass and John Harder—

Of Angling and the art thereof I sing,
What kind of tools it doth behoove to have;
And with what pleasing bait a man may bring
The fish to bite within the watery wave.

—John Dennys, *The Secrets of Angling* (1613)

There is another charm called *sgiunach*
that attracts the fishes plentifully to the angler.

—Robert Kirk, *The Secret Commonwealth of Elves, Fauns, and Fairies* (1691)

I have been an angling all night in my dreams.

—William Samuel, *The Arte of Angling* (1577)

Contents

Introduction

Catch More Fish!

One of the many charming things I've noticed about fly fishing is that most of the time it doesn't work. I'm something of an authority on this peculiar aspect of the sport. When I think of my most successful days on the stream, I naturally concentrate on memories of the fish I caught. Depending on the place and the fish, a really good day's catch may be less than one (any steelhead river), five (a late-August spring creek), a dozen (my local freestone stream), or more than two dozen (some remote backcountry stream or my favorite brook trout pond).

Like most of us, I choose to remember that red-letter number of fish caught and conveniently forget that between any two hookups were scores if not hundreds of casts that caught nothing. Fly-fishing history is a great testament to the nearly total disregard of the fish and to anglers' indefatigable commitment in the face of almost constant rejection made barely tolerable by the occasional merciful acceptance.

And yet. And yet in some strange and often intangible way, we do change and grow and learn. We have been at this sport for at least two thousand years, and for the past seven centuries or so we have been writing more and more about it, exulting and arguing over every gadget and theory that any one of us might cook up and any other one of us might dislike.

Some would say we have made great progress during that two thousand years; others would say we have just refined our failures. I'm confident that we have made many technological and theoretical advances during those many years, but I suspect that what has mattered most about all that energy and effort isn't any imagined "improvement" in fly fishing from generation to generation. Instead, it's the progress each of us makes over the course of our own lives toward becoming better fly fishers. At its best, the sport of fly fishing starts over again each time someone new takes it up. Becoming better is hardly a simple matter.

A few years ago, when Phil Monahan invited me to contribute a history column to *American Angler*, I was attracted to the idea because I saw it as an opportunity to pursue many subjects that I could only breeze through lightly in previous books, such as *American Fly Fishing: A History* (1987). If you're familiar with that book, you'll recognize that in this one here and there I pick up threads from in that earlier one; I ask your forgiveness when I find it necessary to repeat myself, to reestablish context.

But just as I was interested in the chance to pursue these subjects, I'm sure I had more doubts about such a column than Phil did. As much as I enjoy the sport's history, and as important as I know that history is, I'm a realist enough to know that most fly fishers don't care much about it. Would they read such a column?

Besides, *American Angler* was a popular commercial fishing magazine: Did a column on history fit there, anyway? After all, as Phil told me, the magazine had only one goal: "to help people catch more fish."

Offhand, this didn't sound like a very promising stance from which to write what I liked to write. My own idea of what fly fishing brings to our lives was nowhere near so concise as that, and it was a great deal less narrowly focused. For centuries now, fly fishing's most notable thinkers have insisted that the actual catching of fish is only a part, and sometimes a very small part, of why we're out there. How could I write a column about the sport's history that left out so much of the good stuff—art, craft, literature, natural history, philosophies and ethics, sanity-saving humor, strong personalities and their bitter quarrels, theoretical dead ends, and quirky but illuminating streamside adventures beyond counting—that has made us all what we are?

But Phil was optimistic and wiser than I. As I dutifully sent in those first few columns, and as Phil's intermittent rejections taught me (and perhaps Phil) what was and wasn't going to work, it became obvious that Phil's goal—to help people catch more fish—might more accurately have been expressed as "to help people become better fishermen." Phil, I eventually realized, had the same broad view of the sport that the sport's graybeards have championed for centuries. A better fly fisher might or might not catch more fish, but he would without question catch them *better*, which is to say that in a host of ways each fish he did catch would mean more.

In that companionable and enlightened editorial environment, my little history column seemed right at home. So I kept writing it, even if now and then I still asked Phil, "Are you *sure* this is a good idea?"

One happy result of this persistence was that it soon seemed evident that the historical fly-fishing sagas that I wanted to explore merely because they were curious or entertaining might also help people catch more fish. Sure, my little essays would rarely give readers some specific piece of information—fly pattern, trick cast, cool new stuff to buy, outfitter's address, or other advice—that would solve their latest urgent fishing crisis. But I'd always known that history helps us in other ways. It is as true in fly fishing as in any other pursuit that we ignore history at our peril.

Studying fishing history makes me a better fisherman in exactly the same way that reading a biography of Django Reinhardt makes me a better guitar player or watching Ken Burns's magnificent PBS film *Baseball* makes me a better baseball fan (and a better former player). History reveals how generations of our fly-fishing predecessors dealt over the course of their own fishing lives with the same problems and challenges we face today. It reveals how they overcame them or why they failed. In fact, I can't imagine any sort of formal "instructional" fishing lesson that can do a fisherman more good in the long run than witnessing the savviest, most experienced, or weirdest of our predecessors work their way through the exasperating obstacles that so often keep fish off the hook.

Thanks to the column, I've been happy to pursue many historical subjects in my columns and then gather the columns (revised and often vastly expanded from their column form) in such books as *The Rise*, *Cowboy Trout*, and *If Fish Could Scream*.

Fly-Fishing Secrets of the Ancients is the latest in this series. It's about that same great, hope-filled, contentious, heroic, and occasionally daft enterprise of trying to fool a fish. The chapters further expand on some subjects of special interest covered in the previous books and introduce quite a few others, ranging from fly theory to casting technique to technological breakthroughs to the interpersonal imponderables of angling society.

I'll be tickled if you learn some things here that actually do help you catch more fish, but you should reserve the right to read the book with no more ambitious motive than getting to know your fly-fishing ancestors or hearing a new take on some crusty old myth we have constructed about ourselves or just vicariously enjoying some fishing that no longer exists.

For example, chapter eight offers you several options as it presents the nearly epic saga of the longstanding folk "wisdom" that Pacific salmon can't be caught on flies. You can read this chapter as a revelation of the theoretical insights and technical advancements that proved otherwise or as a light but revealing case study in perversely stubborn human nature and stubbornly persistent human hope or, if you are in a sadder mood, as an ironic tale about how we spent a century learning to catch a fish just in time to realize it was no longer there.

The book's tongue-in-cheek title, *Fly-Fishing Secrets of the Ancients*, seems appropriate because it embodies the classic promotional tawdriness that is a happy part of the angler's dream. It brings to mind those great small-print ads in old magazines ("Raise Chinchillas for Fun and Profit!") or the titles of a million outdoor articles ("Bag Your Buck on Opening Day!") or even the mainstream supermarket tabloid headlines ("Lost Boudoir Secrets of Nostradamus!"). We do love a good secret—our own privileged path to glory. Or at least we love the idea that such secrets might exist, even if they never turn out to amount to much when they are divulged to us. I am far from the first to notice that fishing is all about hope.

And what secrets are more seductively hopeful than ancient ones? As today's best-sellers and blockbusters demonstrate, we also love the dream of lost lore. Much of what we read in our favorite outdoor books and magazines has at least a hint of the treasure map about it. The promise that attracts us to the idea of ancient fly-fishing secrets is one of the sport's most enduring traits.

So welcome to fly fishing's own little heroic adventure. Even three generations ago, our ancestors fished in a very different world. Twenty generations ago it was practically a different universe. We're so wrapped up in our own exciting, hectic, demanding, dismaying times that we can barely comprehend what their times were like. If this book helps bring those lost worlds to life for you, it's bound to be worth the trip, whether you catch more fish or not.

Paul Schullery
Gallatin Valley, Montana

PART ONE

The Theoretical Fly

1 Is the Wet Fly Sunk?

For many years, fly fishing had a wonderful story of its own creation and development. When I was learning to fly fish, I read it, or parts of it, in many places. I later celebrated and contributed to it myself. It went something like this.

In the beginning, there was Dame Juliana Berners. This person, apparently a nun of aristocratic lineage, wrote *Treatyse of Fishing with an Angle* (1496). This extraordinary text established the basics not only for fly pattern, rod construction, and other technical aspects of the sport, but also for the attitudes and ethics that constituted good sportsmanship. The dame thus for all practical purposes invented fly fishing and created the wet fly.

As the story was told, that's pretty much all that happened for a really long time. British anglers continued to invent more flies and in other minor ways refine the dame's masterwork, but were uninspired otherwise, and simply cast their flies downstream and let them swing around, again and again, rather robotically. The impression that most modern writers (since the early 1900s) have given us of these anglers is that, though they were nice people, they were probably a little dull and just stuck with what they knew.

As the story continued, however, the dullness vanished rather abruptly in the 1800s. In 1836, Alfred Ronalds published *The Fly-Fisher's Entomology*, suddenly making us aware of the value of imitating specific insects, and in 1857 William C. Stewart published *The Practical Angler*, in which he taught us to cast upstream.[1] In the next few decades, a host

Our fly-fishing ancestors have often been portrayed as simple rustics with only rudimentary skills. In fact, many of them developed extraordinary stream savvy through long and close association with their local waters. From Richard Brookes, The Art of Angling *(London: T. Lowndes, 1766).*

of other British and American luminaries, most famous among them being the Englishman Frederic Halford and the American Theodore Gordon, developed floating flies, and we were cured of our largely thoughtless reliance on wet flies.

Revising Ourselves

That is pretty much how the history of fly fishing was told even as recently as the 1980s. Even today, our history is often still presented as a fairly simple, straightforward tale of fly fishers getting smarter and smarter and discarding primitive, if not foolish, practices. In a certain light, even though we praise and revere the pioneers of our sport, we also condescend to them. They were great, we seem to say, but not as great as we are. In this self-congratulatory view, history is all about the great march of progress toward 8X tippets, graphite rods, and direct flights to the Seychelles.

For the moment, let's set aside the condescension and just stick to the history. In the early 1970s, when I got involved in fly fishing, this happily simple version of the sport's history was already under attack. A few alert writers with an enthusiasm for the unquestionably lovely side of the sport's traditions realized that fishing history could be studied just like real history. Fishing history could be reconsidered and even tested for accuracy. Best of all, fishing history could teach us helpful things about our own fishing.

Once the barrier between fairy tale and historical scholarship was down, these spoil-sport revisionists exasperated the faithful by questioning and even disproving some of the sport's most cherished myths. Facing up to such painful revelations wasn't a happy time for some people, but all in all the process was probably for the best, if only because the real story is so much more exciting and interesting.

We now know that fly fishing wasn't invented in England a few centuries ago. Fly fishing was practiced here and there in Europe for much longer—two thousand years or more. These ancient fly fishers weren't quaint, dull-eyed rustics unable to fish well because they didn't have fluorocarbon and instructional DVDs. They were perceptive observers with unexcelled river savvy and the tools necessary to get the job done.

Dame Juliana, long known by English literature scholars as a doubtful if not mythical historical figure with no demonstrable connection with the writing of the *Treatise*, is still sometimes subjected to the same condescension and misconception as before.[2] And occasional heroic efforts, such as Frederick Buller and Hugh Falkus's provocative recent book *Dame Juliana: The Angling Treatyse and Its Mysteries* (2001), are even made to revive her as a candidate for authorship of the *Treatise*.[3] For the most part, however, she is now properly and respectfully recognized as a beautiful myth.

The same goes for most of the other elements of the grand old fly-fishing fable. Too many of us have been reading the early fishing books for the myths to hold up. We have discovered, among many other things, that fly fishers had been watching, imitating, and writing about their local insects long before Ronalds's admittedly milestone work, that they had been happily fishing upstream, across stream, and downstream for centuries before Stewart's time (Stewart made no secret of this fact), and that those same fly fishers had been making flies float for just as long.[4]

Now that questioning the myths has become acceptable and even fun, fly-fishing history has become more complex, more subtle, and more interesting. Just like real history, though, it is inevitably also becoming less clear. Supposed "inventions" by this or that great genius—fly-fishing writers have especially loved the "great man" view of history—have been replaced by long, slow processes of thought and experimentation with no known date of origin.

This background is necessary for understanding the genuinely strange case of the wet fly. The revisionists have been having a great time with the wet fly.

In his generously encyclopedic book *Trout* (1978), the late Ernest Schwiebert provided us with some valuable context on the wet fly. Schwiebert was certainly not a revisionist, but he was one of his century's most influential fly fishers—a uniquely experienced writer with an enviable global perspective on trout fishing. He cataloged fifteen historical and modern methods for fishing wet flies, from the simplest downstream swing of the fly to more subtle and difficult methods such as the upstream dead-drift and the charmingly named Poacher's Retrieve. He added almost as many more techniques for fishing nymphs—altogether an intimidating array of ways to entice a skeptical trout with a submerged fly.[5] He thus provided us with a comprehensive overview of where a type of fly fishing can end up despite its singularly dissimilar origins. In the beginning, it seems, the wet fly was barely even wet.

The Hypothesis That Jack Built

Among the first modern writers to launch a serious attack on fly fishing's beloved pseudohistory was British bibliophile-angler Jack Heddon. In the early 1970s, Heddon and his friends Tony Sismore and John Simpson created Honey Dun Press to publish new editions of rare fishing books. In 1975, after researching a companion volume that he wrote for the press's beautiful new edition of George Scotcher's rare and insightful *The Fly Fisher's Legacy* (c. 1810–19), he reconstructed the entire angling paraphernalia of Scotcher's day and reached some startling conclusions.

Heddon announced that, contrary to all modern commentators' opinions, fly fishing before the mid-1700s was done almost entirely with flies fished on the surface. He accurately distinguished these floating flies from the modern "dry fly," which is tied and fished according to certain codes and styles to meet modern definitions. But the fact remained that, as far as Jack was concerned, early anglers had little choice but to fish on the surface. He argued that the horsehair lines and small flies used long ago were too light and fine to sink much, if at all. He said anglers fished "on top" (as it was called for centuries) because they had no choice.

Making a really interesting case for this revolutionary new view of fly-fishing history, Heddon pointed out that "Robert Brookes, 1740, was the first person to suggest sinking an artificial fly as much as six inches under the surface. In 1811, Lascelles considered it a special 'tip' to sink flies in conditions of bright sun and clear sky."[6]

Setting aside Heddon's small bibliographical lapse—it was *Richard* Brookes rather than *Robert* Brookes who published *The Art of Angling* in 1740—there is no question that he did a great deal of wonderful homework, including extensive collecting and experimenting with period tackle. He became a leading authority on older fly hooks. He tied many early flies, using authentic period materials, doing so from the often frustratingly incomplete instructions in the early books. He read widely and thoughtfully (I have yet to see the Lascelles title he mentioned). He looked at the whole story of fly fishing with an inquiring, skeptical eye.

Although in the 1970s and 1980s most fly fishers, including most of the popular writers, may not have noticed what Heddon was doing, he was hardly ignored. When he launched this new view of fly-fishing

An early-nineteenth-century brass reel with horsehair line; the ring foot allowed it to be slid along the rod's length and located as the angler saw fit or to be easily removed from the rod for storage or use on another rod. Courtesy of the Chris Sandford Collection, photograph by Andrew Herd.

history in the British sporting press, one favorable commentator, writing in *The Field*, described him as "an eye-brow raiser supreme" who "will trail controversy with him now wherever he goes."[7] Even today, despite having passed away a few years ago, he remains an important, even essential, voice in the study of fly-fishing history.

But, that said, I think it's okay to admit that he overstated his case. It takes nothing from Heddon's stature as one of the pioneers in the modern study of fly-fishing history to say that we now see this story as more complicated than he did. Andrew Herd, whose book *The Fly* (2002) is both the most thorough and the most entertaining history of fly fishing, has taken a sympathetic if more moderate view of Jack's argument. Persuasively agreeing with Heddon that neither the lines nor the flies used before 1700 were capable of sinking much, Herd puts the fly of those days somewhere very near the surface rather than always right on top of it. Flies were sometimes afloat, but they were never more than a few inches deep.[8]

My own very limited experience using horsehair lines suggests to me that a determined angler back then could probably make casts that—through a combination of soggy line, properly approached currents, and heavier hooks—would sink the fly a foot or more. But for reasons we will see presently, that wasn't the style of most fly fishers at the time, anyway. Not only did they have little interest in fishing flies deep, they didn't need to.

If Heddon's argument was somewhat overstated, its grander implications were and still are very important. His turning of fly-fishing history on its head by making the *floating* fly rather than the sinking fly the sport's point of origin was an important restorative. It forced us to think hard about how fly fishing was done centuries ago.[9] And if we're smart, that in turn will force us to think hard about how it's done today.

The Way We Were

We tend to forget how much fly fishing has changed. As I point out in my book *The Rise*, a fly fisher in the seventeenth century spent much of his day *not* casting.[10] He often fished with the wind, placing himself so that the wind would carry the fly out across the stream. This bit of lore, by the way, is further indication that Heddon was right about the relative lightness of earlier lines and flies—an angler could hoist his very long fly rod up, let a light breeze catch the line (silk line worked best for this), and then judiciously direct the airborne fly to the rising fish. With a rod of fifteen to eighteen feet and a line of roughly the same length or even much longer, an angler who was "blow-line" fishing had a reach about the same as many of our modern fly casts.[11]

When the seventeenth-century angler wasn't blow-line fishing with the wind, he might have doing some form of closer-in fishing, "dapping" the fly. Again, we need to remember how different his tackle was from ours. With that same fifteen- to eighteen-foot rod—like the ones Charles Cotton would have used in the mid-1600s—he could shorten the line and accurately dangle his fly over a lot of water, dropping it just upstream of any rising trout he saw. By moving his grip up and down the butt section of the rod, he could further regulate the length of his "cast."

Between the blow line and the dapping, especially on a windy day, such a fly fisher might spend relatively little time doing what we modern

Unlike modern fly fishers, those before the mid-1800s spent a significant percentage of their time not casting, preferring instead to present their flies in other ways. From T. C. Hofland, The British Angler's Manual *(1839).*

fly fishers now do all day long—casting. We can often reach farther than Cotton could, but our flies don't land on the water any more lightly than his did.

It also appears that some anglers in Cotton's time, whether they were fishing on the surface or right below it, gave their flies little or no opportunity to float quietly or drift naturally with the current. In an intriguing account of British fly-fishing technique in 1669, quoted in G. P. R. Pulman's *The Book of the Axe* (1854), the narrator says that as soon as fly fishers get their fly onto the water, they "keep it in continual motion, darting the line into the water like the lash of a whip, then, drawing it along a few paces, they throw it in afresh, repeating the operation until a fish is caught."[12]

Other early writers before 1800 said similar things. Being to a far greater extent at the mercy of the wind, these anglers became masters of the discretely maneuvered line and wisely positioned fly. In the unpretentious little *Barker's Delight: Or, The Art of Angling* (1659), Thomas Barker recommended that even when fly fishing with live insects, you will do best by "drawing your fly as you find convenient in your angling"—that is, keeping the fly moving once it's on or in the water.[13] Two centuries later, in *The Vade-Mecum of Fly-Fishing for Trout* (1851), Pulman argued that the angler must "impart motion to his flies," an activity he labeled "humouring" them.[14]

The reason for "working the fly," as many called it, wasn't just to imitate the known behavior of an insect. It was to make it harder for the fish to get a good look. Colonel Robert Venables elaborated in *The Experienced Angler* (1662): "You must keep your artificial fly in continual motion, though the day be dark, the water muddy, and the wind blow, or else the fish will discern and refuse it."[15]

Venables, by the way, said he used a line as much as twice as long as his rod. Men of leisure such as Cotton and Venables routinely had someone along to handle such awkward details as landing the fish. With that kind of assistance, one wouldn't necessarily miss having a reel, even when it came time to play and beach big fish at the end of an irretrievable line twice as long as your fly rod. You could just back up until the fish was beached and your "boy" grabbed it. Or, if you had a rod with a "loop" on the tip, you could pull line through the loop and bring the fish in that way.

Angling historian and theorist John Betts, who has given us fresh looks at so many elements of old and new fly fishing, also helps clarify this reconsideration of historical angling practice. He points out that when anglers used rods of fifteen or more feet in length, "presenting a fly to fish feeding at the surface was easy if the angler was upstream, above the fish, and with the wind at his back. A 'floating' fly floated because it was suspended at the surface and prevented from sinking. The angler *held* the fly afloat by holding all or most of his line off the water. Whether the pattern would float on its own didn't matter."[16] Right. The advice to keep your line off the water is older than the relatively recent Halfordian dry-fly authors of the late 1800s.

The same insistence on keeping your fly moving, or at least under some tight control, seems to have been common in the less well-known European angling traditions. When the fly fishers of Italy, Bosnia, and other countries first come into our view, through published descriptions of them given in the 1800s, they were fishing rods without reels,

Angling historians have until recently largely ignored the historic influences of European fly fishers, when in fact evidence of fly fishing in several parts of Europe predates the better-known British tradition of the past six centuries. These modern Italian snelled soft-hackled wet flies, tied in Turin, thus represent a recent phase of many centuries of European angling tradition. Tied in the 1970s for use on northern Italy trout streams, these and similar patterns—most often cast on multiple-fly rigs with rods of twelve to twenty-three feet in length—proved effective for many centuries. From the collection of the American Museum of Fly Fishing, photographs by Sara Wilcox.

making frequent casts to likely spots or rising fish, and quite frequently moving their flies around on or near the surface to further attract the fish. It was active, almost athletic fishing, requiring constant concentration and a behavioral ecologist's appreciation for how fish locate themselves in a river.[17]

Getting Deeper

Recent research into the medieval practice of fly fishing suggests how versatile some anglers of that period were—and how adept they could be at reaching deep fish. In the fascinating *Tegernsee Fishing Advice*, a circa-1500 manuscript from the former Benedictine abbey at Tegernsee, Bavaria, the writer recommended weighting the line "with a little lead" when fishing a string of flies in a deep lake.[18]

The same versatility appeared in the better-known British tradition. In the third edition of his *The Experienced Angler* (1668), Venables offered a technique that, in the eyes of posterity, "transforms him from a capable angler to a great one." In a generally overlooked piece of advice, Venables suggested that in order to fish more deeply in slow water, you could make a useful imitation of a "cadbait" (presumably a caddis larva or other bottom-dwelling immature aquatic insect) by placing a "small slender Lead upon the shank of your Hook," covering it with a body of yellow wax and a head of black thread, and fishing it by alternately "raising [it] from the bottom" and letting it sink back.[19]

Though certainly some anglers weighted their fly or line, fly fishing between 1500 and 1800 seems to have been a sport practiced mostly "on top," which meant either on or very close to the water's surface. The "middle" and the "bottom" were the domain of other tools, especially a variety of baits.[20]

Several factors eventually allowed fly fishers to fish deeper and deeper water, but to understand how that came about, we have to keep in mind the difference between us and them. First, an angler in 1700 may have owned only one rod. One day he used it to fish along the stream "bottom" with worms or other bait, the next day he fished the "middle" with a minnow, and the next day he used it to place flies delicately on the "top," or the surface. Most anglers of this period seem to have been generalists who enjoyed and practiced all three methods. Flies were made to be fished on top. Minnows and worms worked really well fished more deeply, so why put flies down there too?

(But it's not hard to imagine that an occasional angler, heading out for a morning of fly fishing after an evening of worm dunking, might have been flexible, curious, or just lazy enough to leave the split shot on the line just to see what flies would do if they were dredged more deeply through a likely run. Anglers may be slaves to the fashion of their age, but they aren't stupid.)

Second, by 1800 or so, fly lines were being made not only of hair, but also of silk, and the nineteenth century saw an explosion of experimentation with composite lines of hair, grass, silk, and even wire. Quite a few of these lines would sink. Some sank surprisingly fast. With new kinds of line, anglers could easily reach fish holding in water that had for centuries been out of reach of conventional unweighted trout flies.

Third, as more and more people fly fished, and as communication among them increased in the great industrial publishing boom of the nineteenth century, the sport's horizons expanded. There was talk of saltwater fly fishing and more talk of fly fishing for larger freshwater fish such as salmon and pike. Larger and heavier flies appeared, many of which must have been the very devil to cast, but with their heavy hooks and their dense, absorbent, and metal-ribbed bodies, some of these flies would have had no trouble reaching several feet under the surface. Also in the nineteenth century, metal-bead eyes and lead underbodies became fairly well known and popular among fly tiers. In 1849, Hewett Wheatley, one of the most original thinkers in the history of fly fishing, described his own fancied-up version of Venables's "cadbait," a fly with a tapered lead underbody. Unlike Venables's simple pattern, Wheatley's featured a partridge-fiber tail, a ribbed, two-tone body, and six legs of silkworm gut—an unmistakable "nymph" imitation.[21]

A small-print footnote in the posthumously published 1864 edition of John Younger's *River Angling for Salmon and Trout* makes clear how serious some nineteenth-century anglers were about weight on their flies. Younger said that in fishing a "deep and strong current" for salmon, a fisherman might add "a grain or two of shot, a gut length or so from the fly, the same as is used in minnow and worm fishing."[22] A "gut length" was usually about fifteen inches. The anonymous editor of Younger's book added a footnote at this point, describing a "fly" developed by "an old and experienced salmon angler" on Scotland's Tweed, among the most famous salmon rivers in the United Kingdom. This man, disappointed that he could not catch salmon in "dull or rough waters," had his professional fly tier "dress him a large fly, on the shank of which he had strapped small beads, with hackles between. The weight of the beads made the hook sink deeply in the water, and the result was that the gentleman for a week or so had first-rate sport, although anglers on other neighboring waters were doing almost nothing."[23]

Fourth, the nineteenth century also witnessed a dramatic increase in scientific studies of aquatic entomology, from which anglers benefited immensely. More knowledge of where insects were and how they behaved inspired broader definitions of fly fishing. Getting deep became part of the game, and though there is still controversy over deeply fished flies, especially those involving large amounts of metal weight in the line or fly, there's no retreat from fly fishing's modern idea of itself as something that's practiced not only on the top, but also in the middle and at the bottom.

An Emerging Realization

Perhaps nothing had a bigger influence on development of wet-fly theory than the realization that aquatic insects "emerged" to adulthood by swimming from the stream bottom to the surface. This period was when the insects were most vulnerable to predation by trout and when artificial flies should be at their most effective.

Today, imitation of emergers is often seen as coming of age with the work of twentieth-century Pennsylvanian James Leisenring, who popularized the technique now known as the "Leisenring Lift." Leisenring's theory, described in *The Art of Tying the Wet Fly* (1941), was that by casting upstream of the probable location of the fish, he allowed his flies time to sink and bumble along the bottom of the stream until they approached the fish. As the fly drifted downstream on a fairly slack line, he would follow it with his rod, "being very careful not to pull against

Pennsylvania angler James Leisenring published his small but influential book The Art of Tying the Wet Fly *in 1941, codifying his own theories and techniques regarding emerging stages of aquatic insects. Recognizing the peculiar vulnerability of these insects as they rose from the streambed to the surface, Leisenring helped alert anglers to the need to concentrate on that stage of the insects' emergence. Photograph courtesy of the American Museum of Fly Fishing.*

Leisenring's wet flies, tied with materials that would "work" in the slightest currents, would have been right at home in the fly books of smart wet-fly fishermen from earlier centuries. Flies on exhibit at the American Museum of Fly Fishing, photograph by the author.

it and cause it to move unnaturally." But when the fly approached the imagined fish, Leisenring would make it "deadly" by stopping the swing of his rod, which caused the fly to cease its downstream motion and begin to swing to the surface, thus imitating an emerging fly swimming to the surface. Leisenring also believed that this approach activated the fly's hackles, which would "start to work, opening and closing," further animating the fly. He was opposed to "working" the fly actively as it rose toward the surface, instead believing that the fly's materials would provide adequate lifelike motion and appeal. As the line continues to resist the current, "the fly rises higher off the bottom and the hackle is working in every fiber." And, in Leisenring's words, "Bang! He's got it."[24]

Leisenring deserved the respect he received for his technique and for the wonderfully nimble flies he tied for it, but we know it wasn't original with him. Something of that idea can be inferred from a number of earlier writers, including John Taverner, who in 1600 reported seeing "a young flie swimme in the water too and fro, and in the end come up to the upper crust of the water, and assay to flie up."[25] And we can see the foreshadowing of emerger imitations in fly-fishing writings as early as Venables's little lead-bodied "cadbait" of 1668. As Ernie

Schwiebert and many others have pointed out, a great variety of older wet flies, including many of the famous North Country soft hackles, were probably excellent emerger imitations, whatever their originators may have thought of them. In the United States, the perceptive but now forgotten angling entomologist Sara McBride, writing in 1876, described the emerging process of mayflies and many other aspects of the life of aquatic insects.[26] Angling historian Kenneth Cameron has described some of the wet flies McBride developed and marketed at that time as "superb imitations of emergers, even to the suggestion of husk in the hair bodies and the air bubble caught in the delicate fur."[27]

The New Wet Fly

During the great revolution in tackle and technique that occurred at an accelerating pace throughout the 1800s, when anglers had so many new opportunities for fishing their wet flies creatively, they naturally disagreed over what was the best thing to do.

Some, anticipating modern debates on the same subject, believed that weighted flies or lines were unsporting.[28] The always entertaining American conservationist and fisheries authority Robert Barnwell Roosevelt wrote in *Superior Fishing* (1865) that he viewed the very thought of placing lead shot on a fly line as "gross a heresy as putting a shot in the fly-hook," which he also abhorred.[29] He objected in part because he was concerned with the issues of tournament casting, which in his time was becoming very popular and required a high degree of standardization among competitors. Weight on a line changed the game significantly and unfairly. But Roosevelt disliked shot on the line or fly also because the additional weight tended to break the solid-wood fly rods of his day in the casting.

Others, contrary to several centuries of advice on the subject, preferred not to "work" the fly at all, but instead to place their faith in the character of the artificial fly—its general buggy appearance, the small waving motions of its hackles and fur as it drifted along, the flash of its ribbing—to attract the fish. Francis Francis, perhaps the best-known British angling expert of the late 1800s, was generally opposed to giving a wet fly much motion because he believed that with only a few exceptions, natural flies "do not dart and spring and shoot about."[30] The American writer Henry P. Wells, writing in 1885, acknowledged

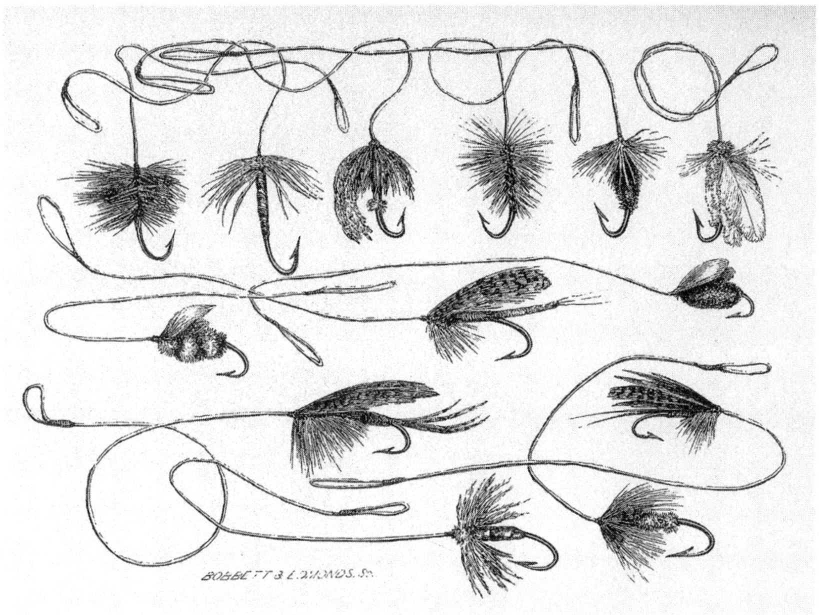

During the 1800s, both England and America experienced a proliferation of angling-related publishing as more and more fishermen wrote about the sport. This selection of wet flies appeared in Henry William Herbert, Frank Forester's Fish and Fishing of the United States and British Provinces of North America *(1849).*

that working a fly was sometimes helpful if the fly's action imitated a "minnow or water-bug," but pointed out that "the truth is we cannot, with any appliance in common use in this country at all events, even approximate to the usual motions of a fly when upon the water."[31]

But the open-minded fly fisher of the late 1800s had an irresistible array of choices available to him: helpful ways to sink, twitch, pull, or lift the fly through the water. Once anglers had been exposed to so many promising techniques, and once they could easily get the tackle that would make it all possible, there was no turning back.

As the years passed, and as more and more fly fishers became serious about the study of entomology, they discovered that some flies do indeed "dart and spring and shoot about" and behave distinctively in other ways that, with enough persistence and ingenuity, could be imitated with an artificial fly. It would be great fun to watch Francis and Wells's faces as they leafed through the pages of Doug Swisher and Carl Richards's 1991 book *Emergers* with its eye-opening photographs of various mayflies and caddis flies making their energetic ways to the surface.[32]

As I finish thinking my way through this story, I realize that, rather in the tradition that Jack Heddon helped establish, I'm going against orthodox opinion in the history of the wet fly. The late 1800s are usually seen as the high point in the long developmental arc of the wet fly, when hundreds if not thousands of colorful, exotically feathered and furred patterns were originated, marketed, and cast upon countless waters. It was the peak of the "favorite fly" era, when whim and serendipity ruled the choice of fly pattern, often independent of the water's biological realities.

At the same time, as I point out in *American Fly Fishing: A History*, this colorful binge of fly making has also been seen as a mistake, a dead-end tangent when fly fishers should have been concerned with getting on with developing more exact imitations of insects. If you buy this view and regard those grand old wet flies as little more than a beautiful mistake, then it follows logically that the decline of the wet fly in the early twentieth century was just a necessary course correction so that anglers could get on with developing dry flies and nymphs.

Seeing the story this way still seems simplistic to me, however. In fact, what eventually fell out of favor was the overdressed, lurid, and formally packaged wet fly of the late 1800s.[33] Some of the older flies—the ones that had a century or more under their ribbing when Victoria took the throne in 1838—tended to keep going after she was gone in 1901. Leisenring's little wet flies of the early 1900s would have looked right at home in the fly book of a Scottish rough-water fly fisher a century earlier.

Just as important, these five "categories" of flies—wet, dry, streamer, nymph, emerger—are not as tidily separable as that. Jack Heddon's message to us was that in our attempts to pigeonhole fly patterns, we are overdefining something whose flexibility we should be celebrating instead. For several centuries, a thoughtful angler might have fished the same fly wet, barely submerged, or afloat. It was a *fly* before we labeled it "wet" or "dry."

For perhaps just as many centuries, some people knew that they were offering their fly to the trout as an imitation or suggestion of an immature aquatic insect. The fly was doing a nymph's job before we labeled it a nymph and an emerger's job for just as long.

And for at least a century before we called them "streamers," there were flies tied with elongated wings and other features meant to mimic the shape or behavior of small fish. I come back to streamers in chapter ten; here it's enough to say that they, too, are a very old idea.

Considering all of that, it seems to me that the continued morphing, hacking, rethinking, and other growing pains of the trout fly in the twentieth century have hardly resulted in the death of the greater idea of the wet fly. Individual patterns and styles may come and go—most of those brightly colored patterns of late Victorian popularity certainly didn't outlast Her Majesty by much—but the underlying practice of fishing a winged fly under the surface seems to be thriving as well as ever.

Back in 1900, the people who didn't want to fish the flies in all the new ways could stay behind if they chose to, contentedly swinging their favorite wet flies through their favorite runs in repetition of one of the sport's most graceful, time-honored, and suspenseful techniques. I have great sympathy for any person who has found what he or she loves best in fly fishing and wants only to stick with it. By 1900, however, what with all the new tackle and techniques available and with so many more developments to come, wet-fly fishing had irreversibly embarked upon a new age.

2 Ragtag and Rumpled

The Mystery of the Ratty Fly

One day last summer I was fishing a small undistinguished local trout stream, and as I released one of its small undistinguished local trout, I noticed that the hackle on my Adams had unwound and was trailing loose. But when I reached for my fly box to replace the ruined fly, I found myself wondering: Did the fish I was releasing tear that hackle loose, or was the loose hackle the reason the fish took the fly? The trout wouldn't tell me, of course, and rather than launch what I knew would be a pathetically quixotic attempt at empirical study by continuing to fish with the damaged fly, I put on a new one.

But the experience got me thinking about one of angling folklore's most intriguing and persistent minor narratives. Spend a little time out on the shadowy margins of fly-fishing propriety, and you're sure to encounter the tale of the ratty fly. Fishing writers and plenty of actual fishermen remember a day when they used a fly the fish loved so much that they gradually chewed it to pieces. In the most extreme cases, the fisherman just kept fishing the same bedraggled fly until there was nothing left of the thing but some fuzzy thread on the hook shank or perhaps some mangled wing fibers. And still the fish took it.

A Comforting Iconoclasm

These stories seem a little unreal the first time you hear them, especially if what they tell hasn't happened to you yet, but plenty of trustworthy people have told them. Ed Van Put, one of the Catskills' leading angling authors and a fish and wildlife technician with the New York State Department of Environmental Conservation, recently related such an experience, also with an Adams, on the Beaverkill: "I had caught a number of trout on an Adams and decided to see how many I could catch without changing the fly. In time, the tail, body and hackle came off . . . but I continued to catch fish. With only the wings remaining, I caught my 37th trout, the beautiful wild brown and largest of the day. I let it go and called it a day."[1] The common implication in these stories is that the rough, half-wrecked fly actually caught fish better than the new, tidy one. This implication appeals to our sense of iconoclasm, of course, especially if we're a little tired of the (let's face it) bullying pronouncements of the angling masters who insist on the highest fly-tying standards. I don't know about you, but many's the day I don't really feel like making sure my hackle is just the right shade of pale watery dun (whatever that is) or my gold ribbing achieves symmetrical microperfection. At these times, it's nice to think that trout will go for something a little less formal and bookishly precise.

Flies do not disassemble themselves in orderly or symmetrical ways. When they continue to catch fish while in such appalling condition, perhaps they are trying to tell us something about fly theory. Photograph by the author.

Nevertheless, the question remains why such accidental and short-lived fly "patterns" sometimes work so well. Flies don't fall apart gracefully. They get lumpy or start dragging loose pieces. The head unravels. Wire ribbing pulls free and sproings out to the side. The body and wings rotate embarrassingly around the hook shank or just scrunch down toward the bend of the hook. None of these developments would seem to help the fly catch more fish, but for some combination of reasons and conditions a surprising number of terribly contorted flies do keep working.

And though it is easy enough to imagine some flies continuing to catch fish with fairly severe structural failures—a streamer that is being worked quickly through the water can still look pretty good even if its hackle collar has unwound and has just become a part of its wing—most of the ratty-fly lore has to do with smaller and more carefully tied wet flies and dry flies.

There are plenty of casual explanations out there. It could just be an off day for the trout, who are in such a generous mood that they'll

From the 1960s to the 1980s, western fly tier Charles Brooks was famous for his admonition that big nymphs needed to be sufficiently rough and ugly to work well. His Montana Stone exemplified that style. Original Brooks fly courtesy of John Juracek, photograph by the author.

take even cigarette butts or dandelion seeds. Or maybe we should see the success of the ratty fly as a modest corrective to keep us humble and realistic when we get a little too puffed up about our imitation theories. Besides, some of the very best fly patterns—the Hare's Ear comes to mind right off—have always featured a somewhat unkempt overall demeanor. The old Casual Dress and Muskrat patterns typify the same approach—keep it loose, keep it buggy, hope for the best.

The Long View

Our neglect of rattiness in our fly patterns is probably more important than we have realized. I think that to an unappreciated extent, the highly refined, tightly prescribed fly patterns we often depend on today are mostly a product of the past century and a half. What's more, I am sure that they don't necessarily represent progress. What they represent instead is the need for the widespread commercial standardization of fly patterns that became necessary in the nineteenth century, when professional fly tying began to move out of the cottage and into the mainstream of marketing.[2] What they also represent is the need for a vastly enlarged angling community, blessed or cursed with a miraculous communications technology, to know that they are "getting it right" when they sit down to tie a fly that has been recommended by someone far away. The rise in popularity of dry flies and each dry-fly pattern's close association with some corresponding insect certainly contributed to a general overall tightening of a fly's outline.

Our long-ago forefathers didn't feel these same needs. If they had, the instructions they gave in their fly-pattern lists would have been a great deal more fulsome and exact than they were. Instead, the typical fly dressing given in books before the early 1800s consists only of the materials in the fly.[3] If the reader of the time was lucky, the author would offer a word of advice about the size of the fly or about making the body slender or about something else. But he would give you nothing about proportion or style and certainly nothing as detailed as what modern books provide with their helpful combination of words and sharp color photographs.

In contrast to the precisely tied and undoubtedly beautiful modern flies, almost every one of the flies I have seen that date from before about 1830 has a consistent looseness of form—they have surprisingly

These wet flies from two centuries ago display a looseness of style and structure that seems to suggest that fly fishers of the time may have been guided by a different philosophy of fly tying than we appreciate today. Photograph courtesy of the American Museum of Fly Fishing.

coarse dubbing (which often provided the fly's "legs" in its errant longer strands), raggedly mixed winging materials, and an overall scruffiness, all of which suggest to me that when it came to fly tying, anglers in the seventeenth and early eighteenth centuries may have operated from an aesthetic stance significantly different than the one we adhere to today.[4] I'm convinced that the earlier flies' rougher traits were not the result of the craft of fly tying's being in a more primitive stage of development. They were a recognition of what worked best on the trout.

Rattiness as a Good Thing

Some anglers accepted the mystery of the ratty fly rather fatalistically. In a charming if neglected little book called *Dry-Fly Fishing in Border Waters* (1912), F. Fernie simply offered, without elaboration or conjecture, the bemused observation that in order for the Black Gnat pattern to work best, "the whole fly should have a rather battered appearance."[5]

Fernie was talking about relatively mild rattiness, of course. A certain indistinctness of outline in a fly pattern—as exemplified by, say, Polly Rosborough's fuzzy nymphs or John Atherton's "impressionistic" dry-fly bodies or Charles Brooks's unruly "maxinymphs"—is nothing new in fly tying.[6] But in our inquiry into the mystery of the ratty fly, we're not talking about mere blurry visual edges here. We're talking about the apparently random and catastrophic disassembly of the fly itself, with chunks poking out in unplanned directions and other chunks simply falling off.

Other anglers besides me have applied more thought to the matter, and the most comforting rationalizations we've come up with to explain the success of such flies seem to involve emergers, whose formalization as a fly type is chronicled in chapter one. The growing appreciation of emergers among anglers in recent decades—based on the realization that a variety of aquatic insects spend critical moments of their emergence looking like neither traditional nymphs nor traditional dry flies—has generated a wealth of wonderful if unorthodox new fly patterns. In defiance of traditional fly-tying conventions, these new creations sprout little tufts of feather or dubbing here and there, or drag an unorthodox appendage—feather, fur, yarn, whatever—behind the body, to suggest a trailing nymphal shuck.

Today, even a quick turn through Doug Swisher and Carl Richards's *Emergers* (1991) or Ted Fauceglia's *Mayflies* (2005) should convince you that flies do indeed pass through a brief but significantly un-"classic" stage in their appearance as they shed their nymphal skins.[7] If you've looked at enough insects at this stage in their life and mentally multiplied them by some sizeable portion of the hatch that may get hung up in the shuck or otherwise fail to emerge successfully (as in Swisher and Richards's "stillborn" flies), it is much easier to understand why even an experienced trout might be attracted to some fairly unphotogenic artificial flies. As Gary Borger states in *Nymphing* (1979), emergers "are a ragtag, rumpled, and disheveled group. The very best imitations are themselves a disreputable-looking lot."[8]

Or, as that most penetrating of angling observers G. E. M. Skues described an emerging mayfly: "One is apt to forget that at the moment of eclosion (which we erroneously designate 'hatching') when it emerges from the envelope which clad its nymphal form, it passes through a stage of untidy struggle not distantly resembling that which a golfer or a footballer displays in extricating himself from a tight-fitting pullover or sweater or jersey."[9]

John Merwin provided me with my first serious lesson in the importance of this "untidy" quality of emergers on the Battenkill in early July 1980. John, the founding editor of *Rod & Reel* (now *Fly Rod & Reel*) magazine and much my superior at catching fish, reported that he was having success just at dark with a slightly sunken fly of startlingly uneven dressing. It looked, as the saying goes, like the materials had been thrown toward the hook from some distance and allowed to adhere however they chose. He gave me one to try, and when I asked him what he called it, he said, "The Brown Yuk" (I forgot to ask him how to spell it). Amazingly, I have saved it all these years and present a photograph of it here. I don't know for certain that John thought it imitated emergers, nor do I know that fish mistook took it for emergers, but they did take it.

Few things help us see the limitations of our theories and philosophies of fly tying than a good look at how anglers in another country handle the same challenges and questions. We're concerned here specifically with the mystery of the ratty fly, but that's only one of the reasons I recommend Peter O'Reilly's *Trout & Salmon Flies of Ireland* (1996), a wonderful testament to both parallel and divergent evolution in fly style from nation to nation.[10] As far as flies that violate our carefully nurtured sense of proportion and balance, the various Bumbles, Buzzers, and Daddys that have long been popular on Irish streams and lochs suggest the extent to which trout approve of hackling and winging styles that might seem absurd to the conservative eye of a tradition-oriented American tier.

For me at least, however, one Irish fly best represents international contrasts of fly style and especially the aesthetic stretch we have to make to understand ratty flies: the Dabbler. Developed in the early 1980s by competition angler Donald McClearn (the original's body was made from old carpet fibers), the Dabbler features a bunch of long

Writer-editor John Merwin gave this successful fly pattern the tongue-in-cheek name "the Brown Yuk" in recognition of its rough appearance. Photograph by the author.

pheasant-tail fibers for the tail and full, somewhat oversized palmer hackling. The wing, which reaches to the end of the long tail, is a "shroud" of bronze mallard fibers lashed on in uneven clumps on the top and both sides of the fly. Dabblers have been enormously successful in Irish competitive fishing, winning many championships for their users.[11]

When my well-traveled angling friend Ken Cameron sent me a Dabbler a few years ago, I immediately liked it and couldn't wait to try it out—perhaps because its rough outline did indeed look vastly more buggy than many tidier flies, but probably also because I found great reassurance in recognizing it as the sort of fly I might end up with when I was actually trying to tie something much prettier.

After a while, as I adjusted to the aesthetic shocks of the fly's proportions, I decided that the Dabbler was pretty, too. Perhaps that is the greater lesson of the ratty fly: if a fly catches trout, we quickly adjust to its visual weirdness or disproportion. Before long, we think it's downright good looking.

E. J. Malone, the great Irish fly encyclopedist who has provided me with current information on the Dabbler, praises McClearn and his

A Dabbler, a modern Irish wet fly popular in competitive angling, tied by angling historian Ken Cameron. Photograph by the author.

Dabbler in *Irish Trout and Salmon Flies* (1998): "Donald has not produced a new fly—what he has done is more fundamental in that his new style consists of dressing old established patterns with a bunch of tail fibers to represent a discarding shuck and a broken wing of straggly fibres which makes a perfect imitation of a hatching sedge."[12]

Here we see the Irish, like the Americans, recognizing the importance of emergers and the need to imitate them quite differently—and more rattily—than we might imitate nymphs or dries. Originally tied in large sizes (sixes, eights, and tens) for loch fishing, the Dabbler has been adapted to more delicate situations. Malone wrote me recently that Dabblers are now "more likely to be found tied on 10's and 12's, with an occasional 14!"[13]

Embracing the Rat

The ratty fly is good for us. It makes us think, and it keeps us off our high horse of overconfidence and overrefined taste. About thirty years ago, a friend of mine from Utah showed me a local dry-fly pattern known as the Hank-O-Hair. It consisted entirely of a few deer hairs laid unevenly along a hook shank and lashed tight to the shank in the middle so that the hairs splayed out in all directions. At the time, I was fully under the influence of the sport's more cosmopolitan thinkers and found the thing kind of offensive. I didn't think such a nonfly deserved a name, even such a silly name as it had received. I didn't doubt that it would catch fish, especially where I lived in the Rockies; little-fished mountain trout could be caught on less impressive "flies" than that. It just didn't fit my idea of how to play the game.

Many years later, however, as I became familiar with the finer points of surface films, read the more recent fishing books on the feeding behavior of trout, and started working on my own book about how trout rise, that simple pattern made more and more sense as an actual imitative fly. The Hank-O-Hair's widely radiating strands of deer hair would have done more than support the hook on the water. From the trout's point of view, looking up at the mirrored undersurface of the stream, those hairs probably gave a pretty good imitation of insect feet pressing into the surface film—the "starburst" pattern of light disturbance in the mirrored underside of the water's surface described so well by Brian Clarke and John Goddard in *The Trout and The Fly* (1980).[14] So simple a pattern, yet it still performed the function it most needed to.

So the effectiveness of ratty flies can't be linked solely to emergers. I think of any number of modern patterns that imitate something other than an emerger with a surprisingly untidy silhouette or defiantly shaggy design. The Iris Caddis, from Blue Ribbon Flies in West Yellowstone, Montana, continues to amaze me not only as a fine fish catcher, but also as a pleasant pie in the face of the dry-fly tradition. It's the scruffiest caddis imitation I've ever seen. It completely lacks the obligatory dry-fly hackle, but it floats really well. It's nothing short of rotund in its scraggly way, and yet it works well during the hatches of many delicate, light-bodied insects. It's an inspiration to us all.

The wise Canadian angling writer Roderick Haig-Brown deserves the last word on the mysteries of rattiness. In 1951, Haig-Brown said that the experience of catching fish on such "tattered and torn" flies was universal among anglers, but he took the experience another step: "I used to think that the explanation was probably in the immediate conditions, in the day and the way the fish were taking. But I have kept these battered flies sometimes and find that they still do well on another day, in another place, under quite different conditions."[15]

Maybe the lesson of the ratty fly isn't well enough learned until we get in the habit of setting the fly aside at the end of its great day and using it again and again.

3 Strange Attractors

Fly Tying on the Historical Fringes

Fly tiers have always been notorious scroungers and scavengers. For many generations, we have been lampooned—perhaps justifiably—for our obsessive quest for raw materials from unlikely sources, and I have to admit that sometimes we're pretty easy to pick out. In the mall, it's that oversized guy hulking sheepishly up and down the aisles of the local fabric store, pawing clumsily through the yarn bins. There by the highway it's the guy staring down at a pungent roadkill, wondering just how desperate he really is for that particular species' underfur.

Even when we can afford to go to the fly shop and buy the very same stuff in cute little plastic bags—which have the advantage of being free of the various tiny passengers so richly associated with similar products harvested in the wild—we're still always on the hunt, scanning roadsides, eyeing unprotected apparel and neighborhood pets, and otherwise trolling through everyday life for the unexpected treasure.

Our persistence has paid off, too. For all our King Midas tendencies, this search we conduct for just the right shade, texture, buoyancy, stiffness, and glossiness of each essential fly-tying ingredient has led us to many wonderful discoveries. A reputation for goofiness seems a small price to pay.

Man's Fat and Mummy Powder

We're hardly the worst. We'll never match our bait-fishing brethren, whose bait recipes sometimes have passed beyond the bizarre into the creepy.

James Chetham's *The Angler's Vade Mecum* (1681) may have established the permanent gold standard for extreme strangeness in fishing tackle. One of his bait recipes begins "Take Man's Fat and Cat's Fat, of each half an Ounce, Mummy finely powdred three Drams" and continues on from there—a recommendation that would give Bram Stoker himself the willies. Chetham also instructed readers to "Take the Bones or Scull of a dead Man, at the opening of a Grave, and beat the same into powder," which, he claimed, made a good bed for your worms, although he admitted that "others like Grave-earth as well."[1] Sounds like the opening scene of a bad late-night movie.

Weird baits aside, Chetham did provide us with helpful information on the origin of one of fly fishing's oddest-named flies, the Cow Dung. This long-popular all-around wet fly has faded from the commercial lists only in the past few decades, and although some later authorities claimed that the fly imitated a manure-loving insect, Chetham believed that the Cow Dung actually matched the manure. As he said, "When Cattel in Summer come into the Fords, their Dung draweth Fish into the lower end thereof." His "Cow-turd-fly" was tied with "Dubbing light Brown and Yellow mix'd, the Wings of the dark Grey Feather of a wild Mallard."[2]

Isn't it interesting that even three hundred years ago, a fly intended to imitate only an undifferentiated blob of bovine excrement was still obliged to honor the stylistic conventions of fly tying by having wings?

But Chetham, for all his baroque charms, has led us astray. What we started out in search of here were unusual fly-tying materials rather than flies tied to imitate unusual things, and we don't have to look far to find plenty of authentic eyebrow raisers.

Forgotten Favorites

The older fly-tying tracts, especially those published before around 1800, persistently recommended some fly-tying materials that we have almost entirely abandoned. In 1760, when the inventive John Hawkins edited a new edition of Walton's *The Complete Angler*, he added a great amount of wise commentary; Hawkins sounds like someone I'd like to fish with. Among other things, he evidently spoke for several of his fellow fly-tying experts when he advised readers to "remember, with all your dubbing, to mix bear's hair and hog wool, which are stiff, and not apt to imbibe water, as the fine furs, and most other kinds of dubbing do."[3] For the authoritative Hawkins, a tasteful mixture of bear and hog wool was a basic ingredient of all dubbing. Must have been great stuff.

The hog's wool in question couldn't come from just any pig, by the way. Certain types of particularly woolly pigs provided British tiers with just the right fibers. Apparently, one of the most desirable of these pig varieties has recently gone extinct, but a few devoted preservationists of rare domestic species and tradition-oriented fly tiers in Europe are working hard to protect the three differently colored races of the Mangalitza pig, an animal that looks literally like a pig in sheep's clothing.

In a whimsical corrective to our tendency to take these fly-tying arcana too seriously, fly-fishing historian Ken Cameron has wondered if the effectiveness of hog's wool was really because the flies smelled like bacon.

Some of the most thoughtful but forgotten fly-tying advice involved taking advantage of previously manufactured goods. Hawkins came

Both urban and rural fly tiers in previous centuries were resourceful and attentive to the opportunities for new fly-tying materials presented by their environments. From Thomas Bewick, A General History of Quadrupeds *(1790).*

through again with the prototype of all modern dubbing kits, advising fly tiers that "a piece of an old Turkey carpet will furnish excellent dubbing, untwist the yarn, and pick out the wool, carefully separating the different colors, and lay it by."[4]

This observation was inspired. These heavy carpets, the product of incredibly complex weaving processes involving a rich and diverse assortment of fibers and colors, must have been irresistible to attentive fly tiers once Hawkins put them onto the opportunity. It makes you wonder how many British homes in the late 1700s had handsome carpets with one corner discreetly obscured under a settee because the man of the house couldn't resist hacking a delectable chunk from it.

Hawkins had yet another suggestion that revealed how sensitized fly tiers were to the way nature creates diffuse and subtle shades of its own. Notice that again Hawkins's insistence that we add some hog's wool to the mix:

> Some use for dubbing, barge-sail, concerning which the reader is to know, that the sails of West country and other barges, when old, are usually converted into tilts [awnings], under which there is almost a continual smoak arising from the fire and the steam of the kettle, which all such barges carry, and which, in time, dyes the tilt a fine brown; this would be excellent dubbing, but that the material of these sails is sheep's wool, which soaks in the water and soon becomes very heavy: however, get of this as many different shades as you can, and have seals' fur and hog-wool dyed to match them; which, by reason they are more turgid, stiff, and light, and so float better, are, in most cases, to be preferred to worsted, crewels, and, indeed, to every other kind of wool.[5]

So first the wool sail cloth was weathered by years of use, then it was further "treated" with smoke and steam (perhaps tea steam, at that), until it achieved just the right shade. In a society in which natural fabrics were subjected to the elements much more than today, it paid anglers to be on the lookout for these uniquely aged materials.

Hairy Situations

The New World has had its own uncannily observant fly tiers. Among those American dry flies that really do deserve the overused adjective *classic*, few rank higher than the Hendrickson, originated by the great Catskill tier Roy Steenrod sometime between 1916 and 1918. Steenrod said that the proper dubbing for the body was obtained from the "fawn colored fur from the belly of a red fox,"[6] but I think it was Art Flick, in his wonderful little *Streamside Guide* (1947), who alerted fly tiers to the specifics behind this prescription. To match the mayfly in question most accurately, you needed the lower belly fur of a *female* red fox because only on the females did that fur become consistently urine-burned to just the right pinkish creamy gray shade.[7]

Flick was right—the fidelity of shade between the Hendrickson body and the fox's belly hair is extraordinary. I don't know what amazes me more about this connection: that nature should achieve just this peculiar tint in two such different ways—a mayfly's body and a mammal's fur stained by its own urine—or that even such superb angler-naturalists as those who developed the modern Catskill dry fly would be sharp-eyed enough to notice the perfect match.

Another R-rated fly-tying material, involving equally famous fly tiers, appeared in the Tup's Indispensable, a long-popular British dry fly reportedly created by the professional tier R. S. Austin perhaps around 1890 and named by the brilliant fly-fishing theorist G. E. M. Skues. Also sometimes called a Red Spinner, the Tup was named because its body required the scrotum fur of a white ram (*tup* was a common term for a ram). According to British fly historian W. H. Lawrie, the body was made of "white ram's testicle fur and lemon spaniel's fur in equal parts, with a little hare's poll fur and enough red mohair to give pinkish tinge or shade."[8] Some authorities have noted that this material is especially difficult to collect.

Though fly tiers have never matched the ghoulishness of the man-fat bait recipes, every now and then someone has proposed using human hair (presumably from live humans) for fly wings. Perhaps the most colorful of these recommendations came from Wisconsin tackle dealer George Leonard Herter, who invented his Red Head Streamer in 1946 and proclaimed that "this is one of the greatest steelhead and rainbow streamers. Good on browns and brooks. Trolled very good for land trout and Coho salmon. Human hair has a very lifelike waving action in the water." For those with access to this material, I might add that Herter used black tying thread and a round silver tinsel body, and he tied the "wing" of red hair "completely around the whole head of the streamer." "The problem here," Herter lamented, "is to find a red-headed woman that will allow you to cut some of her hair off."[9]

From Protoplastics to Silk Stockings

Fly tiers often debate what are the most "appropriate" fly-tying materials. Some of us eagerly use every new synthetic or chemical miracle, but others stick to more traditional materials. I'm not a purist about it, but I do tend to lean toward the traditional view just because I enjoy natural fibers and textures the most. But I realize that the distinction between these two schools of fly tying isn't as tidy as we might like to think.

Part of our enjoyment of traditional, natural fly-tying materials comes from believing that we're honoring the values and aesthetics of earlier generations of craftsmen, especially those who produced so many of our favorite flies and fly styles. The problem with this belief is that as admirable as our devotion to those earlier fly tiers may be, we are probably deluding ourselves that they used those materials because they, too, admired some abstract "tradition" just the way we do today.

In fact, many of the tiers a century or more ago were restless for change, and they never stopped seeking new materials. In the Victorian era, when world trade provided them with many exotic furs, feathers, and other substances, they embraced these new opportunities and created the magnificent array of Atlantic salmon flies—a whole school, almost a guild, of fly tying—that went from being the new thing to being the traditional standard in a matter of a few decades. Some of these same tiers probably would have swapped their soul, or at least their first born, for a few packs of Zelon dubbing or a couple of sheets of closed-cell foam.

Making Do until Plastic Came Along

The evidence of the nineteenth-century fly tiers' interest in reaching beyond "traditional" materials appears in their persistent if often abortive experiments with a surprising variety of materials. In these

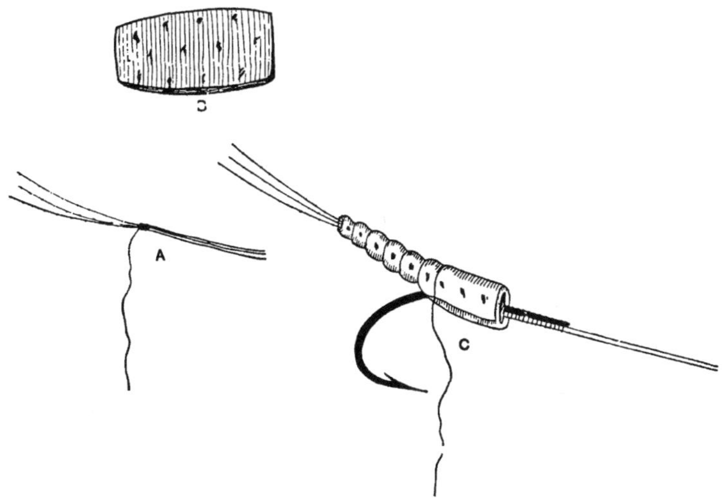

Cork enjoyed a lengthy popularity as a body material for floating trout flies in the late 1800s and early 1900s. It was regularly used to create extended-body mayfly imitations, as shown in these tying instructions. From George Oliver Shields, ed., American Game Fishes *(1892).*

experiments, they employed several promising goods that we might call the "protoplastics." I realize that the term *protoplastics* implies that these materials were in fact plastic when they were not, but considering how casually we apply the term *plastic* to various substances today, *protoplastic* doesn't seem that out of line. The point is that these early fly tiers were experimenting with materials that had some of the same qualities for which we now prize a wide array of synthetics.

I suppose the original protoplastic was plain old rubber, or, as so many writers called it back then, "India rubber." Among the many to put this wonderfully flexible, buggy, and chewy substance to work was Charles Bowlker. In *The Art of Angling* (I'm quoting from the later, 1839 edition), Bowlker recommended a Green Drake imitation tied as follows: "In the first place, fasten near the bend of the hook a small thin piece of white Indian rubber, then warp [*sic*] a little yellow cotton round the shank, the proper length of the body, and wind the Indian rubber neatly over it; fasten under the wings."[10]

In the early 1800s, as silkworm gut replaced horsehair as the most common and popular leader material, fly tiers put it to work in many other ways as well. Stained to whatever buggish color was needed and wrapped (or, as some writers back then preferred to put it, "warped") neatly along the hook shank, gut made a segmented, opaque, and glistening imitation of a worm or larva as convincing as we could create today with modern monofilament. Wrapped over different colors of silk, wool, or fur, it took on the subtle tones of those materials. Other fly tiers even used gut to create realistic legs, antennae, and tails on their flies.

In *Alphabet of Scientific Angling* (1836), James Rennie offered two of the most interesting if lesser-known protoplastics. For one, he suggested that very thin shavings of animal horn could be used to make wings for flies. Bovine horn (as opposed to the more bonelike antlers of ungulates) was a wonderfully adaptable and workable fiber with many domestic uses and appears to have appealed to a number of inventive anglers. For the other, certainly the product of a mind with a special gift for noticing life's most subtle details, Rennie recommended the use of "the thin membrane where the pips lie in the core of an apple."[11] Check this out yourself. The snug little compartments that hold the apple's seeds are lined by a very thin but tough fibrous membrane that can be gently separated from the fruit, dried, and then cut to whatever shape is needed. Angling historian Ken Cameron suggested to me that these

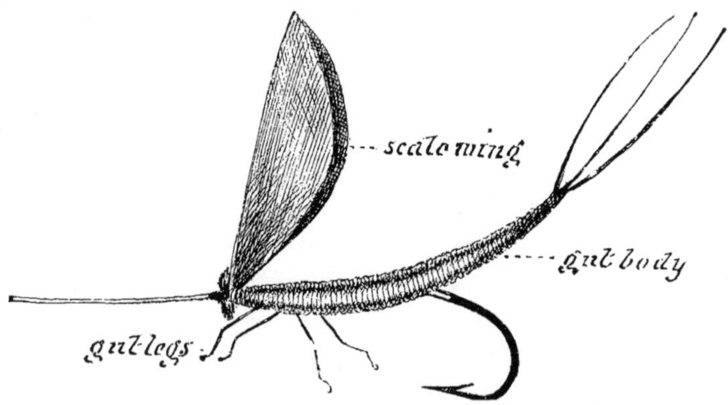

One of fly-tying theorist John Harrington Keene's many fly patterns was an extended-body mayfly imitation created entirely without traditional materials (i.e., feathers or furs). All parts were made either of silkworm gut or fish scale. Note also that the fly was tied on an eyeless hook, with a gut snell extending from under the body. From John Harrington Keene, Fly-Fishing and Fly-Making, *2d ed. (1891), with thanks to David B. Ledlie and the American Museum of Fly Fishing.*

little sheets of fiber were probably noticed back then because people used apples to make pomades for styling hair.

By the mid–nineteenth century, another protoplastic had found its way to the benches of serious fly tiers in the form of "gold-beaters skin," an animal membrane that was apparently much like parchment. Goldsmiths placed this fine, thin membrane between successive layers of gold sheeting to facilitate the process of beating them into gold leaf. Such a wonderful membrane would have been great for fly wings, but as British angler Francis Francis explained in 1867, it also made a great carapace-like covering for fly bodies: "This permits the body colors to be seen distinctly through, gives the glassy shine to the body, and also prevents the body from becoming heavily saturated with water, of course thereby increasing its buoyancy."[12]

A Sense of Scales

It's not clear who first realized that fish scales (especially from pike), properly trimmed and proportioned, could make beautifully realistic fly wings, but their potential excited many late-nineteenth-century tiers, including the British hook innovator H. S. Hall and the famous American fly encyclopedist and commercial tier Mary Orvis Marbury.[13] At first glance, these wings seemed to have all the necessary qualities of transparency, brightness, and general bugginess that had eluded fly tiers for centuries. But scale wings, though offered commercially on flies in both the Old World and the New World, never really caught on. Marbury, writing in 1892, lamented that "they have not proved very popular with fishermen, owing chiefly, we think, to a slight rustling noise they make when cast through the air."[14]

In the mid-1880s, the British fly-tying innovator John Harrington Keene took a harder look at the fish-scale-wing question just before he moved to America and claimed to have discovered a better way to use them:

> At that time I was staying with my father, who was Queen Victoria's fisherman in the Windsor Great Park, and he and I carefully canvassed the whole subject.
>
> One morning, whilst I was still busy with this problem, my father came in with two large Rudd (a

> fish somewhat like a "Shiner") — the largest, I think, I ever saw. They had been taken from a carp pond near the house, and were in the very height of condition. He prepared them for the royal household, and I gathered up the scales that fell from them, intending to make some flies for my own use with the Rudd scales instead of those of a pike.
>
> On cutting one of these through with the shears, I accidentally separated the fine membrane, which lines the underside of all scales, from the hard structure of the outer or upper side. I immediately saw that I had discovered the material I was in quest of, and set to work at once and dissected a score or two of these scales, detaching the membrane, which was easily done after cutting around the edge of the scale with a pen-knife. The properties of this membrane were remarkable. I found it perfectly transparent, and so tough that no effort of mine with teeth or nails was sufficient to tear it, although its thickness could not have been as great as that of the paper upon which this is printed.[15]

Asserting that these lighter membranes, which he made into flies and marketed as the Diaphine Fly or the Scale-Winged Fly, solved the fluttering noise, Keene created several quite realistic flies, including a grasshopper, a large stonefly, and, his special pride and joy, the Indestructible Fly—a large saltwater streamer whose big, long wings were cut from the membrane of a tarpon scale![16]

Why Did the Protoplastics Fail?

Simplistic explanations—for example, that flies with scale wings were too noisy when cast—won't serve to explain why more of these protoplastics didn't take hold in fly fishers' imagination and commerce. A better explanation is that even the most progressive anglers of the time seemed to maintain an innate skepticism. Unlike today's anglers, many of whom are completely detached from such traditions, anglers a century ago lived in a heritage-steeped fishing culture. In the early 1900s, angling writers as distinguished and forward-looking as Theodore

John Harrington Keene, British fly-tying innovator and theorist, immigrated to the United States in 1885 and published widely in the American press. He emphasized the opportunities provided by unorthodox fly-tying materials such as fish scales and silkworm gut. From Wildwood's *magazine (October 1888), courtesy of David B. Ledlie and the American Museum of Fly Fishing.*

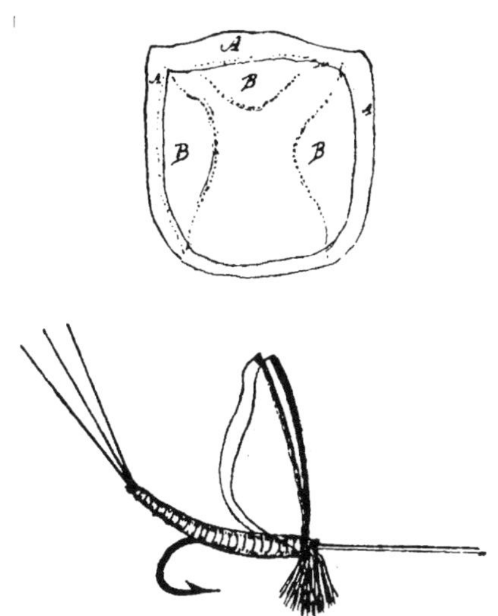

In Fly-Fishing and Fly-Making, *2d ed. (1891), John Harrington Keene's diagram of the scale of a buffalo fish (with dotted lines showing where to cut for wing segments) was accompanied by drawings of several flies tied with these scale wings, including this mayfly imitation.*

Gordon and G. E. M. Skues laughed off most of these experiments. Gordon, writing in 1907, commented on a couple of curious experiments: "One firm of tackle makers went so far as to have the wings of real insects collected and prepared by some secret process to make them tough and durable. Gauzy silk was also tried and there was one fly with patent wings that made a noise in the air like a quail rising from a briar patch."[17]

Perhaps it is true that the protoplastics just weren't good enough. They did indeed present some problems, but perhaps their time just hadn't yet come. The brilliant Skues acknowledged that people had tried everything from "thistle down" to "spun glass" for wings, but he held to his own narrower definition: fly tying still came down to the three basic ingredients of "silk, fur, and feather."[18]

Even when modern synthetics finally began to appear, the fly-tying establishment went through a stage of resistance. In the 1960s, when fly-tying innovator Theodore Rogowski and his friends began to promote the use of small pieces of mesh from nylon stockings to make wing cases on nymphs and emergers, their experiments were happily ridiculed, including a lighthearted critique by columnist Red Smith in the *New York Herald Tribune*. Rogowski kept his good humor about the matter:

> The news was B-I-G, and in fact was printed in a double-column feature of the sports pages in the N.Y. *Herald Tribune* in a syndicated story composed in part by none other than Red Smith. Red, an angler himself, knew that flytyers were apt to snip from the bonnets of ladies, but this, of course, was going too far. Complicity in the project was charged to Sparse Grey Hackle, and Red wanted to warn Sparse by way of the public press that there were things with which an older gentleman did not tamper.
>
> The article was a good one, full of funny lines. It was obvious, however, that Red did not take us seriously, and in point of fact the "silk-stocking nymph is a very real thing."[19]

Tackle shops were soon offering the first of many synthetic variants we now enjoy, and the revolution was under way.

I suppose that the vast majority of today's fly fishers don't give any thought to questions of naturalness or tradition in their flies. Some of us may still struggle now and then with our own personal ideas of authenticity, but most of us are more like the Rennies and Keenes of the 1800s. They were always on the lookout for that next new fly-tying material that would tip the scales—if you'll pardon the expression—a little more in their direction.

PART TWO

Delivery Systems

4 Superfine and Very Strong

The Rise and Fall of Silkworm Gut

One of the most satisfying things about fly fishing is how often nature has provided us with just the right tool for the job. Sometimes it seems to take us forever to notice or discover each item, but pretty much all the raw materials we need are available from the natural world.

Look, for instance, at how many of the colors, textures, and even the shapes needed for tying imitations of stream insects exist ready-made in the furs and feathers of wild or domestic animals. What can possibly be a more perfect match for the iridescence of so many insects than peacock tail fibers? Can anything look buggier than pheasant tail or hare's ear? Early fly tiers eagerly recognized and employed many of those natural resources, and for centuries tiers have been experimenting with new ways to use this bounty.

The same abundance of natural materials has been a blessing to fly-rod builders. A great variety of woods can be tapered into a rod that will cast satisfactorily. Today we're spoiled by the infinite variety of actions that synthetic fibers have given modern rods, but even though wooden rods weren't as susceptible to quite as broad a range of behaviors, they still made countless anglers happy for millennia.

As occasionally happened with this or that particular fly-tying material, however, it took us a long time to discover just the right materials for fly rods. For most of the sport's history, we made our rods from sticks of whole wood (hazel, ash, hickory, greenheart, ironwood, snakewood, lancewood, and more), often using a different, more flexible wood (or whalebone) for the upper sections or the tip. By the early

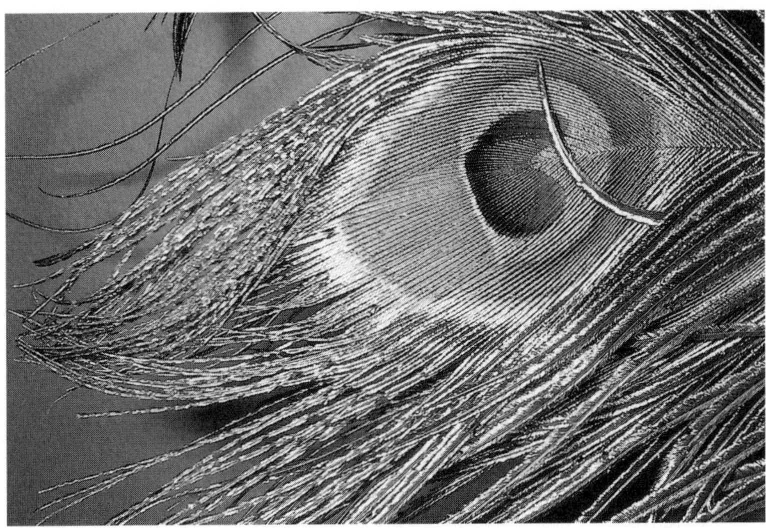

Nature has provided fly fishers with a remarkable array of raw materials ideally suited to the sport's needs. Just as peacock eye feathers were a great natural gift for fly tying, so was silkworm gut a wonderful answer to the angler's need for a better leader material. Photograph by the author.

to mid-1800s or so, though, we eventually found our way to split cane, and the fly rod was as versatile as it would ever need to be for all but our most extreme fly-fishing needs.

It is a testament to the older solid-wood rods, however, that their use continued well into the twentieth century, especially in some parts of England. Tradition and nostalgic malingerers aside, by the 1880s cane ruled among serious fly casters until the quick popularity of synthetic fibers starting in the mid-1900s. And I think it's safe to say that if fiberglass and graphite had never come along, most of us today would be fishing quite happily with rods built of the incredibly dense fibers of Tonkin cane. Natural fibers make great fly rods.

Lines

Other natural fibers made surprisingly good lines. As near as we can tell from an often faint historical record, for more than a thousand years fly fishers relied most heavily on horsehair for their lines and leaders. Other fibers (a hemplike material known as "sea grass" had some popularity in the eighteenth century) also had their advocates, but hair seemed to dominate at least among the fly fishers who bothered to write about the sport until the early 1800s.[1] Darrel Martin, whose beautiful book *The Fly-Fisher's Craft* (2006) is the new standard reference work on the construction of historical fly-fishing gear, says that "the average breaking strength of a single hair was about one pound."[2]

The horsehair fly line differed substantially from a modern line in much more than its material. A number of hairs were twisted or "plaited" together, and these sections were then knotted to one another to produce a line of whatever length was needed. You can probably imagine the imperfections and coarseness of such a line. Besides the knots, the line also featured the errant ends of individual hairs sticking out here and there, as well as the occasional loose loop of one hair that somehow pulled loose or otherwise went astray from the main bunch.

If you think this sounds like an impossible rig to pull through the guides on your rod, you're right. That's why many if not most trout fly fishers rarely used reels (or line guides) before about 1800. The top end of the line was secured to the tip of the rod, and fly fishing was conducted entirely without the retrieval or release of line. The longer rods of those days (discussed in chapter one), often fourteen to eighteen feet in length, gave anglers all the means necessary to shorten or lengthen the reach of their cast simply by holding the rod higher or dropping it lower.

The most ambitious anglers—wanting longer, more precise, and more delicate casts, and being surrounded by such superb examples of how to extend the reach of a thrown line as provided by the buggy whip—learned to taper the hair line, using progressively fewer strands in each section, down to one or a few strands where the fly was attached.

It was here at the end of the line, so to speak, that the qualities of the line material became especially important, and these horsehair fishermen understood how to make the most of their protoleaders. From long experience, they knew everything about hair's qualities, and so they preferred stallion tail hair because mare tail hair was too often weakened by repeated urine saturation.[3] They even saw and exploited the advantages of using different-colored hair for different stream conditions. In *The Experienc'd Angler, or Angling Improv'd* (1662), Colonel Robert Venables said, "I like sorrel, white, and grey best; sorrel in muddy and boggy rivers, and both the latter for clear waters."[4]

By the mid-1800s, silk lines and silkworm gut leaders freed anglers from many centuries' dependence on horsehair, but horsehair remained an attractive alternative for some fly fishers well into the early 1900s. From T. C. Hofland, The British Angler's Manual *(1839).*

The old books contain many quirky recipes for dyes to color the hair as needed. The question of what color a line or a leader should be is a debated issue almost as old as the written record of fly fishing, and it would remain so long after horsehair disappeared from the scene. And only with horsehair did nature give us a leader material with so many color choices built in. Venables, though reasonably content with the natural colors of hair provided by horses, did think that one other color possibly worth bothering with was a "pale or watery green."[5] England lacked Oz's green "horse of a different color," so Venables also gave readers the proper method for dying natural horsehair to that shade.

Up to a certain period, the horsehair fly line was not typically differentiated from its leader by anything except diameter. With its steady stepping down in the number of hairs from "top" (rod end) to "bottom" (tip), it was all of a kind. Angling writers didn't refer to the "leader" as a separate thing until later, when it actually was separate.

In the seventeenth and eighteenth centuries, however, as angling, like pretty much everything else, was subjected to the attention and commerce of an increasingly industrialized society, fly lines changed. Silk (not the gut, but the actual fine product of the silkworm moth's production) became readily available, so anglers and commercial manufacturers experimented with a variety of lines, perhaps the most common type being the mixed silk and horsehair line, and were well on their way to an all-silk line (with continued digressions, such as silk and wire, which must have been as awful as it sounds).[6]

And that was how things stood in the world of fishing lines when again nature yielded a better product: silkworm gut, a natural leader material that, by comparison with horsehair, was so remarkable for translucence, size, and strength that it would eventually dominate the field and anglers' preference to as great an extent as bamboo came to dominate rod building.

Silkworm Sagas

The saga of silk is itself a magical tale of secrets guarded fanatically for centuries, of deadly intrigue, and of amazing persistence on the part of non-Asians who wanted to break China's monopoly on the exotic fiber that made such elegant, kingly fabrics. The Silk Road, which ultimately connected the empires of China, Rome, and any number of in-between kingdoms, became a viable trade route perhaps eighteen hundred years ago, greatly increasing the flow of silk products to the West, where wealthy consumers had for many centuries been occasionally tantalized by the beautiful fabric that arrived intermittently by sea trade.

Once the flow of traffic increased, it was probably only a matter of time before someone smuggled the secret of silk production into the West (despite a death penalty enforced on anyone in China who attempted to do so). It may have happened as early as A.D. 500. It isn't known for certain who achieved that first successful espionage and brought silkworms, their food (mulberry trees), and the necessary knowledge to make silk to the West. Silkworm gut serves as the symbol of the first stage in fly fishing's globalization; from the time of silk's arrival in Europe, the crafts that supported fly fishing could no longer be said to be truly local or even just continental.[7] The written record of European fly fishing from the fifteenth century on includes occasional mentions of silk used in fly tying.

When it came to leaders, it wasn't the actual silk that would be of such interest to anglers. It was the "gut," or more precisely the raw material from which the silkworm spun its silk, that for fishermen was the great treasure of the Orient. Just when the silkworm reaches the growth stage at which it will start spinning its cocoon, it contains two long, thin sacs or envelopes, each holding a tightly bundled mass that when unwound, stretched, and properly treated will make a single strand usually about twelve to fifteen inches in length—just right for a leader tippet or, knotted together, a tapered leader.

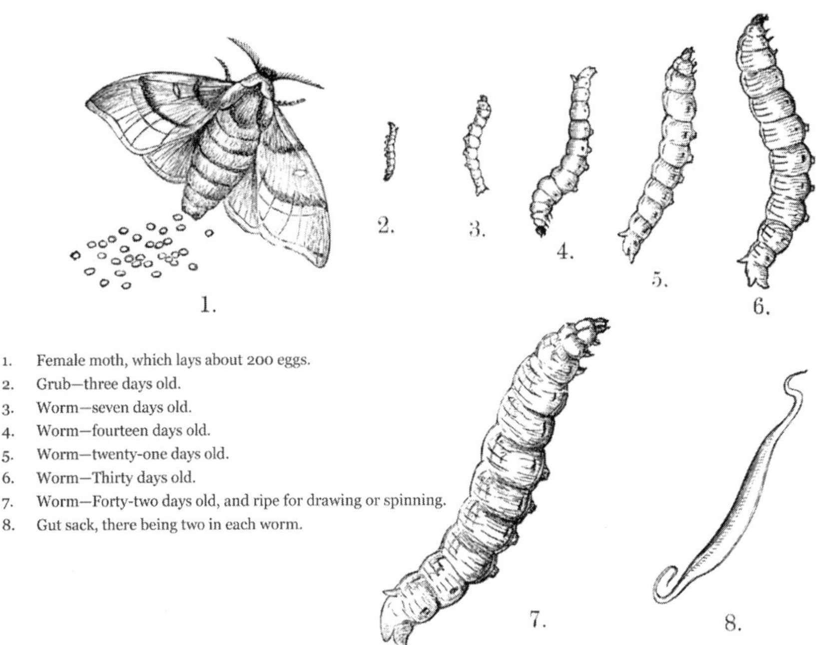

Life stages of the silkworm moth as illustrated in British author George M. Kelson's The Salmon Fly *(1896).*

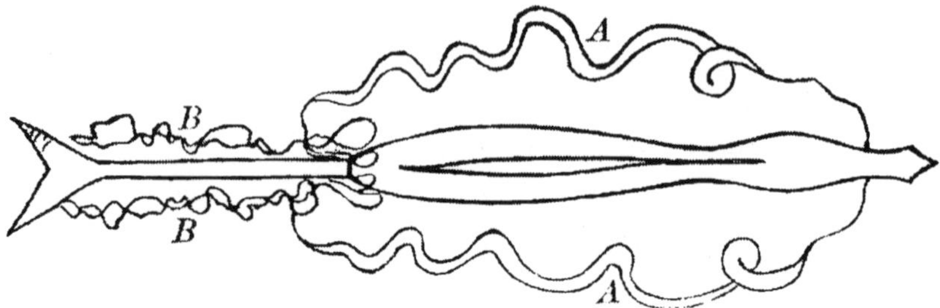

Fig. 18.—Anatomy of the Silk-worm: *A A*, the Silk Sacks, *B B*, the Intestines. (From the "Encyclopædia Britannica.")

This cutaway drawing showing the interior of a silkworm whose "gut sacks" were ready for harvest, originally published in the Encyclopedia Britannica, *was reprinted in Henry P. Wells,* Fly-Rods and Fly-Tackle *(1885).*

Other Guts

A digression is necessary here because of the informality of the language surrounding gut filaments. Silkworm gut is often confused, in casual conversation at least, with a very different material generally known as "catgut." *Catgut* is an almost complete misnomer itself, for it refers most often to strands made from the sinews or gut of animals other than cats. The most remembered historical usage of these strands was in the stringing of musical instruments, although they also served widely in any society needing sturdy string, thread, or cord.

Sinews from waterfowl were among the stringing material used in some instruments in China toward the end of the first millennia B.C. In other nations where people built fine musical instruments, however, the actual gut of various mammals, most commonly young sheep, was the foundation of this craft.

And another digression is necessary in this digression. According to *The New Grove Dictionary of Music and Musicians* (2002), wolf (fourteenth-century England) and lion (ninth-century Arabia) are the most charismatic species mentioned in the historical record as providing strings for musical instruments.[8] The use of lion intestinal material must qualify as the most ambitious possible employment of catgut. Speaking as a sometime musician, I find the idea of music played on carnivore gut enchanting. The knowledge among an audience that the music being heard was quite literally coming from the very fiber of being of such powerful predators—animals that at that time maintained at least some of their being's fiber by consuming the fiber of *human* beings—must have lent a certain heroic or even mystical quality to the musician's presence and performance.

Making strings of mammal gut was, of course, a messy process. It was in effect the absolute opposite of sausage making, emptying the gut of everything rather than stuffing it with something else. Depending on the craftsmen and their local practices, it involved a varying series of lye, water, and alcohol baths that soaked away everything from the lamb's intestine except the actual membrane, which was then stretched tight and twisted, either alone or in groups according to the size of string and depth of pitch required. The finest mandolin string may have used only 2 such membranes twisted together, whereas the deepest bass cord on a double bass viol may have required as many as 120.

Mammal gut strings seem only rarely to have impressed anglers much with their possibilities. The strings swelled when wet, soaking up more and more water. Varnishing them to waterproof them seemed to cause other problems. But there was occasional interest. The great London diarist Samuel Pepys, apparently an ardent angler as well, confided to his diary in March 1667 that "this day Mr. Caesar told me a pretty experiment of his angling with a minikin [a lute string], a gutt-string varnished over, which keeps it from swelling, and is beyond any hair for strength and smallness."[9] At about the same time, however, Robert Venables was less enthusiastic, having tried "the lowest part of the smallest lute or viol strings," which he found to be "very strong, but will quickly rot in the water."[10] This judgment was apparently common because few other anglers left us any mention of using gut strings.[11]

Disgusting Spectacles

The production of silkworm gut was not much less involved and was probably even more unpleasant than the production of mammal gut strings. Silkworm gut was already the preferred leader material among many American anglers by the time Thaddeus Norris described how it was manufactured in his monumental *The American Angler's Book* in 1864: "Silk-worm gut, which forms so important a part of the angler's outfit, is the substance of the worm in an immature state, and is made by steeping the insect in vinegar or some other acid, a short time before it

Silkworm gut leader production was a many-stage process. In this illustration from a German publication of the 1920s, women are soaking and washing small fleece sheets upon which cultivated silkworms had laid their eggs in order to loosen the eggs. The eggs would then be spread on thin cotton frames for drying prior to storage. Months later, the eggs would then be "awakened," warmed, and hatched so that new silkworms could be raised for harvest. Courtesy of the American Museum of Fly Fishing.

is ready to commence spinning its cocoon, stretching it to the required length, and securing the ends until the strand is dry. It is then divested of any extraneous substance by rubbing. It is imported from China, Spain, and Italy, in hanks of a hundred strands, and sold by all the tackle stores, the price varying according to its size, length, and roundness."[12]

For many years, probably up until the early 1800s at least, the production of gut was a nasty little cottage industry that I am sure the purchasers of the final product were just as happy not to know much about. Henry P. Wells was about the only writer of his day with the temerity (or maybe just with the actual information) to describe, in *Fly-Rods and Fly-Tackle* (1885), how silkworm gut was prepared for sale. He reported on an eyewitness account of how each gut strand was handled and processed:

> This manufacture is carried on mainly in Spain, by the peasantry at their own homes, one producing perhaps

> half a pound, another possibly fifty, according to the extent of the mulberry orchard the maker may possess [the worms fed only on mulberry leaves]. With the remains of the envelope still adhering to the dried gut, it is brought in, and sold to the factors.
>
> Their first step is to free the gut from such portions of the ruptured envelope as may adhere to it. Formerly this was done by drawing the gut between the teeth, and thus stripping off this refuse, but chemical processes are said now largely to have superseded this. The eyewitness, to whom I am indebted for this information, describes the old method as a most disgusting spectacle. The rows of women and girls drawing the entrails of this caterpillar through their teeth, their mouths smeared with blood from the cuts inflicted by the thin gut, mingled with the offal scraped from it by their teeth—spitting and drawing, and spitting again—must indeed be far from a pleasant sight.
>
> I would much rather go a-fishing.[13]

Wouldn't we all?

By the beginning of the seventeenth century, then, the silkworm industry was thriving at least here and there in Europe. Although almost all of its production was naturally aimed at real silk—which required letting the worms survive and draw on their gut sacs to create cocoons of fine fibers that were then unwrapped and made into silk—it wouldn't have taken long for at least a few growers to recognize the market for gut and start paying more attention to the needs of anglers, such as those in England. Perhaps some of the silkworm growers were anglers themselves (the Chinese had been using silkworm gut for many centuries for their own fishing, although nobody knows precisely when they started doing so).

The British Get Gut

The arrival of silkworm gut on the British fly-fishing scene must be one of the quietest, slowest technological revolutions in angling history, but a revolution it was. After who knows how many centuries—maybe fifteen, maybe more?—in which horsehair was the most popular material for lines and leaders, change came slowly. Today's fly fishers, conditioned by a worldwide, Internet-energized market to crave and instantly acquire the newest thing, might find it hard to imagine how stodgy and unreceptive earlier anglers could be to any change in their comfortable traditions, even changes that were obviously a big advantage.

By the early 1700s, British anglers started to hear about this wondrous new leader material. It was for sale in England by 1722, but had become popular in Europe well before that. Although James Saunders praised the fishing skills of some of his European counterparts in *The Compleat Fisherman* (1724), he also gave some of the credit for their success to an unfamiliar (to him, anyway) leader material. He said that the Swiss and northern Italians "make a fine and exceedingly strong hair or line, resembling a single hair, which is drawn from the bowels of the silkworm, the glutinous substance of which is such, that like the cat's gut which makes the strings for the viol or violin, of an unaccountable strength, for this silkworm gut will be so strong, that nothing of so small a size will equal it in nature."[14]

And that was true enough. It finally took something synthetic—in other words, something not "in nature"—to replace gut more than two centuries later: nylon monofilament.

Gut struggled in the eighteenth-century marketplace. As late as 1760, London tackle maker George Bowness was still able to offer gut to his customers as a new thing.[15] In 1770, another London tackle maker and dealer, Onesimus Ustonson, was selling "superfine Silk Worm Gut, no better ever seen in England, as fine as Hair, and as strong as Six, the only thing for Trout Carp and Salmon."[16] (I always thought that *superfine* was a modern term applied first to certain controlled substances in the 1960s, but no.) Accolades for silkworm gut from the fishing writers were slow in coming, and well into the 1800s many anglers continued to use their horsehair lines (or mixed lines of horsehair, silk, or grass) in the best tradition of Walton and Cotton. Though the always entertaining and uniquely opinionated David Webster did loop his flies to a long, tapered "gut-line" or leader, he was also still attaching that gut line to a horsehair fly line in 1885.[17]

No doubt traditionalism played a part in this very slow transition from hair to gut, but other factors would have been at work as well. For one thing, early gut availability depended on a scattered cottage industry. Until well-established businesses got into the act, the standardizing of quality and distribution that the better-off anglers wanted probably didn't exist. For another, the gut varied wildly in quality and condition, and the stuff probably seemed absurdly expensive at any price to those many anglers who were used to clipping all the line and leader material they needed from the tails of their neighborhood stallions. And finally, gut was different—it looked different, it cast different, and it had to be treated differently, requiring soaking to soften it prior to each use.[18] It wouldn't have been the first time people decided not to do something new just because it was too much bother.

A large Atlantic salmon fly pattern with a twisted-gut snell. From Henry William Herbert, Frank Forester's Fish and Fishing of the United States and British Provinces of North America *(1849).*

Gut Ascendant

Once accepted, silkworm gut became like every other deeply entrenched element of the fly fisher's equipment and practice. It became what you had to have. The market flourished, and commerce enforced on the manufacturers at least a minimum set of standards. Spanish gut became the gold standard, in the opinion of most anglers. The amusing irony of this preference is revealed in a footnote in the American fishing writer

John Brown's *The American Angler's Guide* (1845), which warned the gut shopper that "inferior qualities of this article are manufactured in China and Italy, but the best is imported from *Alicant*, in Spain."[19] China, the silkworm's native land, was thus disinherited from this important use of gut in the West.

By about 1900, when Wells was writing and when gut was playing its role in such related angling revolutions as the popularization of the dry fly, the discriminating shopper choosing among the grades of Spanish gut had many choices: "Gut is named in the trade according to thickness, as follows, beginning with the thinnest: Refina, Fina, Regular, Padrona Second, Padrona First, Marana, Double Thick Marana, Imperial, and Hera. Flat, irregular gut is known as Estriada."[20] Leon Martuch, one of our veteran modern line-and-leader authorities, has written that Refina at 0X (0.011-inch diameter) had a strength of 2.8 pounds.[21] Rummaging through my fishing vest, I find that my current nylon monofilament at 6X is 3.2-pound test and that my 0X is 15-pound test. Whatever we may feel about silkworm gut as a sporting advantage or disadvantage, and whatever we might prefer for our own fishing, it is pretty plain that by comparison to modern monofilaments, silkworm gut would make catching fish much harder and would require anglers to have a considerably more delicate touch.

Wells also warned his readers that all was not aboveboard in the classification system, a sentiment that every subsequent generation of gut users would echo: "Since the purchaser from the original producer buys by weight, paying the same price for the good, the bad, and the indifferent, it is no easy matter to pre-estimate the prospective profit or loss on his purchase. The larger sizes afford a large profit, while the inferior qualities will not pay cost; so, after the manner of merchants in all trades but that, if any, to which my reader belongs, it is not uncommon to work off the Estriadas, etc., by smuggling a few such strands into each bundle of good gut."[22] Thirty years after Wells wrote, J. C. Mottram complained more specifically and hopelessly in *Fly Fishing: Some New Arts and Mysteries* (1915) of the treachery or inefficiency of the manufacturers. He said that "one tackle-maker's 3X gut equals another's 2X and another's 4X,"[23] a problem that, sad to say, survived long after gut was no longer in use: precisely manufactured synthetic monofilaments are sometimes inexplicably subject to the very same unreliability of advertisement and labeling.

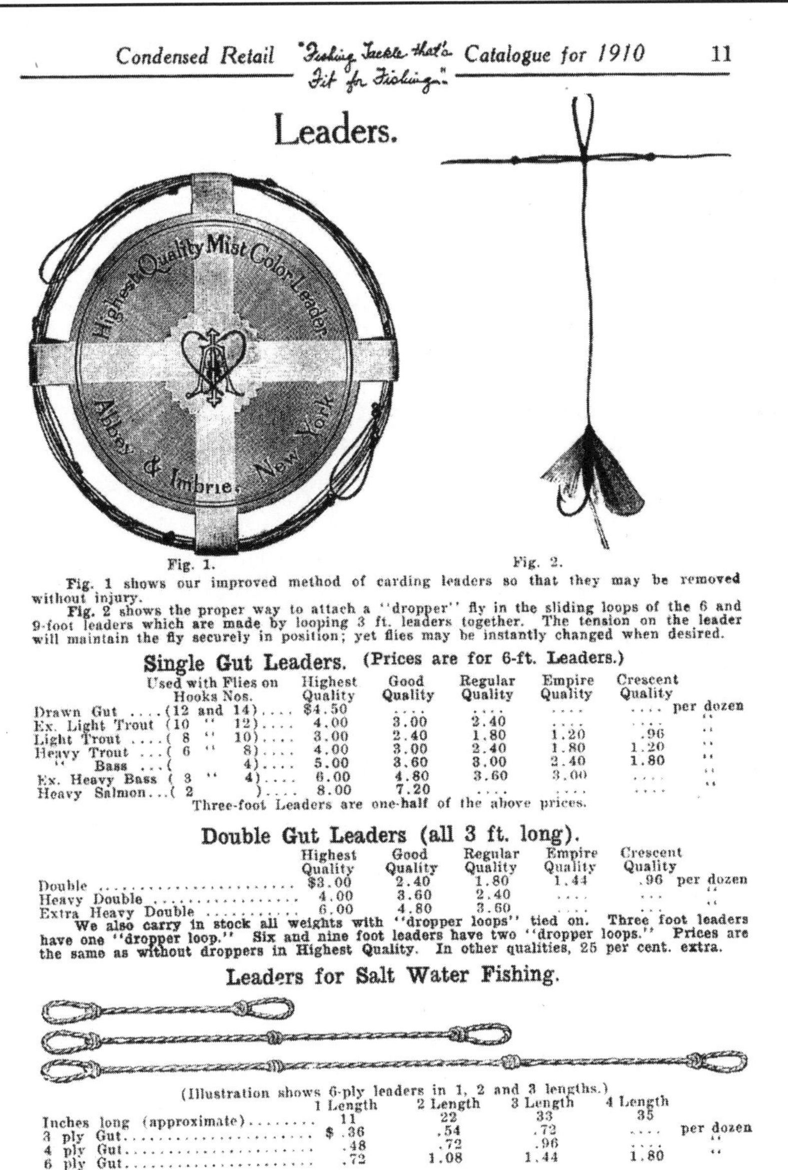

Condensed Retail "Fishing Tackle that's Fit for Fishing" Catalogue for 1910 11

Leaders.

Fig. 1. Fig. 2.

Fig. 1 shows our improved method of carding leaders so that they may be removed without injury.

Fig. 2 shows the proper way to attach a "dropper" fly in the sliding loops of the 6 and 9-foot leaders which are made by looping 3 ft. leaders together. The tension on the leader will maintain the fly securely in position; yet flies may be instantly changed when desired.

Single Gut Leaders. (Prices are for 6-ft. Leaders.)

	Used with Flies on Hooks Nos.	Highest Quality	Good Quality	Regular Quality	Empire Quality	Crescent Quality	
Drawn Gut	(12 and 14)	$4.50	....	....	....	....	per dozen
Ex. Light Trout	(10 " 12)	4.00	3.00	2.40	....	....	"
Light Trout	(8 " 10)	3.00	2.40	1.80	1.20	.96	"
Heavy Trout	(6 " 8)	4.00	3.00	2.40	1.80	1.20	"
" Bass	(4)	5.00	3.60	3.00	2.40	1.80	"
Ex. Heavy Bass	(3 " 4)	6.00	4.80	3.60	3.00	....	"
Heavy Salmon	(2)	8.00	7.20	....	....	....	"

Three-foot Leaders are one-half of the above prices.

Double Gut Leaders (all 3 ft. long).

	Highest Quality	Good Quality	Regular Quality	Empire Quality	Crescent Quality	
Double	$3.00	2.40	1.80	1.44	.96	per dozen
Heavy Double	4.00	3.60	2.40	....	...	"
Extra Heavy Double	6.00	4.80	3.60	....	...	"

We also carry in stock all weights with "dropper loops" tied on. Three foot leaders have one "dropper loop." Six and nine foot leaders have two "dropper loops." Prices are the same as without droppers in Highest Quality. In other qualities, 25 per cent. extra.

Leaders for Salt Water Fishing.

(Illustration shows 6-ply leaders in 1, 2 and 3 lengths.)

	1 Length	2 Length	3 Length	4 Length	
Inches long (approximate)	11	22	33	35	
3 ply Gut	$ .36	.54	.72	....	per dozen
4 ply Gut	.48	.72	.96	....	"
6 ply Gut	.72	1.08	1.44	1.80	"

The 1910 catalog of the American tackle company Abbey & Imbrie featured this page of gut leaders along with instructions for constructing leaders from strands of gut. Note at the bottom of the page the loop-ended, multi-ply gut strands offered for use in saltwater fishing. Courtesy of the American Museum of Fly Fishing.

Gut Astream

So what was it like to fish with gut? The short answer is that for many purposes it wasn't all that different than using modern synthetics. The differences were more matters of degree than anything else.

One difference appeared when the angler geared up. All anglers were necessarily in the habit of soaking the felt pads in their leader tins with water or glycerin and placing the day's extra leader and snelled flies in the tin to soak and soften until needed. But that was a matter of form, as was drying and dressing one's silk fly lines after each day's fishing. It gave the days a more measured pace, perhaps, and maybe enforced a little additional deliberation or meditation on the angler. Once the fishing began, the differences were more subtle.

As I have already suggested, by comparison with today's technomiracle leader materials, gut was far less strong. It was more easily damaged and thus weakened, and perhaps it had a shorter life expectancy (monofilaments don't rot, for one thing). But once it was wet and ready for use, it tied some great knots. That was the most interesting thing I noticed the first time I tried it myself. Knots seem to cinch down with a comforting finality that I rarely sense even with my favorite nylon monofilaments.[24] Though some nineteenth-century users of gut thought it treacherously slippery, its ability to hold a knot well was one of the attractions that allowed it to compete with early nylons for quite a few years. In 1952, Ray Bergman attributed gut's superiority over the nylons he used to gut's absorbency; even after it was soft and ready for use, it continued to soak up a little more water, thus making its knots gradually more secure after you tied them. At that point, Bergman still preferred gut for dry-fly fishing because nylon was not yet being made with the relaxed suppleness that even heavier diameters of gut had.[25]

Attentive readers will already have noticed that gut, like everything else to do with fishing, functioned or failed in light of individual opinion and the vicissitudes of angling fashions. Reading accounts of gut as it slowly became accepted or in its heyday or reminiscences of it now is like reading a hundred different eyewitness accounts of a pivotal World Series game; everyone saw it differently. Roderick Haig-Brown, writing as late as 1964, accurately predicted that gut was in its last commercial years, but also admitted somewhat wistfully that "silkworm gut casts much better than nylon and I believe it is less visible to the fish than nylon of equal diameter, two very important advantages."[26] But Leigh

Perkins, retired CEO of Orvis and a fly fisher for upward of seventy years, says that the 3X gut they had to use when he started fishing "had the strength of wet toilet paper."[27]

It was, at last, not just the inadequacies of the material that did it in. Horsehair would seem pretty miserable as a fishing line today, but it was good in its time, and that time lasted many centuries. A tool is good as long as its users are patient, believe in it, and aren't compelled to desire ever better tools.

No, it was more even than its physical limitations that made gut easy prey for synthetic substitutes. It was also the pace at which the sport of fly fishing was changing and the pace at which our ever-more technological culture was racing toward new things.

Nature didn't design the silkworm's gut bundle for fly fishers; this gut worked only for anglers using larger-size flies. An angler using 0X or 1X silkworm gut could have reasonable confidence in controlling most trout. Keep in mind that little more than half a century ago, prior to the small-fly revolution that was symbolically launched in America by Vincent Marinaro's *A Modern Dry Fly Code* (1950), 1X was, for most everyday anglers, a respectably fine leader.

For very large fish, anglers relied on multiple strands of gut, twisted together to form heavy-duty leaders. Atlantic salmon fly tiers relied on the same twisted-gut strands to create eyes for large flies even in the early 1900s. Courtesy of the American Museum of Fly Fishing.

Gut strands could be twisted or braided together into industrial-strength lines that would handle very heavy fish; the problem was on the finer end of the spectrum. No amount of searching through the silkworms' immense mileage of natural production was going to reveal commercial quantities of gut that combined the fineness of diameter and strength that fly fishers increasingly required to handle the progressively smaller flies that seemed necessary under twentieth-century fly-fishing conditions. Just as changes in fly theory, especially the rise of dry-fly fishers as a separate school of angling, had helped bring silkworm gut to full popularity, continuing changes in that same school of angling would help push it off the stage.

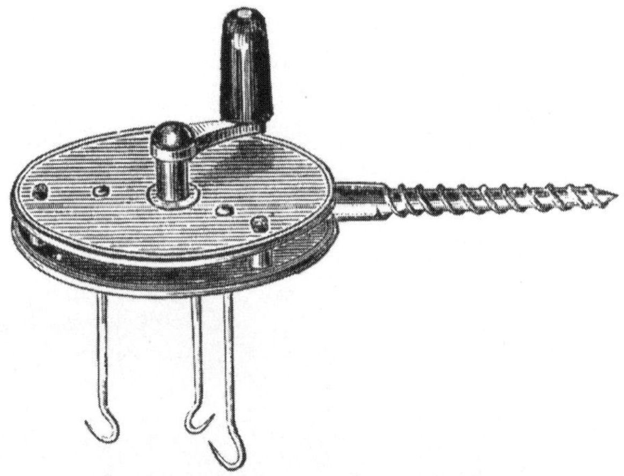

GUT TWISTING ENGINE.

A simple gut-twisting device from the late 1800s allowed for the combining of three gut sections into one much stronger strand. Manufacturers had no equally successful options for meeting the demand for very fine and yet very strong strands of gut. From George M. Kelson's The Salmon Fly *(1895).*

Silkworm gut manufacturers had long recognized that the raw product simply couldn't deliver the fine diameters that some anglers desired. Even before 1900, they developed a simple and efficient means for "drawing" gut by pulling it through progressively finer diamond-edged holes in metal plates. They could thus scrape a strand of gut down to 5X and even 6X. But the strength of such fine strands was measured in small fractions of a pound, and some anglers complained that shaving gut down removed "the whole of the tough outer skin" or reduced the gut's translucency or otherwise compromised its fishability. Not all these opinions were justified, of course, but many weighed against the process. As early as 1913, Samuel Camp stated in *Fishing with Floating Flies* that "drawn gut was at one time extensively used by dry-fly fishermen, but it is now generally recognized that fine undrawn gut is quite as efficient and the additional strength gained by its use is a distinct advantage."[28]

That pronouncement proved to be spectacularly wrong. By 1940, most commercially available gut (Spain was still the leading producer) was drawn.[29] Drawn gut, for all its shortcomings, was still the best thing there was.

The End

Not for long. Dupont patented nylon in 1938, and although nylon's introductory years were plagued with complications and failures on a scale that the birth of the silkworm gut industry never approached, the new lines and leaders that soon began to appear showed incredible promise, and gut's days were numbered. These days, aside from a few traditionalists and reenactors out there trying to reconstruct earlier fishing experiences for one reason or another and tiers of traditional fly patterns that require either gut snells or twisted gut eyes, fishermen have forgotten gut and for the most part have no interest in remembering it.

I suppose that's okay, and I'm certainly not going to propose bringing it back. Nevertheless, of the elements of older angling times that we've left behind—solid wood rods, brilliantly colored wet flies that don't imitate anything, lovely hand-crafted creels, silk fly lines, eyeless hooks, and the rest—silkworm gut is one of the most charming. It brought yet one more little piece of the natural world to the game, a piece with a remarkably exotic history. Like wooden rods, whether solid wood or split cane, it gave the acts of preparing to fish and casting a fly a slightly different feel. Watching that first knot I tied in silkworm gut as it snugged down into itself isn't an experience I will soon forget. I had never tied a knot in a formerly living thing before, and it's different. The needs of the gut, like the needs of the bamboo fly rod, give the fishing a just enough different mood and pace to remind me how subtle this sport is and how susceptible to our moods is its essential

The replacement of gut with nylon and subsequent synthetic fibers greatly expanded the angler's options, allowing for easier use of progressively smaller flies and lighter tippets for sizeable fish. This photograph by the author shows Bob DeMott straining a 6X tippet on Armstrong Spring Creek, Montana.

authenticity. I expect that in the future, just as I sometimes go streamer fishing or nymph fishing, I will dedicate the occasional day to fishing with silkworm gut for the fun of it.

And there is an amazing larger story here, of which the silkworm gut saga is only a small part. This story involves the extraordinary extent to which American fly fishers have depended on Asia. From 1890 to 1960, say from the time of Theodore Gordon to the time of Vincent Marinaro, our most highly regarded fly rods were made of bamboo from China. Our leaders were silkworm gut, again from both a biological source and a practical application originating in China. Our best fly lines were silk, from the same brilliant cultural source. And we hackled many of our most popular wet flies and virtually all of our dry flies with the feathers of long-transplanted Asian jungle fowl. There's no question that all of these contributions to our fly fishing passed through the hands, industries, and theoretical filters of quite a few other nations and cultures before our famed and anonymous anglers could make their casts on American waters. But a startling amount of what made up American fly-fishing technology originated in the Far East. It would be worth someone's time to study the parallel indebtedness we may hold to Asian cultures in the modern angler's attitudes toward sport and the wild nature on which it depends.

The replacement of bamboo rods, silk lines, and gut leaders with near equivalents made of synthetic materials had great appeal not only among anglers but among the various manufacturers who no longer had to depend on not always reliable supplies of raw materials from other nations. Although it took some time to get domestically produced inorganic materials working right, these materials provided the average angler with a more efficient set of tools—whatever costs there may have been in the aesthetics that were and are so important to many of us. That Asia has not always been a popular part of the planet in the minds of many Americans probably made the transition seem all the more important.

From our supposed eminence among the earth-orbit tools of modern angling, we might tend to condescend to earlier fly-fishing technologies, but we should also find them inspiring. Some of fly fishing's most renowned theorists and commentators, including William Stewart, Alfred Ronalds, Frederic Halford, G. E. M. Skues, Thaddeus Norris, Theodore Gordon, George LaBranche, Odell Shepard, Ray Bergman, Roderick Haig-Brown, and Preston Jennings, to name only a few, did most or all of their milestone work casting nothing but silkworm gut leaders. By all accounts, they had the fulfillment of a lifetime of fun doing it. Perhaps this fact should heighten our respect for what they accomplished, but it should also give us a somewhat higher opinion of gut, too. After all, if the stuff was so awful, how could it have connected so many great fly fishers so productively to their flies and to the trout they sought?

5 Straps and Ladders

How Many Flies Are Enough?

When I started fly fishing in the early 1970s, I fished quietly and with very little company for a couple years before I discovered that some people used more than one fly at a time. My initial reaction to this revelation was, "Can we *do* that?" For some reason, no doubt having to do with my very limited sources of information on the sport, I had just presumed that "fly" fishing was singular, as the name implied. Otherwise, it would have to be called "flies fishing," wouldn't it?

Of course not. Within the generous limits provided by the fish and game laws, we anglers can do whatever we want and call it whatever we want to. Over the past two centuries, many of fly-fishing history's greatest authorities had fished their whole lives with multiple-fly rigs. I just didn't know enough about what I didn't know.

I wonder if my reluctance was influenced by the great fishing writer Joe Brooks, whose *Trout Fishing* was published in 1972, the year I began fishing. *Trout Fishing* was my very first fly-fishing book—a gift from my brother. It is a superb condensation of the world of fly fishing for trout. To me, then, it seemed not only friendly but infallible, and when he described his own feelings about the question of multiple flies, I would have been inclined just to buy his view. He said that a gillie at Loch Leven, Scotland, gave him instructions on fishing four wet flies, keeping the highest two flies "skipping across the surface, the next one just under the surface, and the tail fly a bit deeper." He said it worked, too. "Whether it was the combination of the extra flies, the dancing of the bobbers over the surface, the sight of several rather than one fly, that excited the trout, I don't know. But there, as in many other European lakes and rivers, I found that multiple wet flies often produce more than a single fly."

But the experience didn't make Brooks a convert. "Nevertheless, I usually fish only one fly, because I like the art and pleasure of casting so much, and the finesse of real casting technique is not possible with multiple flies, which all too easily become snarled in each other."[1] Which is pretty much how I still feel about it. I enjoy the clarity of focus and targeting that comes from trying to put a single fly in the right place. But there is no denying that multiple-fly rigs are often very effective and that we have tried some amazing fly arrangements over the past few centuries with equally amazing results.

The Bavarian Option

I find it intriguing that the earliest published British fly-fishing texts have so little to say, or even to imply, about using more than one fly at a time. It's easy enough to read the best-known of those writers, including such seventeenth-century luminaries as Thomas Barker, James Chetham, and Charles Cotton, and imagine that they were exclusively one-fly guys.

But this issue is yet another reminder that fly fishing back then, being ancient in origin and fundamentally local in practice, was defined very differently depending on where you lived. For one notable example of such local and regional variations, we need only turn to Bavaria in 1500 and *Tegernsee Fishing Advice*, a manuscript at the Bavarian State Library in Munich that prescribed the fishing procedures used by Benedictine monks at the Tegernsee abbey. Thanks to the recent scholarly publication of this remarkable manuscript by historian Richard Hoffmann, we can now picture these fellows fishing their *vederanglen* (feathered hooks) on "lines with as many as fifteen hooks, each suspended from a short 'branch' line."[2] For lakes, they weighted the line; for rivers, they probably didn't.

The Tegernsee fly patterns and the order in which they were to be attached to the line were firmly established matters. One of the most enduring elements of the multiple-fly tradition is that many anglers have seen the rig as a whole. They didn't change individual flies; they changed whole sets of flies. By the beginning of the 1800s, an angler

In all ages, anglers are individuals, each following his or her own local and personal code of practice. We can only guess how many preferred to cast a single fly or three or ten. From The Fisher's Garland for 1823 *(1823), a book of angling verse by Robert Roxby.*

might set forth for the day with several such sets, or "casts," looped around his hat—handy for when the cast of the moment seemed to be failing him.

A determined example of the "cast" school of fly selection was provided by T. E. Pritt in *The Book of the Grayling* (1888). One of the things that makes Pritt's book so interesting is that he was by disposition a serious hatch-matcher (he would probably have called himself an "imitationist") who believed in and participated in studying the behavior of individual insect species. One of the great formalizers of the modern soft-hackle fly style, Pritt knew his stream's insects.

And yet he saw the grayling as generally exempt from such studies: "So long as aquatic fly is abundant, Grayling will take it usually in preference to anything the angler can offer them; and, unlike trout, they are by no means particular that the angler's imitation should represent a fly with which they are acquainted, though they show a decided preference for certain favourite patterns of fanciful flies; all that is necessary, apparently, being that their attention should be directed to the surface of the water by the occasional appearance of a natural fly." Accepting the grayling on those terms, Pritt offered his readers five different favorite "casts" of three flies each—just as a trout-fishing writer might have provided his readers with a list of favorite individual fly patterns. One of the casts was his own favorite, and the other four were the favorites of four other prominent anglers and friends of his. "I have only to remark," he said confidently, "that if the fly-fisher for Grayling fails to rise fish in any river of England with the five casts here quoted, nothing short of an earthquake will bring them up."[3]

Bobs and Droppers

By the nineteenth century, the terminology of the multiple-fly rig was an established matter of local practice. The fly on the very end of the line had the most different names, including *point fly*, *stretcher fly*, *trail fly*, *tail fly*, *leading fly*, *bottom fly*, *lowermost fly*, or (no surprise here) *end fly*. (Even in the nineteenth century, some writers still referred to flies as "hooks," so the fly on the end of the line would be called the "tail hook" or "stretcher hook.")

The flies that were suspended on very short lines from the main line were most often called "droppers," for the obvious reason that they "dropped" from the primary line. They were named in order of their distance from the tail fly: first dropper, second dropper, and so on. If there were three flies, the first dropper was often called the "middle fly." In 1906, the famous American fly tier Theodore Gordon said that in a cast of three flies, the fly in the middle had the "worst position on the cast," meaning it was least likely to catch a fish.[4]

It was in constructing dropper tackle that the older horsehair lines, already discussed in chapter four, found favor among some anglers. By the early 1800s, silkworm gut was replacing horsehair as the most popular leader material, but even a century later there were still holdouts who favored hair. As late as 1907, Gordon, though himself a thorough convert to gut, explained why some people still preferred hair: "Horsehair still has its advocates in some parts of England, the dales of Yorkshire, for instance. There four small flies on hooks tied on hair and with single hair casts, are used by old-fashioned anglers. They claim hair falls straight and lightly on the water, that the droppers stand out better from the cast, and that it is less conspicuous than gut. They may

This carefully staged studio photograph of British angler Ewen Tod in about 1903 reveals more than the angling fashions of the day. The huge creel is some indication of how well the fishermen of that era assumed their multiple-fly methods would work. From Ewen Tod, Wet-Fly Fishing Treated Methodically *(1903).*

be able to get better hair than we can procure in this country, but from my own experience I should say let hair alone; it is a delusion and a snare."[5]

Droppers were also called "bobs," a reference to how they were sometimes fished. British angling writer H. C. Cutcliffe explained in *Trout Fishing on Rapid Streams* (1863) that when fishing, he would sometimes allow the stretcher to sink, but would hold the line tightly enough to keep the droppers hanging in the air, "bobbing and dapping about on the surface of the water."[6] George Bainbridge, in *The Fly Fisher's Guide* (1816), emphasized that successive droppers needed progressively longer lines to dangle from, "in order that they may all play upon the water together, without sinking the main line."[7] In other words, as the line angled up from the water, the droppers attached higher up the line wouldn't bob on the water surface unless their individual lines were longer. This configuration was what Joe Brooks described doing in Scotland.

Most writers didn't say you needed to differentiate the length of line between droppers, and most said that the dropper line needed only be two and a half to three inches long. It's hard to believe that many anglers, busy on a stream with feeding fish at hand, worried too much about an inch one way or another.

The majority vote among nineteenth-century authorities was that the first dropper should be attached about a yard up from the tail fly, though some recommended more than sixty inches. Prescribed distances between the first and second droppers ranged from about fifteen inches to two feet. Some said that the distance between the second, third, and additional droppers could be less, as little as twelve inches.

Which Flies, Where, and When?

I'm impressed with the extent to which these anglers understood the value of a hovering dropper dipping into the water again and again. It's another proof, if we need it, that our ancestors were not naive bumpkins mindlessly casting pretty but unrealistic wet flies over equally naive fish. Anglers based this dropper-bobbing technique on actual streamside observation and knew which mayfly species they were imitating. Cutcliffe, for example, said that the March Brown mayflies were "strong on the wing; they dip themselves, and just when they please, rise from the water and dip again; they are not easily washed under water, as more delicate flies are."[8] Bobs worked.

Cutcliffe wasn't isolated in his view; despite what now seem to us like significant limitations in their tackle and in their scientific knowledge of insects, these people were often terrific self-taught naturalists, and many were dedicated hatch-matchers. In *The Angler and the Loop Rod* (1885), David Webster spoke for generations of anglers before his time when he pronounced, "It is not enough, therefore, that the angler, in selecting his cast for the day, should merely consult his season's list of flies; he should ascertain for himself, by actual observation, what insects are then on the water, and so be guided in his choice."[9]

Even among anglers for whom the "cast" of two or more flies was a unit to be fished or replaced as a whole, there were firm theories about what types of flies should occupy each position on the cast. At least since the time of Cotton's great essay on fly fishing in 1676, simple Palmer patterns were recognized as an excellent choice to use as a searching, experimental fly when it wasn't yet clear what the fish would take, so Palmers were often recommended as a tail fly, to be left on even if the droppers might later be changed. As Alfred Ronalds put it in 1836, "The Palmer is never totally out of season, and is *a good fat bait*."[10]

There was also agreement that the tail fly had to be the biggest, or at least the heaviest, of the flies on the cast. In *A Book on Angling* (1867), British angling writer Francis Francis said, "Always put the heaviest fly on as the tail fly or stretcher; for if, this practice be reversed, the heaviest fly, receiving the greatest momentum, goes first, and is apt to double over the lighter one, and thus the drop will fall over the stretcher, and a foul will be the consequence; or to avoid this so much force will need be used that the flies will alight in anything but gossamer fashion."[11]

It's hard to overstate the importance these people placed on active observation; there was nothing mechanical about this fishing. Webster, Francis, and the others described an intensely proactive fishing style in which this or that dropper or set of droppers was experimentally replaced as the day went on and the angler had time to study the stream and the fish's choices. This was serious work done by thoughtful, alert fishermen.

How Many?

In the 1839 edition of *The Art of Angling*, the highly admired and often republished British expert Charles Bowlker probably represented the mainstream of angling practice as well as anyone when he said that "an experienced fly-fisher will use three or four flies at the same time."[12] The likewise revered Scottish authority Thomas Tod Stoddart agreed in *The Angler's Companion to the Rivers & Lochs of Scotland* (1853), but seemed more flexible: "Trout-flies, when fished with, are used, according to the caprice of the angler, in pairs, threes, or fours, seldom singly. In small waters, two hooks are sometimes thought sufficient. I seldom, under any circumstances, employ fewer than three."[13]

Some dissenters preferred fewer flies. The Scot John Younger, writing in *River Angling for Salmon and Trout* (1864), said, "I have always hated the confusion of fishing with more than a pair of flies, and would rather nip off the dropper and fish with only one than fish with three, and be more sure of success, too."[14]

Whether American anglers read British books or the first American fishing books, they received about the same advice. The British expatriate Henry William Herbert, who wrote under the pen name "Frank Forester," approvingly quoted a friend on the matter in 1849: "You say 'the flies should be three in number.' Not always—there are exceptions, many exceptions. In confined streams, where there are bushes, weeds, &c., one fly is as much as can be managed or used. Also, in streams where the fish are very numerous, one fly is plenty, particularly with the light tackle, which a gentleman and angler should use. In clear water, lakes and ponds, three flies are the proper number."[15] Forester's friend spoke for America's first generation of serious sporting journalists. George Gibson, George Washington Bethune, and their pals, who were writing about fly fishing eastern American streams in the 1830s and 1840s, adhered to the British orthodoxy in the number of flies they used even as they launched our first known experiments in matching the American hatches they encountered.

But mainstreams are often less interesting than the strange little side currents. With so many people casting so many flies, it was inevitable that strangeness would abound.

Some alternative approaches to casting many flies at once fall outside the conventional definitions of fly fishing, such as "cross-line" fishing. As a pair of anglers stood on opposite banks of the river, their lines connected across the water. With as many as fifty flies suspended from the line, they could cover tremendous stretches of water at once. It must have been especially exciting if three or four big trout grabbed hold at once.[16]

But even the more traditional fly casters stretched the definitions of fly fishing. Or, considering the Tegernsee experience of a few centuries earlier, it might be more accurate to say they *re*stretched the definitions. I am especially intrigued by the approach of a Captain Clarke of the Royal Navy, who, according to Stoddart, didn't even use droppers. He built his flies right into the entire length of his gut leader. As he tied together the segments of silkworm gut (which were rarely more than twenty inches long and were knotted together in a taper), he literally tied a fly into the leader at each knot, "simply dressing the upper flies over the joinings of the different lengths of gut, instead of appending them at fixed intervals as droppers,—consequently they will be ranged along the lower casting or foot line, at a distance from each other averaging fifteen inches; and should the above-mentioned portion of the throwing tackle measure ten feet, they will amount in number, inclusive of the trail hook, to seven or eight. This tackle, the author of the treatise in question recommends as highly serviceable when employed on rapid streams or under a strong wind."[17]

This description reminds me of the common short-cut method we still use today to add a second fly to an existing leader-and-fly combination. We just knot a two-foot section of tippet material onto the bend of the hook rather than mess with a dropper line of any kind. One would think that the leader coming out of both ends of the fly would interfere with the hooking of fish, but the method does seem to work okay.

The oddest, indeed the least understandable, local technique I've read about was developed in my own neighborhood in the late 1860s or early 1870s. I recently read an unpublished manuscript account of a trip to Yellowstone National Park that probably occurred in 1872. The writer, a Montana pioneer named Edwin Beard Hendrie, left a description of his preparations for the trip to Yellowstone. You'll just have to trust me that from the context of the rest of his account, it's clear that by "hook" and "permanent bait" he meant "fly." He clearly did mean flies, but that is about the only thing that is clear in the tortured prose of this account. But stick with it; I think he was doing something odd enough to be interesting.

> So I concluded that I would make a nest of hooks having permanent baits, that I could cast and catch fish for them [i.e., his companions on the trip], as I seemed to be the one selected for that purpose.
>
> I took a three foot leader and on the ends placed a twelve inch hook and leader with permanent bait and in the middle another one ten inches long, and between the two put one each side of eight inches in length, making five leaders attached to the main leader, and used that as

> a casting hook. In that way I would sometimes pull out two at a time and at others at least one. As the divide between Idaho and Montana was flat for a distance of a quarter of a mile at least, with the streams running in both directions for one mile into the Coeur D'Alene Lakes, and the others from our state into the Missouri River, I found that was a very good way of arranging the hooks, as my after experience in the Yellowstone proved to me and has since proven.[18]

I try to picture this rig as a central line festooned at various places with droppers of various lengths apparently extending out in different directions, so that the overall effect would be rather treelike. Exactly what the drainages of the various rivers he mentioned had to do with anything is unclear; I think he was trying to say that his party traveled by a route that gave them lots of opportunities to try out his "casting hook."

Back in the mainstream, however, several nineteenth-century angling authorities were known to fish with eight, ten, or even more flies.[19] These longer "casts" were known as "ladders" or "straps," and although they could lead to exasperating tangles, the people who used them were ardent in their defense.

The type specimen as well as the most eloquent champion of fishing such straps was David Webster, a strange mixture of throwback and innovator. In his book *The Angler and the Loop Rod* (1885), published after almost all serious fly fishers had adopted reels, rods with metal guides, and silk lines, Webster advocated a much simpler and older system. His solid-wood rod was thirteen and a half feet long and had only a woven horsehair loop at the tip through which he released and retrieved line by hand (no reel). His horsehair "casting-line" was eighteen to twenty feet long, and attached to it was a "gut-line" of sixteen or seventeen feet; both were tapered. But it was his flies and his way of casting them, more than anything else, that make him stand out today.

Webster always used nine flies, spaced evenly along the "gut-line." He recommended, however, that beginners start more modestly: "Until he attains to some degree of expertise in casting, the beginner should use a short rod of ten or eleven feet, with a hair-line of twelve or fifteen feet, and length of gut in proportion, carrying no more than half-a-dozen flies. To simplify matters a little at first, let him select for practice an open stretch of water, free from bushes, trees, or whatever else

With ten or even more flies on the line, an angler could "comb" a stretch of water with an instant hatch of identical flies—or simultaneously present a variety of flies to the fish and thus shorten the time it took to determine which fly they were most willing to take. From T. C. Hofland, The British Angler's Manual *(1839).*

would endanger his tackle or wreck his hopes; and, getting the wind in his favour, endeavor to cast out from the channel side towards the bank."[20]

Perhaps the most surprising thing about Webster was that he was a strong advocate of upstream fishing. This did not make him unique among fly fishers, of course—there had been many upstream practitioners of the sport for generations—but it does make it all the more remarkable that he fished all those flies in the riskiest possible direction.

At first blush, the idea of casting such a Very Large Array of flies out across a river has an immediate appeal. Wet-fly anglers used terms such as *sweeping* and *combing* for the casting of several flies. Webster's strap of flies would indeed take a pretty comprehensive survey of the water, almost like an entire hatch of artificials. But with so many flies, if you weren't really good at line control, you could find yourself in an awful mess really quickly.

And it got worse when you hooked a fish, especially if the fish took one of the droppers far up from the tail fly. In a recent phone conversation with me, angling historian John Betts, who has built and fished extensively with a variety of replica old tackle, told me that when you hook a fish on a rig with lots of flies, you must keep above the fish because "if he gets upstream of you, then all the flies get involved." The ever quotable Cutcliffe makes the same point: "Some use more than three flies, and if the wind is not high, you may put on as many as you can manage to throw properly; but more than four are sure to become a nuisance by entangling the collar, and hitching in just everything you do not want to do; and at most disagreeable times, as when playing a trout with the bob fly, your stretcher catches in a stake in the middle of a deep stickle; or just when your fish, being tired, you are about to lift him over some little bush, you find your numerous flies each hooked in the branches of a black thorn, placed as if on purpose to molest you."[21]

Webster's book offered hints on how to avoid or overcome these problems, but he was one of those authors about whom we wonder: Was this fellow so uniquely gifted and skilled at his chosen techniques that we mere mortals shouldn't even try to do what he did? We may not be able to answer this question, but the historical reality is that his straps and ladders did not endure among the average fishermen. Perhaps he was just better at it, or perhaps the rest of us are just too intimidated to get that good at such an odd method.

Changing Ways

Or perhaps the multiple-fly cast lost ground among anglers for other reasons. Webster's book came out just as the dry fly was emerging as the new sporting standard among many influential British fly fishers; he must have looked even more antiquated among all the new trendsetters with their fancy split-cane rods and new fly patterns tied on eyed hooks. Dry-fly fishing, with its emphasis on a single, precisely aimed fly cast over a specifically targeted fish, seemed to many to be a much more rigorous and fulfilling technique than the older wet-fly style that was, even then, known as "chuck-and-chance-it." Fashions changed, and those anglers who took on the dry fly as their new passion would have not only abandoned their old wet-fly casts, but soon initiated a condescension toward and even disapproval of such "outdated" and even

This illustration of two frogs apparently testing the strength of an Orvis gut cast of three flies (note the two droppers) appeared in countless advertisements and catalogs in the late 1800s and through much of the 1900s. Courtesy of the Orvis Company.

"unsporting" wet-fly methods. Wet flies and multiple-wet-fly fishing didn't disappear, but they lost significant ground among many of the sport's leading commentators.

To our benefit, most of the huge numbers of people who still fished with wet flies didn't really care what the snobs thought anyway and continued to catch lots of fish in a way they found suitable. My friend Bud Lilly, whose early fly-fishing experiences in Montana now stretch back more than seventy years, tells me that in the 1920s and 1930s he and his dad routinely fished with two or three large wet flies during Montana's salmon fly hatch, and if the opportunity afforded itself, they'd impale a couple of real salmon flies on each fly hook; we regular anglers are often much more open-minded than might appear if you only read the standard reference books written by our professional taste makers.

Today we continue to generate new theories to support our methods. It has long been said, for example, that as a three- or four-fly cast comes by, the trout's attention is first caught by the highest dropper, which activates his appetite enough that he sucks in the tail fly. Or that the tail fly appears to be pursuing the droppers, thus triggering a similar pursuit, in competition, by the trout. We have all kinds of theories of what's happening out there and what sort of little subaquatic drama the series of flies is setting up in the trout's view.

These days, at least here in the American West, we are especially fond of using a dry-fly dropper as a strike detector for a sunken tail fly. I don't know how old this technique is, but its precedents are obvious in all the generations of anglers who fished wet flies as anchors for bobbing droppers.

Even after the formally defined dry fly arose in the 1870s and 1880s, serious dry-fly anglers sometimes fished mixed rigs. In 1903, R. B. Marston, the distinguished long-time editor of the great British periodical the *Fishing Gazette*, described just such fishing. In a letter to the wet-fly specialist Ewen Tod, Marston described using some of Tod's flies: "I fished all three flies first dry and then wet. I also fished with two of the flies dry and one wet, or one dry and two wet, and this in the rapid broken water of the streams as well as on the pools. It is a great mistake to think dry-fly fishing must be confined to slow smooth water. Wherever the natural can float there the artificial can float if properly made, and oiled, and used. It is most interesting to watch your fly coming down dancing on the waves, and then disappear when the brown head of a trout breaks the surface, also to see it pulled under when a trout takes one of the wet flies."[22] Marston was, admittedly, an all-round angler who resisted the more obnoxious elements of dry-fly purism, though he was also a veteran dry-fly man. He is a good model for us today: devoted to the conventions and wisdoms inherited through centuries of smart wet-fly fishermen, yet savvy enough to keep his eye open for new things.

It all comes down to personal preference. Though I have often tried fishing two or more flies, most of the time I have stuck with my original skepticism about such extravagance. It is an entirely subjective choice, I know, but, for me, tossing a row of flies out there seems a little too indiscriminate; I feel I should try them one at a time rather than all at once.

Nevertheless, reading through all this great advice from all these excellent anglers makes me wonder what would happen if I put together a rig of three or four dry flies, maybe all Adams or Elk Hair Caddis. I've never seen that done, perhaps because it's not even legal in many places anymore. But if it were, and despite my stubborn preference for the one-fly cast, I have to admit that the idea of watching so many dry flies glide over a good pool at the same time sounds better than watching just one.

6 This Most Salutary Reform

The Slow Rise of the Eyed Hook

One of my proudest possessions as a fly fisher is my copy of the second edition (1886, same year as the first edition) of Frederic M. Halford's *Floating Flies and How to Dress Them.* I acquired it some years ago during a flush-feeling period when I had accumulated an unseemly volume of credit with a favorite out-of-print book dealer. From the two-color (red and black) type on its title page to its dozens of delicately precise engravings of fly-tying methods to its ten "hand-coloured" plates of flies, it is a joy to own—and to gently read.

Because I tend to make marginal notes in my books, I more typically prefer either cheap later facsimile reprints or simple photocopies of older books. I can carry on my conversation with the authors with no guilt in these newer, cheaper books, scrawling comments here and there, underlining curious points, and otherwise doing the sorts of things that would make librarians weep if I did them in a valuable book.

I would never dream of marking the pages of an older book (some previous owner did mark up my Halford a little). I enjoy having these few inviolate books, the ones that were printed when the author was alive and his words were fresh in anglers' minds.

And make no mistake about it: though today we may see Halford as a rather hidebound fisherman, intolerant of any way but his own, he must not be read that way. He must be read for the excitement of the day the book was published, when the dry fly was just as he, George Selwyn Marryat, and their associates were just then envisioning it. He must be read for the clarity, confidence, and graciousness of his prose

Frederic Halford's series of books on dry flies, commencing with Floating Flies and How to Dress Them *(1886), became the leading advocates of eyed hooks in a fly-fishing culture that was accustomed to many centuries of flies tied on snelled hooks. From Martin Mosely's* The Dry-Fly Fisherman's Entomology *(1921).*

and the handsomeness of his books. He must be read for the obvious fun his crowd was having 120 years ago as they launched this new and rigorously formal style of fly fishing on a largely unsuspecting world.

It might seem odd to us today, considering the momentous nature of their enterprise, that Halford's book did not begin as, say, Vincent Marinaro's *A Modern Dry Fly Code* would some sixty-four years later—with an eloquent literary flourish, invoking mythic imagery to celebrate what was to come. Instead, as an indication to us of how much things have changed since Halford's time, his opening chapter had the mundane title "On Eyed-Hooks." This was because his work was part of a revolution founded on what to us would seem the most trivial of details, but to his readers was a factor of immense proportions: "Before many years are past the old-fashioned fly, dressed on a hook attached to a length of gut, will be practically obsolete, the advantages of the eyed-hook being so manifest that even the most conservative adherents of the old school, must, in time, be imbued with this most salutary reform."[1]

This prediction was concisely put, but was in fact more an expression of his determination to advance the angling community's slow transition to eyed hooks than on any real certainty that such a transition was inevitable. Anglers, especially fly fishers, had known about eyed hooks for a very long time. What seemed to Halford and to us today as only common sense looked quite different to most anglers before and during his time. The eyed hook was an idea whose time had come only if you were among the few anglers not perfectly comfortable with the older way of doing things.

Snells

Through most of written fly-fishing history, flies were almost always tied on hooks without eyes. At least from the 1200s until the late 1800s (that being the portion of our history for which we have much of a written record), the fly tier began by first lashing a section of horsehair or, later, silkworm gut to the shank of the hook. These hooks (known aptly as "blind" hooks) often had a "spade" or flattened end where the eye would be on a modern hook in order to facilitate and stabilize the placement of the line.[2]

Typically, this short section of line—which roughly equated with the modern tippet—was looped at its other end so that it could be easily attached to a corresponding loop on the end of the fly line, which was also composed of hair, grass, silk, or some combination thereof. Anglers carried as many flies as they wanted, usually in some type of "book" whose pages would accommodate the "snelled flies."

As mentioned in chapter five, many anglers carried whole leaders ready for use, each already rigged with two, three, or more snelled flies. Unlike modern anglers, who most often change from one fly to another, an angler of one hundred or more years ago often saw his flies in sets that were routinely fished together—perhaps one set of flies for the afternoon of a certain season and another for the evening of that same season, or one set for certain water conditions and another for other conditions. At any time, of course, one could change just one fly in the set, but I have been impressed with how often earlier fishing writers thought in terms of changing the whole leader.

With a few centuries of practice behind it, the nineteenth-century snell was undeniably a very efficient way to manage the construction,

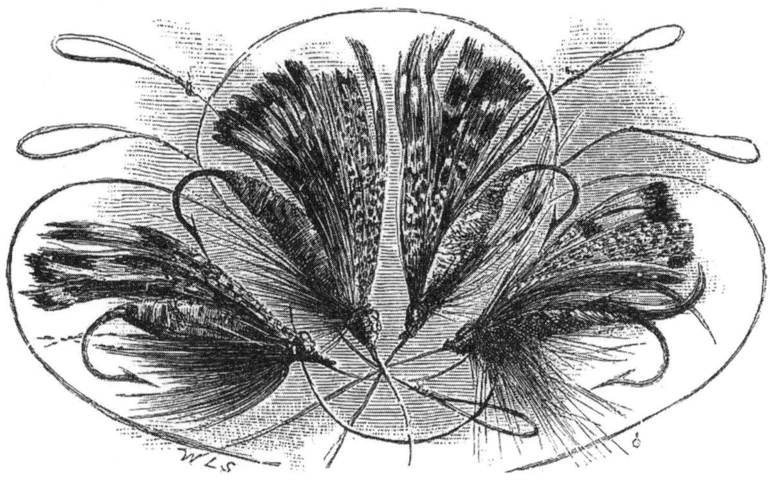

The often ornate and unrealistic snelled wet flies favored by most American fly fishers in the late 1800s were too effective simply to vanish when angling fashions changed; the transition to the new, more imitative patterns inspired by Halford and others would take several decades. From Alfred M. Mayer, Sport with Gun and Rod in American Woods and Waters *(1883).*

use, and changeability of flies. Once the hair or gut was securely wedded to the hook shank with a good wrapping of silk, the fly was tied over it in the conventional manner. The hair or gut extended straight out from the fly, a much tidier visual transition from fly to line than could easily be accomplished with a leader knotted to an eyed hook. Champions of the snell over the eyed fly said that having the gut come straight out from the hook also made the fly "swim" more truly lined up with the fly line and that flies with eyed hooks were more likely to swing this way and that on the "hinge" provided by the knot.[3]

Though some of us still remember seeing snelled flies for sale somewhere—usually in a dusty corner of an old hardware store that dated from that era when hardware stores carried almost everything you needed—we were more likely to see snelled bait hooks than snelled flies. The former are still readily available in many tackle shops. And in almost all cases, at least since the 1920s or so, such hooks have had both eyes *and* snells. In American angling's most traditional and practical circles, snelling is still dying a very slow death.

For good reasons. Once you got the hang of using the loops (which many modern anglers still use to attach their fly line to the butt of the leader or their tippet to the leader), it was a faster way to change flies than learning and tying some annoying knot that involved first threading the line through the eye of a small fly.

It was a mighty secure way, too, at least when the snell was put on properly. Snells were no more likely to fail than are modern knots. Pre-1900 fly-tying instructions sometimes included the advice that you should gently bite down on the end of the gut snell a few times along the section that would be lashed to the hook shank. Doing so would leave a series of nice grooves for the tying silk to nestle into as you wrapped it around the gut and the hook shank, ensuring a secure grip and making most fishermen's knots seem treacherous and unreliable by comparison. Or so it apparently seemed to almost all anglers until the late 1800s.

What troubles many modern anglers when they learn about historic snelled flies is the thought that when the leader on a snelled fly grows frayed or weak, the fly is more or less useless. By contrast, if the tippet attached to an eyed fly should begin to wear, we can simply clip off the fly, replace the tippet with a new one, and retie the fly to it. Once a snelled fly of days past had lost its hair or gut loop, it could not so easily be put back to use.

Early Eyes

In the greater history of the fish hook, eyes of one sort or another are genuinely ancient, dating back thousands of years and showing up here and there in the archeological record among the countless hooks made by resourceful people around the world, whether of bronze, bone, ivory, or wood. There has been nothing novel in the idea of putting some kind of hole or notch or other contrivance on the end of the hook shank to enable one to run a line—made of hide, sinew, thread, grass, hair, whatever—through it or around it.[4]

Nor was the eyed hook new to fly fishing at Halford's time. Every now and then during the past three or four centuries, literate fly fishers were exposed to eyed hooks. In *A History of Fly Fishing for Trout* (1921), John Waller Hills reported that Frère François Fortin's *Les ruses innocentes* (1660) contained the "first illustration I know of an eyed hook."[5] I

be for euerie fish, here may ye see the figures of your instruments and hookes.

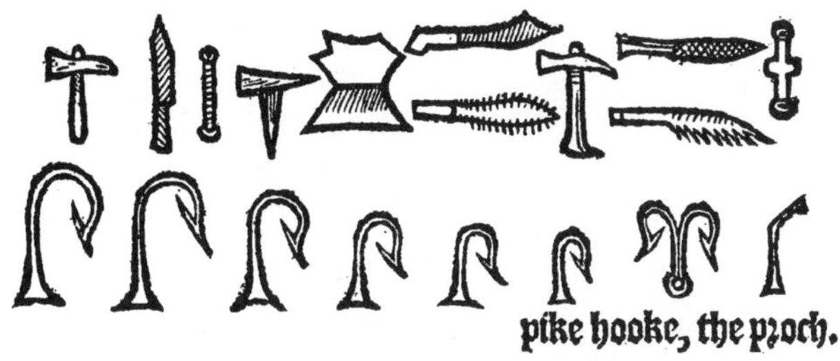

pike hooke, the proch.

Now when ye haue made thus your hookes of al sorts,
then must yee set them to your lines, according in

A simple double hook, with its bend serving as an eye, as illustrated in Leonard Mascall's A Booke of Fishing with Hooke & Line *(1590).*

have never seen the latter book or a copy of this illustration, and Hills's very interesting book is unfortunately not illustrated, so I don't suppose many other people have, either.

Even earlier, however, a British fishing writer had revealed, at least in a general way, an awareness of the eyed hook. Leonard Mascall's *A Booke of Fishing with Hooke & Line* (1590), though now often disregarded because Mascall copied so much of his text from the more affectionately remembered *Treatyse of Fishing with an Angle* (1496), contained a simple woodcut of a double hook with an eye, apparently used for pike. Like modern Atlantic salmon double hooks, this one involved a single piece of wire bent back double on itself, then bent into hook shape on both ends. The "eye" was just the natural result of the doubling over of the wire. In modern parlance, it would be called a "loose double" because the shanks, though side by side, were apparently not soldered together.[6] Mascall gives us no reason to think this hook was ever to be used for fly fishing, but there it sits in plain view of thinking readers—right next to a few coarse woodcuts of fly-type hooks like those in the *Treatyse*—with its nice circular metal eye.[7]

By far the most notable, even famous, eyed hooks in the early British fly-fishing literature must be those that appeared first in the 1760 edition of Walton's *The Complete Angler*, edited by John Hawkins.[8] Hawkins provided a series of wonderful engravings by H. Roberts (the

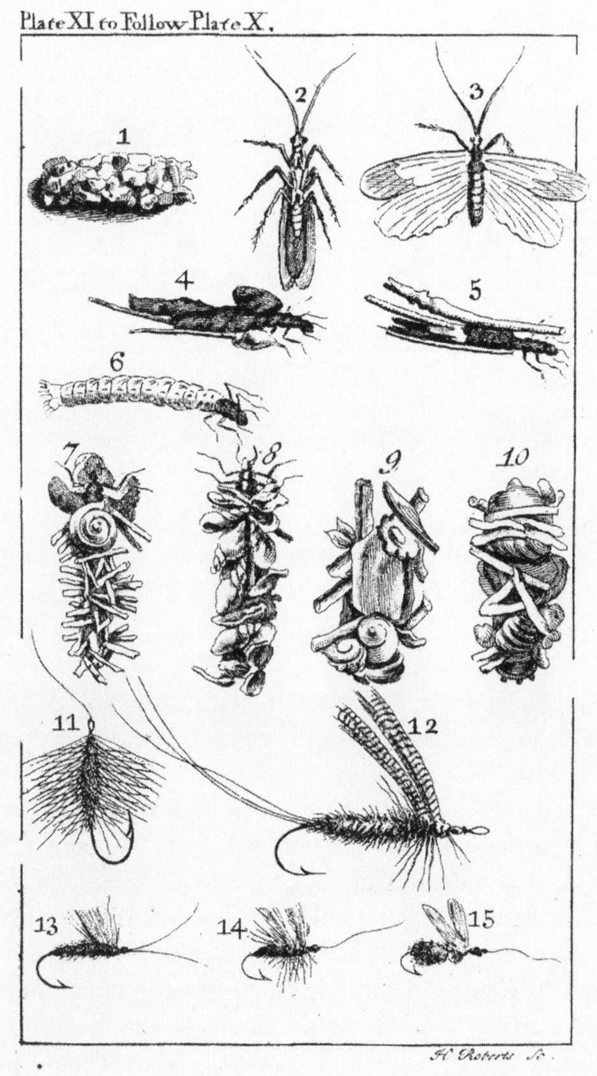

In 1760, John Hawkins published a new edition of Izaak Walton's The Complete Angler, *with several remarkable illustrations, including this "plate" of natural insects (including caddis cases) and artificial flies. The earliest clear depiction of British trout flies, this plate shows two flies with eyed hooks. Number 11, the Palmer, and number 12, the Green Drake, feature eyes (as does another palmer in a separate plate elsewhere in the book). The eyes were not usually made of metal; Hawkins made the eyes from a loop of hog's bristle. From Isaak Walton,* The Complete Angler, *edited by John Hawkins (1760).*

artist is not named), certainly the highest quality and most helpful of such illustrations yet to appear in a fly-fishing book. Among other things, these engravings showed a fly tier at work, an angler's hands splicing rod sections together, several excellent insect illustrations (including some drawings of caddis cases that would have as long a life when copied in later publications as would the artificial flies), and an impressive array of other tackle, including the best illustration of a reel to that date. The flies shown are "the first six believable illustrations of artificial flies to be found anywhere in angling literature."[9]

The eyed-hook flies in the Hawkins edition of Walton, apparently a Great Dun and a Green Drake, were shown with straight eyed hooks. At least one of the edition's engravings, showing the Great Dun with a strand of line coming through the eye, seems almost certainly to be a metal eyed hook.[10] But Hawkins himself seemed to favor hog bristle as the best material to use to construct the eye on the blind hooks of the time, so I assume that most of these early eyed fly hooks had a nonmetal eye.

A question remains: Even if the eye on the hooks was a hair-loop or a gut-loop eye, rather than a metal eye, why didn't it become more popular among anglers? Wouldn't even a gut-loop eye be a big improvement over a snelled hook?

The Rise of the Eyes

Whether it was the influence of the nearly incessant copying and reprinting of the Hawkins engraving of flies, the use of eyed hooks in other kinds of fishing, the independent innovation of new generations of anglers, or some combination of these factors, by the mid-1800s the eyed hook was a coming idea. Hewett Wheatley, whose *The Rod and Line* (1849) perfectly exemplifies the very notion of independent innovation, was obviously already a regular user of eyed hooks by that time, illustrating several of his beetle and moth patterns tied on them.[11]

A few years later, in 1862, the prominent American fisheries authority and fishing writer Robert Barnwell Roosevelt (who was known among fishing readers as "Barnwell") made it sound as if eyed hooks were already pretty common things in the United States:

> There is a Limerick hook now made with the shank turned over so as to form a loop into which the gut is inserted and the trouble of tying the gut is avoided. They have come into general use among the Irish and Scotch fishermen, and are a great aid to the man that ties his own flies. The gut in ordinary fly fishing wears out just above the hook, a difficulty that is entirely removed by this improvement, and it is by no means ugly or ungainly as might be supposed. This is no new discovery, but has been practiced with common American hooks for a considerable period, and might be advantageously used in many kinds of fishing, and applied to all hooks.[12]

It is a little difficult to tell what Barnwell meant by some of this description. It sounds as if he was saying that American anglers often independently bent an eye onto the shank of a hook that didn't have one when they bought it. In any case, the novelty was apparently wearing off the idea of the eyed hook by the 1860s, though I suspect that Barnwell was overstating the abundance of eyed hooks at that time.

A parallel development among Atlantic salmon fly fishers demands attention here. While Wheatley, Roosevelt, and apparently others were discussing eyed hooks for trout, more and more Atlantic salmon flies were being tied not with eyed hooks, but with blind hooks with gut-loop eyes (usually multiple strands of gut were used for greater strength). Angling historian Andrew Herd says that this method arose in the "first quarter of the nineteenth century." Unlike the metal eyed hook, the gut-looped Atlantic salmon fly seemed to become quite popular very quickly, although, as Herd amusingly explains, it was not unanimously accepted: "Naturally, it was seen as a great threat to world order and some fishermen fought a rearguard action against such a perversion of nature's laws for almost another thirty years. Despite this, the gut loop became standard on salmon flies by the end of the third quarter of the century. Gut eyed salmon flies persisted long after it became the rule to tie trout flies on eyed hooks, and they only started to become difficult to find in the 1920s."[13]

My own experiences in cataloging and caring for large numbers of flies during my five years as director of the American Museum of Fly Fishing reinforces my impression that Herd has the timing right. Just as the Halfordian dry fly moved from being the latest thing to being the correct, traditional thing in a very short time, the full-glory Victorian Atlantic salmon fly, replete with a great complex mass of unusual materials and colors, became firmly entrenched as the "right" and even "traditional" style of fly for salmon anglers very quickly, and there was substantial resistance to anything that might threaten its preeminence. I remember wondering, as I worked with the museum's fly collection, how these beautiful gut-loop eyed patterns remained popular for so long when the rest of the fly-fishing world had long switched to eyed hooks. It is a telling example of how individual traditions, styles, and habits *within* the fly-fishing culture can change at significantly differing rates.[14]

Henry Hall's Hook

In his fascinating biography of Frederic Halford, Tony Hayter says that when Halford first fished the Test in 1877, he did not use eyed hooks, but that they were already on the minds of some very influential anglers of the generation following Wheatley's. Halford's great mentor and silent partner in his early dry-fly theorizing, George Selwyn Marryat, was already using them when Halford came to the Test. Farlow, a prominent British tackle maker, later said they had been offering eyed hooks to anglers since the 1850s.[15]

According to Hayter, however, these still early stirrings weren't the impetus behind the hooks that Halford, Marryat, and others finally took to their hearts and built their new dry-fly passion upon. In 1876, a circa-1800 manuscript by W. H. Aldam was published as *A Quaint Treatise on "Flees, and the Art of Artyfichall Flee Making."* The book contained a set of actual flies mounted on special pages, and two of those flies were "tied on eyed limericks specially made by Bartleet of Redditch."[16] Two thoughtful fly fishers, Henry Sinclair Hall and George Bankart, impressed by these well-made hooks, recognized the possibilities and spent the next three years developing a reasonably fine-weight and necessarily small fly hook. Commissioning Hutchinson of Kendal to produce the final version, they took delivery of their first acceptable order in March 1879. Hall, a schoolmaster and textbook author, has been credited as the leading light in this development, earning himself a comfortable and permanent place among fly fishing's important historical innovators.

A Halford dry fly tied on an eyed hook, as pictured in Halford's first book, Floating Flies and How to Dress Them *(1886).*

Serious students of the dry fly in the next few decades would look back on the development of an eyed hook that was small and light enough for dry-fly fishing as, in the words of one commentator in 1900, one of "the two biggest advances of the nineteenth century in trout fishing,"[17] the other being the dry fly itself. As I suggested at the beginning of this story, however, this development wasn't that simple in the minds of anglers. One man's technological miracle was another man's unnecessary nuisance.

The Conversion

Just as it took anglers a long time to abandon horsehair lines in favor of silk lines and gut leaders, it took a long time for them to let go of the snelled hook. Even the most progressive professional fly fishers and fly tiers struggled to break old habits and adjust to new ones. In the United States, no less a fly-tying pioneer than Theodore Gordon—angling theorist and ardent proponent of the new dry-fly fishing ideas of Halford and his chalk stream friends—made the transition slowly. Writing to the British *Fishing Gazette* in 1904, he predicted that "the eyed *versus* plain hook controversy will never be settled. Many anglers dislike exceedingly the business of knotting, and cling to the old short snell and gut loops. This is not neat, but it is certainly convenient."[18] A full twenty years after Halford's first book was published, Gordon wrote in *Forest and Stream* that he now used "eyed hooks as often as hooks tied

The great American fly theorist Theodore Gordon, shown here in a famous photograph with a mysterious and unknown female fishing companion, was representative of many late-nineteenth-century American anglers who displayed allegiance to both the traditional snelled hooks and the newer and increasingly more fashionable eyed hooks. Photo/Image property of Catskill Fly Fishing Center and Museum, Livingston Manor, New York.

on snells."[19] Like others, he continued to struggle with the adjustment and said so.

Perhaps even more revealing is the view from Vermont, where Charles F. Orvis was running what was perhaps America's most respected and prestigious mail-order fly business. Orvis's son Albert, responding to a letter from a customer in 1910 about the rationale behind eyed hooks on trout flies, pondered the pros and cons at some length:

> In regard to the use of the flies tied on the Eyed hooks the advantage over the snells is that when a fly gets worn at the point of contact with the hook the snell may be retied to the hook and then the fly will be as strong as ever. Another advantage is that the leader may be made without the loops and have just drop snell attached so that there will be less ripple when drawing the snell or leader through the water. This is a point in favor of eyed hooks when the water is very still and clear.

> We can make the leaders with the drop snells for use with eyed hooks when so ordered or a gut snell for droppers can be adjusted to looped leaders and the eyed fly attached to this snell.
>
> If one has their flies reinforced as you have had some of yours I think they will wear as long as the material of the fly and there is no advantage in using eyed flies.
>
> It is certainly much easier to attach regular snelled flies than the eyed hooks and this is the reason that the regular snelled flies will be largely used. When we who can get out fishing but seldom we do not want to stop to "putter" with that eyed hook and when a fly gets weak we just pull it off and attach another and say to ourself that we will economize on something else when the fish are not rising.[20]

That both Gordon and Orvis—two of the day's savviest and commerce-wise fly fishers—thought that snelled hooks might not ever be totally replaced and might even continue to dominate the market, suggests how devoted many anglers were to their comfortable old ways and how powerful a hold the eyeless hook had on fly fishers even when confronted with such an excellent and versatile alternative.

Why So Slow to Catch On?

We have already seen some of the reasons the eyed hook had such an uphill struggle among fly fishers. In practical terms, many anglers weren't sure the eyed hook was even an improvement. Whether gut or hair, the line was no stronger on an eyed hook than it was on a snelled one. Sure, you could keep using the eyed hook after the gut or hair got frayed, but how many people really cared about that? Apparently not very many, or at least not enough to force the change.

Legitimate questions about the eyed hook implied that it might not even be as good as the snelled hook. Many were convinced that the snelled fly swam better and that eyed hooks tended to swing around too much on the leader. True or not, such received wisdoms quickly take on a life of their own and become part of the sport's common knowledge.

But I think much more was going on than these practical fishing matters. For one thing, people are comfortable with what they know. At a time when fly fishers weren't yet swept along in the modern tides of commerce, constantly confronted with beautiful new rods, reels, lines, and fly patterns every few months in the pages of gorgeous catalogs, they were a considerably more stodgy crowd than they are today.

There was also the matter of personal taste. I haven't seen clear proof of this factor in the literature, but I suspect that some eighteenth- and nineteenth-century anglers, getting their first look at an eyed-hook fly, were probably offended by the ungainly mass of metal eye and gut knot where the snelled fly had only the smooth emergence of the gut from the fly's body. Just as the bead in a modern bead-head nymph seems to some anglers a violation of the aesthetics, proportions, and realism of a fly pattern, all this new hardware sticking out the front end of their favorite fly pattern may even have troubled some of fly fishing's more serious imitationists back then.

A bigger and even more basic issue has to do with the eyed hook's actual availability to anglers before 1879. During the first couple of centuries that eyed hooks were occasionally shown to fly fishers in early fishing books, those hooks were still out of their reach. For most of the time that the eyed hook was known but had not yet become popular among fly fishers, its limited acceptance probably had much to do with the difficulty of manufacture.[21] As long as many fly fishers either made their own tackle or relied on some local craftsman to do so, the making of a hook was a more personal matter, subject to problems having to do with the quality of the materials, the skills of the craftsmen, and the demands of the market. If fly fishers or other fishers were predisposed to skepticism over the eyed hook, there would be little incentive for the hook maker to go out on a limb and try to push a new and largely untested (either in actual fishing or in the market) kind of hook. Even if you could get it right, it took much more work to make one. Adding an eye—not an easy task, especially in the smaller sizes—to each hand-bent, hand-sharpened, hand-barbed, and hand-finished hook would have been an iffy proposition even for an adventurous small business-man, especially when anglers were not disposed to try new things any-way. One didn't add such a thing to one's inventory without substantial reason and high expectations of sales.

This circumstance also reveals a significant difference between the fly fisher of, say, 1500 or 1700 and the fly fisher of Halford's time. When people fished using techniques and tackle inherited from their parents, they were using tools rather like the other tools in their lives—tools that nobody saw any need to change. Unlike us, these people did not live in a scientific and technologically sophisticated world where a high premium is placed on innovation and "improvement." In the less fevered commercial atmosphere of previous centuries, it was more likely that the rare new product had first to prove itself, angler by angler, before earning a guarded acceptance among the tribe.

It also should be no surprise—in fact, it was predictable—that the eyed fly "took" most firmly among the anglers who could afford the sport's finer touches. Once this market demanded eyed hooks, eyed hooks came out of their long dormancy and took over.

This is not to say that in Halford's time fly fishing suddenly left the poorer classes and became solely the province of the wealthy. Remember that Cotton and some other sixteenth-century anglers could afford not only a hired boy to carry their stuff and help land their fish, but also the leisure to fish recreationally and hang out in the local taverns for extended bouts of drinking and swapping fishing stories.

It is to say, though, that over the past few centuries, fly fishing has gravitated more and more toward the top end of the available market—a movement that modern fly-fishing magazines would seem to prove has continued today. In other words, the higher degree of dependence on technology, information, and privilege required by the Halfordian dry fly—in terms of rod construction, line construction, hook construction, entomological study, access to the "right" sorts of water, and so on—required a fly fisher with the resources to support the habit.

If you want to see how this class distinction worked in angling society, take a quick reading tour through angling writing when Halford was becoming England's most famous fly fisher and was even being celebrated by Americans as a great new angling pioneer. On that tour, you will notice the sizeable number of non–chalk stream fishermen who viewed his celebrity and his methods with a mixture of amusement and disregard, and who continued happily fishing with snelled flies on, in, or right beneath the surface. Read, for example, E. M. Tod's *The Wet-Fly Treated Methodically* (1903) or, in American writing, James Henshall's *Favorite Fish and Fishing* (1908), for skeptical antidotes to the self-congratulatory mood of the dry-fly enthusiasts.[22]

Although the emergence of the "dry fly versus every other kind of fly" rivalry in fly fishing never devolved into actual class warfare, it was in part a social movement on both sides of the Atlantic. In our desire to

In some specialized markets, snelled flies persisted almost to the present. I purchased these Montana-tied woven-hair trout flies in the 1980s in a small Montana shop. Note that the flies have both snells and eyed hooks. Photograph by the author.

think of ourselves as "just regular fishermen," we fly fishers still like to invoke images of fly-fishing heroes among the common folk: an impoverished Theodore Gordon tying his flies through the cold Catskill winters or the humble lifestyles of the great bamboo rod builders of the late 1800s and early 1900s. But those gifted people weren't the operational center of the dry-fly movement in America. Instead, they were the often brilliant artisans whose existence was justified and supported by well-heeled customers in the city, men who identified and enjoyed the exclusivity of the dry-fly school. There may be nothing bad in this distinction, but there is surely nothing simple in it, either.

More than anything else, the dry fly symbolizes the growing compartmentalization and specialization that has since taken place among that large group of people who once were all just thought of as anglers. We live in an age when the compartments have become so spread apart that it's easy to go through an entire angling life—say, as a fly fisher—with virtually no meaningful contact with the several other concurrently flourishing angling traditions on American freshwaters. Indeed, it's even become possible to be one type of fly fisher and have little or no contact with the other types.

With such powerful commercial and social forces at work, it surprises me that snelled hooks didn't last longer than they did.

7 The Hatch-Matching Nondebate

The justifiably celebrated publication of a magnificent new edition of the late Ernest Schwiebert's *Nymphs* in 2007 is a fine occasion to ask one of fly-fishing's most urgent and enduring questions again. I'm speaking of the question many of us silently ask ourselves each spring as our vest settles heavily (oof!) onto our shoulders: Do I really need this many flies?

Schwiebert's answer to that question seemed always to be an emphatic and italicized, "*Yes!*" For half a century, from the publication of his equally significant milestone book *Matching the Hatch* (1955), he was our most distinguished champion of angling entomology and the fly patterns it inspired. As an eloquent proponent of the quest for better fly patterns, he had his work cut out for him. I still remember the fuss that arose thirty years ago when he published an article on ants with *forty* essential patterns. Even some hard-core hatch-matchers thought that might be setting our collective sites a bit high.

The Reassurance of History

A quick glance at the literature of fly fishing suggests, however, that Schwiebert had history on his side. Ever since the *Treatyse of Fishing with an Angle* introduced its twelve immortal fly patterns in 1496, we have promoted progressively longer lists of patterns. From the early 1800s on, uncounted fly-fishing books have been just annotated lists of flies, with hardly any instruction on how to cast them, fish them, or do anything else.

Personally, I love reading about flies. After all, fly patterns are one of the sport's greatest and most reliable comforts. No matter how

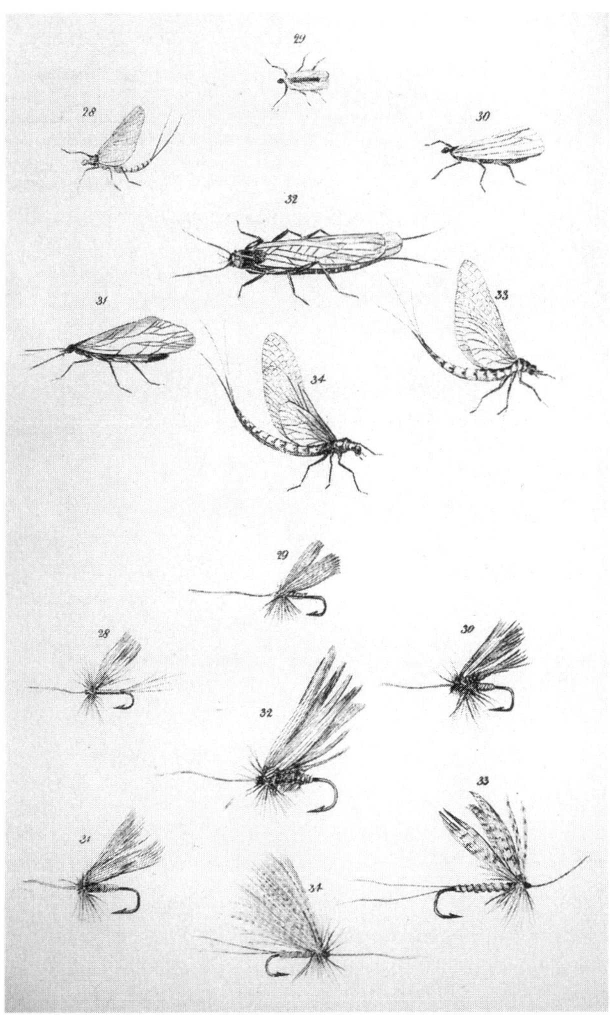

Countless fly-fishing books have offered prescriptions for imitating trout stream insects, and the lists of necessary imitations have grown progressively longer with the passing centuries. This page from British writer John Jackson's The Practical Fly-Fisher, *2d ed. (1862) conveniently portrays seven insects on the top half, with their corresponding imitations below them.*

unsuccessful I am, I can always stop, open any of six (eight? ten?) fly boxes, and happily paw through the tidy regiments of patterns that restore hope.

As a historian, however, I wonder. If you're a fishing authority who loves creating lots of new fly patterns, you're naturally going to want to write about them. But if you're suspicious of the whole fly-pattern game, you aren't likely to write books anyway, much less read those written by others. Such skeptics might remain invisible in the published literature no matter how abundant they are on the rivers.

As it turns out, they aren't invisible even in the literature. I think most of us who read the old books are so conditioned by the idea that fly fishing is all about a steady march toward improved imitation that we read right over distracting opinions to the contrary. In fact, for most of the sport's history, the fly fishers who stuck to a few flies or even to one fly were probably pretty common. Just for the flavor of their times, let's meet a few of them.

Imitating What?

Among the well-known expert British chalk stream fly fishers in the early 1800s was Colonel Peter Hawker, who was said to fish through the season with only two patterns on his cast: a Yellow Dun tail fly and a Red Spinner for a dropper.[1] About the same time, Stephen Oliver, in his unjustly neglected *Scenes and Recollections of Fly-Fishing* (1834), admitted that although he used quite a few fly patterns, he knew he could get along with just two or three favorites.[2] Such opinions were not unusual in those days.

And just in case you think this minimalist approach was possible because the fish were so much easier to catch back then, forget it. Anglers such as Hawker and Oliver were fishing streams that had been hammered by smart anglers for centuries.

William Stewart, the combative and famously skilled fly fisher whose book *The Practical Angler* (1857) did so much to codify upstream fly fishing, had no faith in the "exact imitation" creeds then being promoted by many of his contemporaries in the mid–nineteenth century. Admitting that "this opinion is still held by the great majority of anglers in Scotland, while in England it is all but universal," Stewart insisted that you really only needed three or four of his soft-hackle "spiders" and

British chalk stream anglers of the mid-1800s were intensely interested in the insect life of their exclusive rivers, but they defined the sport of fly fishing in a variety of ways—including the use of their skills to cast live insects just as they cast imitations. This photograph shows a group of anglers at Stockbridge on the River Test. From Herbert Maxwell, ed., The Chronicles of the Houghton Fishing Club, 1822–1908 *(1908), courtesy of Andrew Herd.*

three different winged flies. You fished them as a set of three, on or near the surface, and if "varied in size according to the circumstances, [they] will at any time kill as well, and even better, than the most elaborate collection arranged for every month in the year."[3] Stewart routinely lugged home heavy creels to support his argument.

It's easy to get lost in labeling these viewpoints. All these people were obviously trying to imitate small stream insects at least vaguely, so they all were "imitationists" in that sense. The difference was in how much emphasis they placed on precision of imitation and, thus, how many fly patterns they thought necessary. Very few fly-fishing writers of any meaningful authority in the past five centuries claimed that fly pattern was completely irrelevant. There was just a wide range of opinion about which of the fly's features—its size, color, shape, how closely it resembled a given insect, how it was presented, what conditions prevailed on the stream, and so on—mattered most.

By the early nineteenth century, leading British angler-naturalists were acutely aware of the appearance and behavior of many of the insects that inhabited their trout streams. From Alfred Ronalds, The Fly-Fisher's Entomology *(1836).*

For all their heated debates and controversies over imitation theory, at least some fly fishers never lost their sense of humor. From Reverend Henry Newland, The Erne, Its Legends, and Its Fly Fishing *(1851).*

That said, it appears that a great many nineteenth-century American fly fishers—who had to deal only with the relatively undiscriminating appetites of bass and brook trout—were even less devoted than their Old World counterparts to strict theories of imitation. A number of American writers did take the time to explore the questions involved, and a relatively small number of anglers did take on the challenges of a few eastern spring creeks where the questions were no doubt more urgent.[4] I suspect that for most American fly fishers, however, imitation-related questions were fairly academic until the arrival of the brown trout and the popularization of dry-fly fishing.

Even then, there were strongly diverging schools of thought. Between 1870 and 1910, Robert Barnwell Roosevelt, Sara McBride, Mary Orvis Marbury, John Harrington Keene, Theodore Gordon, and some others exhorted their fellow anglers to undertake serious entomological study and create patterns to match, but other equally skilled and vocal angling theorists took fly theory in different directions, emphasizing what we now think of as presentation over imitation.

Pink Ladies and Whirling Duns

The most famous American example of a few-fly generalist may have been George LaBranche. In *The Dry Fly and Fast Water* (1914), LaBranche devoted a substantial chapter to his ideas of imitation, which for him meant that, first, you put the fly in just the right place, and, second, the fly behaved exactly right. His third priority was the fly's size, fourth was its "form," and fifth its color.[5] Who is to say that, by his own lights, he wasn't an imitationist?

His philosophy, however, freed him from worrying much about fly pattern. Because the fly's size, color, and shape were relatively lower priorities for him, LaBranche admitted that despite all the hundreds of dry-fly patterns he could choose from, "I rarely use over six. If I were compelled to do so, I could get along very well with one—the Whirling Dun."[6] It has been said, perhaps inaccurately, that LaBranche successfully fished through an entire trout season and an entire salmon season using only his Pink Lady dry fly.[7] Whether he did or not, it's not unreasonable to assume he wouldn't have minded much if he had to.

This diversity of opinion over how many fly patterns one needs has continued. In England in the 1930s, fly-fishing theorist E. W. Harding said that at "one end of the scale is the man who uses but a single pattern of fly, and at the other is the man who carries boxes full of flies. Between them is the average fly fisher," but Harding doubted that even the average fly fisher used many patterns. He observed that "although there may not be many avowedly 'one-fly' or 'few-fly' men," the majority of fly fishers "do not habitually use more than a very few of the patterns which they take with them to the river."[8]

In 1953, only two years before Schwiebert's groundbreaking *Matching the Hatch* appeared and further advanced the cause of the serious angler entomologists, the impeccably credentialed A. J. McClane advised American dry-fly fishermen that "it is generally accepted that an angler can get along with four or five different fly patterns and catch trout anywhere. You can do a very competent job with an Adams Quill, a Light Cahill, Brown Bivisible, Royal Coachman (hairwing), for instance, provided the fly behaves like an insect after you throw it on the water."[9] LaBranche was still alive at the time, but I don't know if he read this ringing affirmation of statements he made almost forty years earlier.

Delightful Uncertainties

Ernest Schwiebert and his hatch-matching colleagues have made their case superbly and have backed it up not only with surprisingly good science, but also with many convincing tales of taking difficult fish on just the right fly.[10] They don't need me to argue their side here.

But the one-fly, few-fly, and generalist-fly experts don't write as many extended tracts about their view, so I'll summarize it as I see it. To them, hatch-matching is a kind of scam we have perpetuated upon ourselves, albeit a very gentle and happily self-serving one that does us no real harm. In fact, we love it for several reasons that, even if not as scientific as we think, are still important. Here they are.

Each new fly pattern brings fresh hope on fishless days. We love fly patterns, and we enjoy being beneficiaries of today's amazingly gifted fly-tying craftsmen. If we also tie our own flies, we enjoy the creative challenge and the joy of catching a fish on our own pattern. We may even secretly crave the small glory of developing a famous fly pattern ourselves. Last, and perhaps most important, even the skeptics admit that sometimes getting the pattern exactly right really does matter to the fish.

Since the time of Theodore Gordon more than a century ago, New York's Catskill Mountains have been famous among fly fishers for the development of imitative patterns. This photograph by the author shows Bill Cass on the Willowemoc in the Catskills, 1978.

Most of us get such a kick out of trying new flies that if we stuck to one pattern, no matter how good, we'd be missing out on a great deal of what makes fly fishing fun for us. A "one-fly" tournament is fun because of its novelty and challenge, not because we would rather fish with the same fly all the time. As so often happens, fly fishing comes down to these personal choices. We fish as we most enjoy fishing. I once wrote a little novella, *Shupton's Fancy*, that explores what happens when a fly fisher actually stumbles onto a fly pattern so perfect that he needs no other. He discovers, as I think most of us would, that such a miraculous fly is not a simple blessing.

The arguments pro and con are circular and more than a little self-fulfilling. If you read between the lines of enough fly-fishing books, it eventually becomes apparent that working really hard at imitating specific insects will help you catch more fish—especially if your presentation skills are also top grade. The real message of all these position holders in the hatch-matching dialogues seems to be that there aren't any shortcuts. If you're not going to bother with many fly patterns, you'd better be a really terrific caster, and if you're not going to bother to be a really terrific caster, no amount of scientifically derived and expertly tied flies will save your bacon when the fish get choosy.

If there is one lesson implicit throughout the debate over imitation, it's that whatever approach you personally choose, you need to get really good at it if you want to catch a lot of fish. Whether you choose to emulate Schwiebert, LaBranche, or some combination of their traits, what you most need to emulate is their hard work.

I personally know hatch-matching experts so skilled that they can toss away all their fly boxes and use nothing but an Adams dry fly and a Pheasant Tail nymph all season and still outfish me. So, just to hedge my bets, I'll probably continue to be open to suggestions from all corners. Fly fishing is a sport, which means its intellectual underpinnings are incredibly complex.

Idaho's Silver Creek is typical of modern fly fishing's most demanding trout streams, where generations of anglers have tested their skills and experimented with new fly patterns. Photograph by the author.

Let me close with two opinions, the first from Andrew Herd, whose magnificent book *The Fly* (2003) set a new standard of intellectual penetration and good homework in a comprehensive history of the sport of fly fishing. After digesting the sport's literature and spending much of lifetime exploring the sport's opportunities, Herd concludes his book with a profoundly skeptical comment on the question of fly pattern:

> I have listed the developments which I think have been innovative, but unfortunately the majority of the new flies we see are the sad products of collusion between competing magazines anxious to fill pages and what amounts to a new profession of author/developers, many of whom are motivated to churn out endless new patterns for financial gain. In my opinion, ninety-nine per cent of the new patterns we see are completely superfluous and they do fly fishing a disservice by confusing beginners and obscuring real innovation. I know this is a particularly harsh view and I am sure it won't win me many friends, but I recently asked the editor of one of the magazines in question how many patterns he actually used and his reply was six. Feel free to draw your own conclusions, but I don't think that many of the thousands of patterns we see released every year will still find places in boxes even twenty years from now.[11]

The second opinion is from LaBranche, who, even though his personal choice was to carry very few flies, understood as well as anyone how complicated our interests are. In a comment that was half wisdom and half whimsy, he summed us up pretty well: "No matter how great the faith an angler has in a single pattern, it will naturally be difficult for him to confine himself to its exclusive use. So much of his sport depends upon its delightful uncertainty, that if he does confine himself to the use of the single pattern, he will, of a consequence, be denied the pleasure of congratulating himself upon the acumen he has shown by the selection of the fly which is taken, after the favourite has been refused."[12]

PART THREE

The American Evolution

8 Pacific Salmon and the Myth of Uncatchability

In February 1850, a wealthy British outdoorsman visiting Sacramento, California, sent a long letter to *Bell's Life in London* about his adventures hunting and fishing in the Sacramento Valley. On June 22, 1850, *The Spirit of the Times*, the leading American sporting periodical of the day, reprinted the story "Salmon Fishing and Deer Stalking in California" by "An English Sportsman." Among many other experiences, the writer told of his successful fishing for salmon in the Sacramento River. Fishing with "Blacker's London trolling rod, with a stout reel and line," and using an unspecified "bait," he had made only a few casts from his hired yacht in midstream when he hooked a fish. "I immediately jumped into a small boat and called the cockney to join me and pull for his life and we started in pursuit. After going down stream some 200 or 300 yards, he [the fish] dashed up again with lightning speed, and after about an hour's hard fighting, I landed him safely. He was in the finest condition, fresh run and weighed 36 lb. On the same day, I killed five more, weighing respectively 15 lb., 23 lb., 32 lb., and 43 lb." Only a couple sentences later, still talking about what he regarded as the same type of fish, he said, "High up the river I have caught seven and eight a day with a fly."[1]

It is in brief and all-too-vague reports like this one that we find the written origins of fly fishing for Pacific salmon. The writer described the capture, using bait, of several fish so large they were certainly chinook salmon—the largest Pacific species—then immediately referred to taking other salmon on the fly farther upstream. Can we assume

Today's fly fishers are so adept at catching large Pacific salmon that it is difficult to imagine that their ancestors believed the fish could not be caught on flies. This photograph by Dale Greenley shows Oregon guide Gary Lewis with a king salmon on the Sixes River, Oregon.

that these others were also the same species? Perhaps not. At this time, neither anglers nor naturalists were especially clear on who was who among the West Coast's migratory salmonids. Elsewhere in his article, the English Sportsman did refer to "salmon trout weighing 5 lb. to 20 lb.," so he was at least aware of one distinction among the local salmonids.[2] As the century wore on and more and more anglers tried to catch these fish, *salmon trout* was one of the terms sometimes applied to steelhead, as distinct from the five species of Pacific salmon. Even then, however, the term was used loosely.

So what did this man catch on flies? Was he really successful in taking the big chinooks on flies, or did he just not care enough or know enough to make a distinction between species? Without more information, we can't know for sure, but he does represent a very early round in a chronic, repeating so-called milestone in western angling history: the so-called discovery, generation after generation, that some of these so-called salmon would take flies.

What makes this episode and the ones that followed it all the more curious is that for more than a century, starting at this same time, the reigning centerpiece of the folklore of Pacific salmon fly fishing was a charming but poorly documented story retold countless times in countless forms that established the common knowledge among sportsmen that these fish simply would not take a fly.

Birth of the Myth

The earliest published version of the story that I have seen appeared in an article entitled "The 'Genus Salmo' and Other Fish Taken in the Rivers of the Pacific," published in *The Spirit of the Times* on July 17, 1852: "After reaching fresh water, the salmon of the Columbia no longer feeds, as is the case with the European salmon, and no persuasion will ever persuade it to rise to the fly, a circumstance perhaps, we are partially indebted to the peaceful settlement of the boundary question; for it is said that the officers of the British Man-of-War Modesto, which was sent at about that time to look around, became highly disgusted, and that Capt. Gordon wrote home to Lord Aberdeen that the d—d country wasn't worth having, for the salmon would not bite."[3]

Another early version of the story appeared in 1886, in Captain L. A. Beardslee's chapter "The Salmon and Trout of Alaska" in the book *Fishing with the Fly*, edited by Charles Orvis and A. Nelson Cheney. As Beardslee told the story, "When the news that the Yankees had purchased Alaska, and thus become owners of the land north as well as south of British Columbia, was communicated to the Scotch Admiral of the English squadron at Victoria, Vancouver's Island, he ejaculated, *'Dom the country! Let 'em have it; the blausted saumon won't rise to a floi.'*"[4] This tale, with its hilarious dismissal of a vast, resource-rich portion of the North American continent as worthless because its salmon didn't measure up to a British gentleman's sporting whims, has flourished ever since. With each retelling, the rank and identity of the speaker vary, the land being disregarded moves around (in the two examples I've given, article author "Chinook" was talking about the U.S.–Canada boundary, and Beardslee was talking about the whole land from there to Alaska), and the wording of the quotation seems never to be precisely repeated from one telling to the next.

But perhaps the most amazing thing about the story isn't its durability or even its flexibility. The most amazing thing about it, at least from today's perspective, is its finality.[5] Ever since that time, opinionated people beyond counting have been absolutely and irrevocably convinced that no Pacific salmon—ever, anywhere—would or will take a fly. Such a confident pronouncement seems absurd to us.

For just one modern example of why it seems absurd, consider me. Though I have cast on a number of West Coast streams, my serious experience of fly fishing for the Pacific salmons with flies is limited to a few days in a few Alaskan locations. Even in that brief and rankest of amateur experiences with these fish, however, I have caught all three species that I have fished for—sockeye, chum, and pinks.[6] The pinks were such aggressive feeders that I could hardly have avoided catching them; they attacked the fly like bass chasing florescent frogs. How could an inveterate tackle-fumbler like me catch these fish so readily when those very smart, very experienced anglers of the mid–nineteenth century believed that catching them wasn't even possible for the most expert anglers?

Well, there were in fact some pretty powerful reasons for this belief. Anglers could believe such a thing for so long in part because there is just something in human nature that is susceptible to grand myths and willfully simplistic pronouncements. Let's face it: we outdoorsmen and most other people interested in natural history have always had a weakness for attractive yet fundamentally silly nature lore. Over the centuries, sportsmen have clung to a remarkable collection of wondrously preposterous fairy tales—pickerel are spontaneously generated by pickerel weed; bears can't run downhill; eels grow from dew drops; cats always land on their feet; lightning never strikes twice. We have a million of them, and at the same time that we poke fun at the old ones that we've abandoned, we're busy making new ones that are just as silly. It's what we do. Maybe it's what makes us so lovable.

I have already alluded to another reason why our angling forefathers struggled with the catchability question. Like so much wildlife in the 1800s, many fish had several informal names. Local tradition quickly established quirky neighborhood names for the fish in nearby rivers. The name "spring salmon" might refer to a species, or it might just be a seasonal label applied to whatever fish showed up then. A

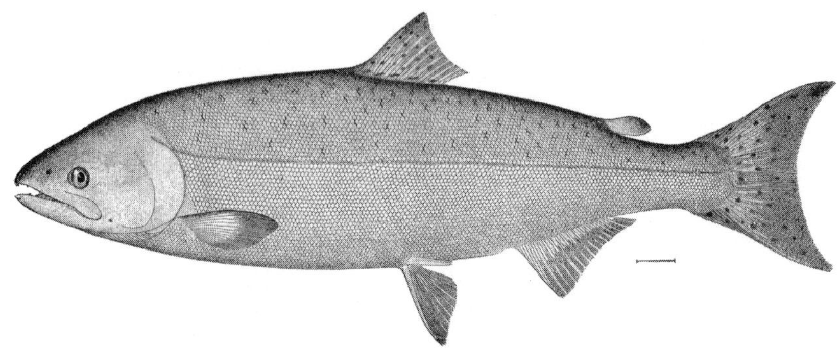

King salmon. From Edward W. Nelson, Report upon Natural History Collections Made in Alaska Between the Years 1877 and 1881 *(1887).*

"salmon trout" might be a steelhead or a resident rainbow or a sea-run cutthroat or a dolly varden or something else.[7] Or not. Who knew? Hardly anybody. Who cared? Almost nobody. This meant that any report of anyone catching anything was muddled by uncertainty.

It's not as if the experts and professional naturalists were always much help in dealing with this problem. The later nineteenth century saw a great surge in taxonomical trophy hunting as scientists divided well-known animal species into finer and finer subdivisions. Each new species required a name, and a name was an opportunity to provide either one's self or one's colleagues with nomenclatural immortality.

I date the symbolic peak of this tremendously involved exercise in creating new species to 1918 and one of my favorite stories in the history of wildlife biology. In that year, Clinton Hart Merriam, one of the foremost zoologists in America, published a monograph in which he divided the grizzly bears of North America into eighty-six species—an exercise in fantasy biology that has since collapsed in on itself so totally that we now recognize only two possibly distinct brown bears.[8]

In the great explorations and scientific surveys of the American West, each new species "discovery" was promptly published. Fish species names proliferated and were laid on top of the welter of common names. Getting any of it right was usually dependent on the local sportsmen's uneven or nonexistent reading habits. Looking back on all this confusion today and trying to piece together an accurate account of which fishermen were actually catching which fish require us to rely

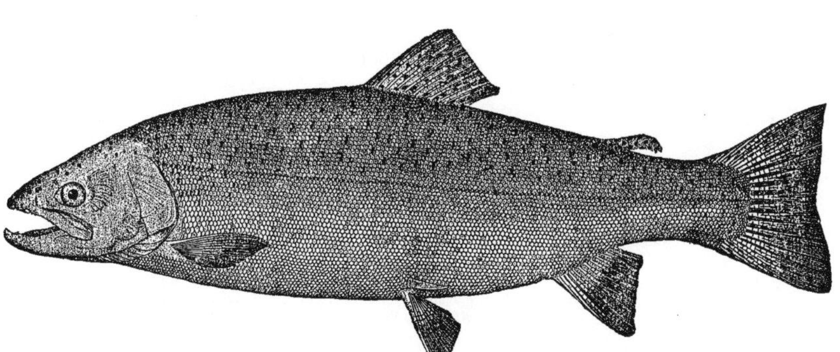

Many generations of western anglers struggled over the nomenclatural fundamentals of the Pacific salmons and were likewise confused by the exact identification of the steelhead, which was often referred to as "salmon trout" and other names. Steelhead portrait from George Oliver Shields, American Game Fishes *(1892).*

both on the cooler heads who sometimes intervened in those days and on our own best guesses.[9]

Many of us have watched this same confusion play itself out on modern streams. In Yellowstone National Park, I have watched anglers land cutthroat trout, take one look at their vaguely brownish-yellowish flanks, and declare them "brown trout." Another sad fact we must admit about ourselves is that many of us really don't know much about the fish we catch, and we know even less about the fish we catch when we're on vacation. Many cutthroat trout are kind of brown; that's good enough for the casual angler, who doesn't even know why anyone would consider such species distinctions worth bothering with.

Rediscoveries

Sporting historians now regard *Forest and Stream* as the grand-daddy of the modern outdoor magazines. Though preceded by several important periodicals, such as *The Spirit of the Times*, quoted earlier, *Forest and Stream* was for general purposes the most authoritative outdoor periodical of its century. As the *New York Times* is the "newspaper of record" for American politics and culture today, *Forest and Stream* was almost from the time of its launching in 1873 the foremost reporter

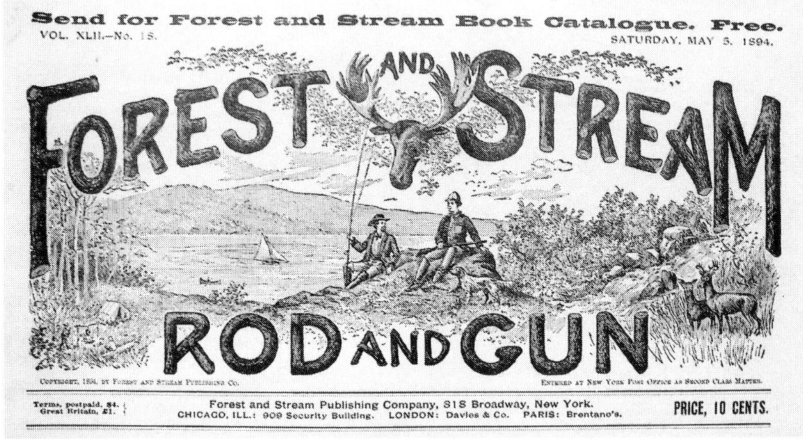

Starting in the 1870s, Forest and Stream, *the leading American sporting periodical, reported on many West Coast fly-fishing adventures, often revealing the uncertainty surrounding anglers' identification of Pacific salmon and steelhead. Courtesy of Montana State University Library.*

and commentator for the society of American outdoorsmen. It fully and competently reported any important development—whether in game management, outdoor publishing, firearms manufacture, tackle technology, wildlife conservation, natural history, or any other related subject—in good part because for many years of its long life *Forest and Stream* was under the brilliant editorship of George Bird Grinnell. Now sadly forgotten by several generations of sportsmen, Grinnell was one of the real giants in the American sporting tradition. A leading naturalist and anthropologist, a widely traveled sportsman, cofounder with Theodore Roosevelt of the Boone and Crockett Club, author of a long list of popular and authoritative books, and celebrated father of Glacier National Park, Grinnell did more than almost anyone else to shape the sporting community we belong to today.[10] Thanks to his vast network of information sources and his many connections with the scientific community, newsworthy developments having anything to do with the sporting scene routinely debuted in *Forest and Stream*'s pages. And ironically, considering that *Forest and Stream* was published on the opposite coast, it was most often in its pages that we can now watch the periodic rediscovery and flourishing of fly fishing for Pacific salmon.

Almost as soon as *Forest and Stream* appeared, it featured the occasional flurry of articles and letters from the West Coast about salmon fishing. Writers in the 1870s proclaimed their success at catching Pacific salmon with flies; other writers questioned if they were catching salmon or steelhead, which were generally known to take flies. In the August 5, 1875, issue of *Forest and Stream*, however, the editor made the following firm statement: "It used to be denied that the salmon of the Pacific would take a fly, but the ignorance on this subject arose principally from the fact that strangers did not try them at the proper seasons and places, while the resident anglers, like our friend 'Podgers,' *et al.*, who were in the habit of taking them with flies, were altogether reticent on the subject. The files of *Forest and Stream* give all the information necessary to an intelligent understanding of the matter, describing fly-fishing from Puget's Sound to San Francisco." This statement was followed with an extended reprinting of a letter from Livingston Stone, a nationally prominent fisheries authority and employee of the U.S. Fish Commission. Stone described witnessing an acquaintance catch a twenty-and-three-quarter-pound salmon from California's McCloud River, "just in front of our house."[11]

Without question, Stone knew the difference between salmon and steelhead, but those who write about these episodes today, with their greater knowledge of the species involved, tend to discount almost all such reports. I don't. I'm still skeptical about many of the early accounts, and I assume most of them involved steelhead, but let's be fair. Stone was an acknowledged fisheries expert, and among the many reports coming in from a variety of California rivers about salmon taking flies, his story must rank high on any credibility scale.[12]

I have no choice but to assume that some nonsteelhead were being taken by at least some of these fishermen in the 1870s because we now know that, given the right circumstances, all five species of Pacific salmon do take flies, and because the odds seem overwhelming that some of these anglers just had to luck into the right circumstances now and then.

That said, I also enjoy the perspective offered by Bruce Ferguson, Les Johnson, and Pat Trotter in their pioneering book *Fly Fishing for Pacific Salmon* (1985). Discussing the early years of fly fishing for steelhead on California's Eel River starting in 1890, when San Francisco fly tier John Benn made the river his home, these authors describe how the early steelheaders were probably alerted to fly fishing for the salmon

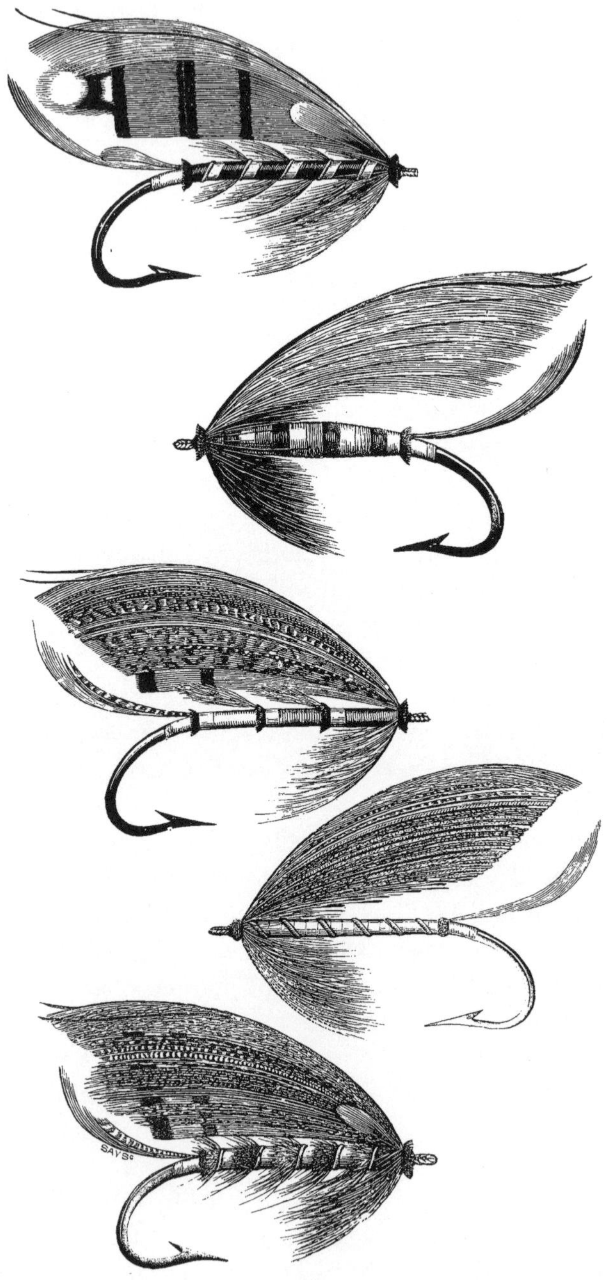

The often elegant flies developed over many years by European and eastern North American anglers proved only occasionally effective for Pacific salmon. From George Kelson, The Salmon Fly *(1896).*

that ran in the same river: "Fly fishermen, still under the influence of eastern and European techniques, usually fished steelhead with small, brightly dressed wet flies. It must have been a sight to behold when a gentleman angler would suddenly find himself contending with a 40-pound chinook salmon that had grabbed his No. 10 Professor and chugged off across the pool. Most of these encounters ended with the salmon parting the gut leader with a casual shake of the head."[13] There's no reason to imagine that similar encounters didn't occasionally happen wherever enough people cast enough flies into salmon rivers.

Salt Water

The fly fishers of the 1870s did leave us some firmer evidence of their success, however, and it was in a direction that would dominate much of West Coast fly fishing for salmon for several decades: salt water. In 1876, Cleveland Rockwell was a member of a survey party working at the mouth of the Columbia River in Baker's Bay. In a story published in *Forest and Stream* on October 30, 1879, Rockwell described rowing his dingy from the survey ship to a rocky shoreline. He had an unfamiliar "two-handed English salmon rod of ash with lancewood tips, one hundred yards of braided line, and the best flies, all furnished me by a valued friend."

Like many other narrators of sporting adventures, Rockwell claimed primacy, stating that "no salmon had ever been known before to take a fly on the Columbia river." He soon hooked a fish and gave us a breathless account of the slapstick struggle that ensued (I quote from the original *Forest and Stream* article).

> What a thrill of excitement accompanied striking the hook into the solid tongue of that first salmon! and how my heart rushed up into my throat as the alarmed fish made his first frantic rush for liberty! There was an old log or spar with a ring-bolt in the end, projecting above the water and its bottom fast in the mud, and this spar was not two rods from the rocky bluff. With what agony of apprehension I saw my salmon making for the spar with the line singing through the water! Turn him I could not, though the good rod was nearly bent double,

In 1876, topographer-artist-angler Cleveland Rockwell, long-time officer with the U.S. Coast Survey, successfully fly-fished for Pacific salmon in salt water at the mouth of the Columbia River. Image theb3579, National Oceanic and Atmospheric Administration's People Collection, Oregon Historical Society.

and holding the rod with one hand I seized an oar with the other and tried to scull the boat near enough to pass the rod over the spar as the fish went behind it. Alas! the salmon was too fast for me, and in a desperate moment as the salmon was drawing my tip around the spar, I cast the whole rod as far as I could throw it the other side of the spar, where it sank in [word unclear in original] fathoms of water. I stood for a moment in despair at what I had done; then took up the oars and pulled for the schooner. After getting my sailing master in the boat and a long pike pole, to which I lashed my salmon

> gaff, we pulled off again to the scene of disaster, and almost immediately succeeded in fishing up the rod. The line had been run out clear to the barrel of the reel. Of course I had lost my first salmon and probably half my line, and slowly and in sorrow I reeled it in, when whizz! out flew the handle from my fingers, and away went my salmon fresh for a second heat.
>
> The salmon and I fought it out on "that line" all aorund [*sic*] the harbor, and half the military post was down on the shore to see the fun, and when finally I thrust the gaff into his shining belly and lifted him into the boat, a cheer went up from the shore, which with the salmon thrashing around in the boat made me feel quite proud over the adventure. He weighed twenty-five pounds.[14]

If Rockwell's friend who lent him the tackle was there watching that day, we can only imagine what he said when he saw Rockwell pitch his expensive salmon rod and reel into the ocean.

But Rockwell's bumbling triumph presaged several generations of gradually more sophisticated saltwater fly-fishing exploits up and down the West Coast. By 1919, when A. Bryan Williams published his book *Rod & Creel in British Columbia*, he could include a brief, separate chapter devoted to "fly fishing for salmon." It was almost entirely about cohoes (Williams said that "spring salmon," or chinooks, were "occasionally" caught as well), which, by then, were well known for taking flies. He stated that trolling flies had long been the favored method, but that casting flies to the best locations had become more popular.

> The best places, however, to fish for salmon in salt water are at the mouths of any small creeks up which they go to spawn. If there has been a dry spell the cohoes and some springs congregate there waiting for enough water to go up. Not only can you catch salmon but an occasional big trout can be caught. The end of September and beginning of October is the time to try such places.
>
> As soon as there has been a good freshet most of the fish go up the streams and you can then get them in fresh water.[15]

Cleveland Rockwell's drawing of officers fishing from a boat at Fort Canby on the Columbia River. Oregon Historical Society photograph no. bb003565

This last observation is a tantalizing one that I return to later. Other writers in the early 1900s echoed these sentiments. Anglers were working their way to a better understanding of how and, perhaps more important, where and when to fly fish for saltwater salmon.

It seems generally agreed that it was in the 1930s that this sport reached a kind of maturity. In those years, Seattle angler Letcher Lambuth, one of the most innovative West Coast fly fishers of the time, began studying various species of ocean baitfish in an aquarium and developed a series of streamers to match them. The American Museum of Fly Fishing has a number of Lambuth's polar bear–hair coho streamers, and it is easy to see why their long translucent wings were a big improvement over traditional wings made of feather or bucktail. Some of Lambuth's reminiscences of his fishing in the 1920s and 1930s were finally published in 1975:

> At the height of the run the fish will frequently be jumping in every direction as far as the eye can discern

Seattle angler Letcher Lambuth, a leading West Coast fly-fishing innovator and fly-pattern theorist in the 1920s and afterward, developed numerous salmon-fly patterns. Photograph courtesy of the American Museum of Fly Fishing.

> the splashes. Frequently the jumping fish will not take the fly. We explore for those disposed to feed by casting to the side from the slowly moving boat, allowing the line to swing into the wake and then stripping in. Sometimes the fly is taken when thus trolling. More often, as the fly is stripped in, the bow wave of the fish suddenly appears near the fly and the ensuing few seconds as the angler manipulates the fly and the fish makes up his mind to strike are moments of exciting suspense. Suddenly there is a boil or splash, a surge as the hook is set, and the reel whines.[16]

The periodic rise and fall of interest in this fishing since the 1930s has been well described in the Ferguson, Johnson, and Trotter book. In fact, that book itself is one of the most important steps in the popularization of saltwater fly fishing for salmon. Its authors not only documented the many developments in recent fly fishing for salmon in

Letcher Lambuth developed his coho streamers with wings made of polar bear hair in the 1920s and 1930s. From the collection of the American Museum of Fly Fishing, photographs by Sara Wilcox.

salt water, but also advanced the sport with, among many other things, a concise photographic field guide to the relevant natural ocean food items of salmon, which they complemented by a generous selection of corresponding fly patterns. Saltwater fly fishing for salmon is now widespread as fly fishers have thoroughly explored many of the coastal travel routes of the migrating fish and continue to refine both techniques and tackle.

In our greater story of the "Pacific salmon won't rise" myth, however, all of this exciting saltwater fly fishing is little more than an aside. I suspect that although Captain Gordon and his contemporaries might have been curious about the exploits of Rockwell, Lambuth, and many other saltwater fly fishers, they would not have been moved enough by them to reconsider their position on the worthlessness of Pacific salmon. Catching salmon in the ocean wasn't the point for those British sports. In the most strict, traditional sporting terms, catching them in salt water was irrelevant. It didn't really count.

If we are seeking to track the myth that salmon won't "rise to a floi," we are necessarily concerned with the traditional Old World and eastern American definition of the term *rise*. When those proper gents spoke of salmon rising to a fly, they meant in rivers. Even more important, they meant "rising" the way Atlantic salmon rose—up through some considerable distance in the water column to the kinds of flies cast in the kinds of ways that the traditional Atlantic salmon anglers had for so long deemed "right."

Pacific salmon were indeed very often unwilling to do any such thing, and before considering how Americans responded to that problem, we require a digression into theoretical natural history to consider some of the complications of comparing Atlantic salmon and Pacific salmon as sport fish.

Life Stories

A variety of natural-history factors have been invoked to explain why, under so many circumstances, Atlantic salmon and steelhead are more willing to move considerable distances to take a fly than are the Pacific salmon. These factors provide reasonable conjecture rather than demonstrable conclusion, but that's the point, isn't it? It's all a guessing game.

George Kelson, a leading British Atlantic salmon fly-fishing authority of the late 1800s, epitomized the tackle and technique preferences of traditional salmon anglers at the time of the first serious attempts to develop methods to take Pacific salmon on flies. From George Kelson, The Salmon Fly *(1895).*

All of the fish mentioned—Atlantic salmon, steelhead, Pacific salmon—stop feeding when they leave the ocean and enter rivers on their spawning migrations. Like every other "rule" in nature, this one isn't perfect. I have friends who have caught steelhead with great numbers of freshly eaten insects in their stomachs. But it is generally true that the metabolic processes associated with the consumption and digestion of food cease when these fish enter freshwater. This complete cessation of feeding was well known even in the early days of Pacific salmon sport fishing. In *The Sportsman's Gazetteer and General Guide* (1878), Charles Hallock invoked the "fact furnished by J. W. & Vincent Cook, proprietors of the Oregon Packing Co., on the Columbia River, who have stated that out of ninety-eight thousand salmon examined by them in 1874, only three had anything in their stomachs, and these three had the appearance of having just left salt water."[17]

Considering the predisposition of these fish not to eat, we should all be amazed that we ever catch any of them in freshwater. However, folk wisdom has long suggested, first, that the feeding instinct or impulse may still be triggered now and then, even though the fish's system has no use for the food, and, second, that fish attack things for reasons other than the need for nutrition, including protection of a territory or a mate, simple annoyance, or, if I may be even less formal, just for the hell of it. Whatever we may or may not know about salmon physiology, we know less about the personalities of individual fish, and in that great imponderable of individuality is a mystery best expressed by Lee Wulff: "Why does a salmon rise? Why does a small boy cross the street just to kick a tin can?"[18] Lee Spencer's wonderful and hugely patient observational studies of steelhead in Oregon's Steamboat Creek reveal fish after fish rising to what are obviously nonfood items (at least we might presume that it's obvious to the fish that a stick or a leaf isn't food) and either nudging them or taking them in and spitting them back out.[19] We are left wondering if such behavior is brought on by the steelhead equivalent of ennui or some vague need for target practice or some other evolutionary imperative at work, but we just don't know.

As far as why Atlantic salmon and steelhead seem more willing to take flies under more circumstances than Pacific salmon are, students of their natural history might suggest that it can't be entirely a coincidence that those two species are the ones that, if they can survive the hazards of the spawning run, will live to spawn again, sometimes even three or four times. One of the very few unexcepted absolutes in salmon natural history is that every individual among the five species of Pacific salmon dies after spawning. Perhaps, a plausible conjecture suggests, the fish species with the prospect of an extended biological future are less likely to have quite as complete a behavioral disconnect from feeding impulses as are fish species that are racing sure death to the spawning grounds.

Other conjectures connect the Pacific salmons' relative willingness to take a fly to each species' individual life histories. Coho salmon, for example, usually spend two years in freshwater before migrating to the ocean. It has been proposed that this period gives them a deeper habit or "memory" of river feeding that lingers through their saltwater phase and is reactivated when they again arrive in their home river.

Cohoes have been, after all, the species most often celebrated among fly fishers.

Cohoes were the species that A. Bryan Williams emphasized as most promising for saltwater fly fishing in his 1919 book, and he emphasized them again for freshwater fly fishing: "In fishing a pool for salmon it is best to start at the head of the pool and fish down. Cast across stream at an angle of 45 degrees and let it sweep round with the current slowly, giving the fly a moderate amount of movement. Get the fly down as deep as possible as a general rule. There are, however, times when a fly worked quickly on the surface will kill better, but such cases are the exceptions."[20] Just a few years after Williams wrote this advice, a nineteen-year-old Roderick Haig-Brown caught his first coho on a fly in a small tidal stream on Vancouver Island; it took a Silver Wilkinson, a traditional Atlantic salmon fly. Judging by how often the few West Coast fly-fishing writers of that time mentioned cohoes, other anglers had to have similar experiences.

The cohoes tend to be the most commonly mentioned species in these early accounts. Chinook salmon, however, migrate from freshwater into the ocean at a much younger age and then spend proportionately more time in salt water. Thus, according to this hypothesis, any tendency for river feeding is more thoroughly muted in them. The big chinooks were certainly the species that those British sports most wanted to hook, which further explains why they were so disappointed. The chinooks looked up through ten feet of river water and saw the pretty little Atlantic salmon flies swinging over, but had absolutely no reason or need to go all the way up there to get them.

At the opposite extreme from the chinooks, the little pinks, whose entire life span is only a couple of years, go the shortest distance into the ocean from their home rivers and spend the least amount of time there. They tend to spawn in lower reaches of their rivers, still close to the sea, and perhaps retain the feeding urge for all those reasons. At least such reasoning came to my mind as these eager little salmon attacked my hot pink woolly bugger that day north of Juneau a few years ago.

Theories abound; proofs are hard to come by. They're all fascinating and mostly up for grabs. When those early fly fishers started trying to catch Pacific salmon on flies, all they knew was that it was really hard and that sometimes, for some reason they didn't yet understand, flies worked. Seeing tremendous numbers of those big, shiny, tantalizing fish rolling into the rivers each year was no doubt exasperating and drove many anglers to give up. For others, however, the sight of that potential sport just made them try harder. The fish looked so perfect. How could it *not* be possible to catch them on flies?

Captain Gordon Was Right, Sort Of

Based on a reading of the accounts of all those years of Pacific salmon fly fishing, it now appears that in order to achieve any level of consistency at fair-hooking the fish, Atlantic salmon fishermen had first more or less to abandon the notion so precious to them that there should be a way to cast a fly so that the fish will rise to it. We can track the growing success of Pacific salmon fly fishing by the step-by step development of tackle and techniques that signaled the abandonment of that hope and the acceptance of the reality that these fish required more personal service. The history of Pacific salmon fly fishing in rivers is largely the history

Atlantic salmon anglers, like this 1890s era individual playing a large salmon, were accustomed to fishing for salmon that were occasionally willing to rise considerable distances through the water column to take a fly. West Coast anglers had to adapt their techniques to salmon that, although they looked quite similar, behaved very differently. Courtesy of the American Museum of Fly Fishing.

of getting deeper more quickly and of developing a working knowledge of each river's salmon runs, holding waters, and all the other quirky factors that seem so important in almost any kind of sport fishing.[21]

In their historical review, Ferguson, Johnson, and Trotter say that success required specialized tackle all the way from the angler's hand to the fish's mouth.[22] As bamboo rods replaced the older solid wood rods, and as manufacturers began to cater to the needs of big-river anglers who needed more power, fly fishers had the wherewithal to reach the fish. As flies were reconsidered and tied to sink (whether with lead wrapped around the hook, with the early bead heads, such as Jim Pray's Optics, or by some other means), it was possible to approach deeper and deeper fish.

But Ferguson, Johnson, and Trotter place the real emphasis for success on new lines. The replacement of silk lines with modern synthetic lines, built-in fast-sinking densities "dredged" pools deeper than anglers had imagined possible only decades earlier.

It must also be said that the West Coast fly-fishing crowd dedicated themselves to cultivating some extraordinary fishing skills as part of their long, dedicated quest to reach and catch both steelhead and salmon. The Golden Gate Casting Club seems to have been the most influential presence in this quest, gathering many of the most talented and inventive fly fishers in the region and providing the laboratory they needed to refine their considerable abilities. The San Francisco Fly Casting Club and the Portland Casting Club were also very important, producing their share of expert fishermen and champion distance casters.

It is no disrespect to all these accomplishments, however, to suggest that those early British sportsmen were right. No amount of fly fishing in the nineteenth-century style was going to catch them more than the occasional Pacific salmon. The beautiful big salmon those chaps could see finning in deep holes and rolling in the open currents just weren't susceptible to the established methods. And because these anglers practiced such methods with a nearly religious conviction, I seriously doubt that they would regard themselves as having been proven wrong by today's Pacific salmon fishermen, even though today's fishermen can bring plenty of fish to the fly. The Atlantic salmon fishermen's practices did not develop in a sporting culture that prized innovation, much less such utter breaks with tradition as lead-core shooting heads and fluorescent fly patterns. Fly fishing wasn't just a matter of catching fish on a fly. It was a matter of catching fish on the fly in the right way.

Even in recent years I have seen eastern American Atlantic salmon fly fishers turn up their noses at the lead-core lines and other specialized gear required to take Pacific salmon; the issue still isn't just about hooking fish.

And there are other differences between these salmon-fishing traditions. The Atlantic salmon is a very expensive fish, and its fishing is in good part an elite or at least an exclusive social practice, centuries deep in guides and lodges and fiercely restricted fishing rights. Pacific salmon on the West Coast of the United States were and are almost all swimming in public rivers, and the fly fishers who figured out how to catch them were not a particularly upscale crowd. Many of the proudest parts of the Atlantic salmon tradition, such as its glorious craft of fly tying, grew out of the sport's high cost. If there is a corresponding symbol of West Coast salmon fly tying—at least before the past thirty or so years, when fly tiers have adapted and adopted older traditions so beautifully—it may be Jim Pray's Optics, which may look, to some at least, more like the product of a plumber's workshop than a fly dresser's cabinet.

The social lessons here are mixed, of course. Exclusivity provides the economic conditions and incentives that keep Atlantic salmon rivers alive, whereas the overused Pacific salmon rivers of the West Coast have long suffered, sometimes fatally, from the tragedy of the commons.

Other parts of this story drift into ethical ruminations. Although all the Pacific salmon are known—at least some of the time—to inhale a fly voluntarily or even aggressively, that's not the only way we catch them. Now that we have the equipment to reach them even in deep water, we also have the ability simply to feed a fly right into a salmon's mouth. Repeatedly drifting a fly through a group of salmon can and does result in salmon being involuntarily hooked in the mouth—they are "fair-hooked" without having taken any active part in the process. Traditional sport fishing for almost all fish species implicitly required the fish's active participation; the fish had to be tricked into wanting to eat the bait, or lure, or fly. We're doing something different here.

A variation on this new ability to hook a nonparticipating salmon is casting the fly beyond the group of fish so that the line, rather than the fly, drifts again and again through the fish until the line or leader enters a fish's mouth. As the bellying line drifts downstream, it draws itself sideways across the back of the fish's jaws until the hook reaches the jaw's hinge and becomes embedded. Again, the fish is "fair-hooked"

Jim Pray created his series of Optic flies in the 1940s. These flies, heavily weighted with a large metal eye, were among the breakthroughs necessary to allow anglers to reach deep into fast-flowing coastal streams. From the collections of the American Museum of Fly Fishing, photographs by Sara Wilcox.

because the fly, embedded just outside the fish's mouth, is close enough for both traditional sporting ethics and usually whatever laws are in effect about such things. In Alaska, this tactic goes by the charming term *flossing*.[23]

I've flossed an Alaskan salmon or two. It didn't seem like an important sin, and the fish was really exciting to play and land, but I knew I wasn't quite meeting my own definition of fly fishing. We owe it to ourselves and to the salmon to think hard about what we're doing in these situations. Such adjustments and compromises of older rules are often the way fly fishing evolves, and such evolution is often an edgy and even controversial matter.[24]

A New World, Found and Lost

To appreciate the progress that fly fishers made in figuring out how to take Pacific salmon in the first half of the twentieth century, there's a book you really ought to read. It is odd that the small specialty of Pacific salmon fly fishing should include an authentic literary gem in its modest library, but Russell Chatham's *The Angler's Coast* is just such a book. First published to apparently slight sales in 1976, the book was lavishly reprinted in 1990.[25] The first edition is getting hard to find, but I recommend the second edition, anyway, both because it is handsomely produced and because it contains many, many photographs that demonstrate beyond any doubt that the old myth should have died in the 1950s.

Myths don't work that way, of course. They hardly ever die, certainly not abruptly. They may outlive their usefulness and fade, but they tend to hang on for a long time in dusty corners of our collective memory, just waiting their chance to reassure, entertain, or mislead us again. In any case, mere proof of a myth's falsehood has never stood much chance against the mysterious cultural durability such beliefs have.

At least for anyone who cares to know better, however, Chatham's book is the answer. Though the salmon-fishing stories in his book are to a great extent autobiographical, the central figure is Bill Schaadt, who between the 1940s and 1980s became, not just in Chatham's view, "perhaps the greatest fly-fisherman who ever lived."[26] The stories of Schaadt's exploits on California's Eel, Russian, Smith, and other rivers,

Bill Schaadt, regarded as one of the greatest of Pacific salmon and steelhead fly fishers, with a king salmon from the Smith River in northern California in about 1969 or 1970. Photograph by Dan Blanton.

profusely illustrated with photographs of anglers grunting to hold up enormous chinook salmon, indicate a problem solved. The fish, the big ones that weighed thirty, forty, and even fifty pounds—the descendants of the ones that Captain Gordon had eyed so wistfully and hopelessly—were taken on flies.

There is, by the way, something happily reassuring about photographs in a book like this. Even if you trust the author completely, somewhere in your darker doubts must linger a question: Can things like this really happen? They sure never happen to most of us. Could fishing anywhere, ever, have been this incredibly good? Photographs settle those questions and bring a solidity to the story. The startling photographs in the 1990 edition of *The Angler's Coast* reveal a significance in Chatham's text that I had not realized I was missing. When I saw all those pictures, the book became, in addition to an adventure story and a testament against the blind greed that has destroyed so many wonderful California rivers, a historical document of grand proportions, rather like Eliot Porter's book of photographs of Glen Canyon before the dam was built.

About a century passed between the time of the first pronouncements that Pacific salmon wouldn't take a fly and the time that anglers perfected methods for taking even the biggest and least accessible of those fish. The answers weren't mystically complicated, but they took a great deal of hard work to find. Pacific salmon fishing didn't reward passionate devotion to traditional angling methods. It didn't require aristocratic fly rods and reels or elegant, time-honored fly patterns. Instead, it demanded the vision to develop the special casting skills, the variety of very heavy lines tailored to each individual reach or hole in the river, and the smart persistence that most big, difficult-to-reach fish require. By the time of Schaadt, Chatham, and their growing number of companions and counterparts up and down the coast in the second half of the 1900s, the Pacific salmon was neither unreachable nor uncatchable. The fishing was still often difficult, but no more so than Atlantic salmon fishing could be. It was just different.

Sad to say, it would turn out that the difficulty of catching the fish wasn't the worst thing these anglers had to worry about, but rather the destruction of the river habitats and the overdevelopment of the river valleys, things that have more or less ended the terrific fly-fishing opportunities that are so well chronicled in Chatham's book. In a very short time, the stories he tells went from being simply a celebration of good times among nature's abundance to being a eulogy for a beautiful spectacle stolen from us. It's nice that fly fishers worked out their methods before the rivers were ruined, but it just makes the loss all the more tragic.

Truth

The historical loose end in this tale is the origin of the myth that Pacific salmon wouldn't take flies. What, if anything, did Captain Gordon say, and why did he say it?

When Roderick Haig-Brown captured his first fly-caught coho, mentioned earlier, his companion immediately told him that he had just disproved what that "other Englishman" had said long before

(British-born Haig-Brown had immigrated to Canada only a year earlier). For decades, Haig-Brown encountered the story again and again. He said, "It didn't sound like very good history to me," but thirty years later, in the 1950s, he finally traced it to an unpublished manuscript in the British Columbia provincial archives.[27] The manuscript was something of a memoir left by Roderick Finlayson, who had been in charge of Fort Victoria on Vancouver Island in late summer of 1845 when Captain Gordon (whose ship was actually named the HMS *America*) visited. According to Finlayson, he and Gordon hunted deer, but it appears likely that Gordon never actually tried fly fishing for Pacific salmon. Finlayson said their deer hunting was unsuccessful:

> The Captain felt very disappointed and was anything but happy. I said to him I was very sorry we had missed the deer etc., and also remarked how beautiful the country looked. He said in reply—"Finlayson, I would not give the most barren hills in the Highlands of Scotland for all I see around me." . . . In the morning we had a nice salmon for breakfast. The Captain seemed somewhat surprised and asked where the salmon was had. Oh, we have plenty of salmon was the reply. Have you got flies and rods, said the Captain. We have lines and bait was the answer and sometimes the Indians take them with the net, etc. No fly, no fly, responded our guest. So after breakfast we went to fish with the line, from a dingey. When we came back we had four fine salmon, but he thought it an awful manner in which to catch salmon.[28]

In a later, privately published version of the same episode, Finlayson apparently modified the tale somewhat. In describing the occasion of their fishing experience, Finlayson reportedly wrote about Gordon as follows: "Another day he was preparing his rod to fish for salmon with the fly, when I told him the salmon would not take the fly but were fished with bait. I then prepared fishing tackle with bait for him, and he went in a boat to the mouth of the harbour, where he caught several fine salmon with bait. His exclamation on his return was, 'What a country, where the salmon will not take the fly.'"[29] This version indicates that Gordon did have fly-fishing gear with him and perhaps that Vancouver Island wasn't the only place where he had tried to catch Pacific salmon.

If so, then his offhand dismissal of the salmon of this vast sport fishery was at least based on a little more experience than his conversation with Finlayson.

Nevertheless, if this is all there is to the story, and if the myth was somehow launched by Finlayson's relating the conversation to others, who put it into print, then it's a pretty thin origin story. Not only did Gordon never directly connect the British Empire's keeping of the territory to the quality of fishing, but he wasn't even faintly qualified to make the statement in the first place, having fly fished so little, if at all, for Pacific salmon.

There must be more to learn. Did Gordon talk to other local anglers who had themselves tried to fly fish for these salmon? How, precisely, did this casual comment by Gordon become so well known? According to "Chinook," quoted at the beginning of this chapter, Gordon eventually wrote to the earl of Aberdeen, foreign secretary and later prime minister of England (who, according to Finlayson, was Gordon's brother) and specifically made the statement in writing in that letter. Maybe that letter was published, or perhaps the earl of Aberdeen made reference to it in some writings or speeches of his own. There is more searching to do.

So far, such a search is well beyond my means, and the various British friends I have pestered about this question insist that they have actual lives and aren't willing to occupy themselves permanently looking for this particular needle in the British archival haystack.

In the meantime, British fly-fishing historian Reverend Robert Spaight has tossed an entertaining monkey wrench into the works by suggesting that the statement may not even have originated with Gordon and may even predate Gordon's visit to Vancouver Island by as much as a decade. According to one historical account, the statement might have been made by William Lamb, the Second Viscount Melbourne, who was both uncle and first prime minister of Queen Victoria.[30]

This information causes me to wonder if the myth of the uncatchable salmon is, like so many other things about the sport of fly fishing, without a single point of origin—at least without a point that we can definitely identify. By the 1830s or 1840s, any number of gentleman anglers from either Europe or eastern America might have had a chance to cast a fly on those wonderful Pacific Coast rivers. Their combined informal lament over the reluctance of all those big beautiful salmon to cooperate may just have worked its way into the public conversation over time. Perhaps it was only the most notable of those people whose comments were written down, and thus only those comments survived to modern times.

But it sure would be nice to know where it all started.

9 The Long Haul

Where Did the Double Haul Come from, and Why Didn't It Get Here Sooner?

Surely one of the most entertaining moments in the long history of competitive fly casting occurred in 1937, when Marvin Hedge, a big Portland, Oregon, angler with a remarkably athletic casting style, stepped to the platform of the British Casting Association in London. But the moment is best savored today if we pause for some historical stage setting.

Hedge was in the vanguard of a revolution in casting technique and technology, and deserves to be remembered because he and his pals had so much to do with how we fish today. To give you a sense of proportion about this revolution, consider that in 1934 in St. Louis, Hedge established a new American distance fly-casting record. Like many athletic records, this one had crept up slowly, inch by inch, over the years and stood at 125 feet. But on a sweltering Missouri day, in a Bob Beamon–like moment, Hedge surpassed that seemingly extraordinary distance by *22 feet!* This wasn't a new record; it was a new world.[1]

In 1937, Hedge's European conquests began in France at the invitation of the great French hotelier and angler Charles Ritz. In Paris, Hedge outcast the European champion, Albert Godart, by nine feet. But when he moved on to London, the British were still skeptical. As Hedge prepared to cast, he saw that the judges had placed their boat in its accustomed spot at the far end of the casting pond, well beyond the distance reached by British casters. Hedge politely called to them that they were in the way of his cast, but they apparently dismissed his remark as bravado and told him to get on with it.

Pioneering American tournament caster Marvin Hedge in action in the 1940s. Photograph courtesy of Gwen Wethern and The Creel.

He did. His line sailed out, draped itself across the judge's boat, and continued to unroll well past the amazed officials. The fly landed in the water right in front of the honorable secretary of the British Casting Association, who shouted, "Hey! I say there! It's sinking! *It's sinking!*"[2]

The cast was almost 170 feet—the British record was 123—and to add injury to insult, the judges disallowed it, apparently because of their own interference. Hedge had to settle for a 151 footer as his official best that day, but the British casters were impressed and couldn't wait to learn his "secret."

The Secret

Hedge's secret, besides his great skill and his finely tuned equipment (he painstakingly polished his lines with graphite dust before every session, to reduce friction), was the double haul, often then known as the "double-line haul." And although some later writers have mistakenly credited him or one of his contemporaries with "inventing" this fundamental part of modern fly casting, there is no question that he was enormously important in its popularization.

Where did it come from? Hedge and others of his day had memories of seeing anglers double hauling on big western steelhead rivers even in the early 1920s. The technique seems to have been around for some years even before he, rodmaker Bill Phillipson, and a few others made it famous in the 1930s and 1940s.[3]

Reaching back into the fainter and fainter memories of these pioneering modern distance casters isn't really the best way to track this story. We'd do better to come at the story from the other end—from the days before the double haul existed and even before it was possible. Maybe once we have a better idea of when it became practical, we'll be able to guess when it became real.

Shorter Rods for Longer Casts

In his superb new book *The Fly-Fisher's Craft: The Art and History* (2006), Darrel Martin chronicles the gradual development of fly rods and lines since medieval times.[4] The written record of fly fishing over the past six hundred or so years is often spotty in such particulars as casting, but it does give us a general idea of how we got here.

But we have to read it sympathetically and get past our graphite- and fluorocarbon-induced sense of superiority if we want to understand the sport's earlier generations. I must repeat a point I made earlier in this book: although it's true that at first glance our angling forefathers may look like hicks with sticks, they were really good at catching fish, including savvy, hard-fished trout in easily accessible streams. Earlier anglers weren't innocents. They just had simpler tackle.

In fact, for most of the past two thousand years, their outfits resembled the cane-pole rig I learned to fish with as a child. Even in the 1700s, the typical British trout fisher's fly line was just a little longer than his fly rod and was firmly attached to the rod tip. People who fished for big salmon or maybe pike might use a reel (they called it a "winch"), but I suspect that it was well into the 1800s before the majority of trout fishers bothered with one. If a trout fisher wanted a little

Published illustrations showing fly-casting techniques are extremely rare in books prior to the mid-1800s. This somewhat stylized and amusing woodcut published in 1834 seems to show an angler making an energetic backcast. From Stephen Oliver, Scenes and Recollections of Fly-Fishing, in Northumberland, Cumberland, and Westmorland *(1834).*

more line control, he might have a small loop of heavy cord at the rod tip through which his line ran down to his hand. This was the "loop rod," endorsed and celebrated by David Webster in his book *The Angler and the Loop Rod* (1885), mentioned in earlier chapters. It allowed a little handier retrieval of some line when playing a fish.

Even without a loop rod, however, the system wasn't bad. People fished farther away simply by using longer rods. Fifteen- and even twenty-foot rods weren't uncommon for larger fish, and every now and then in the eighteenth- and nineteenth-century books you'll find a reference to rods longer than that, presumably used by hefty anglers who could hoist and manage such a thing for hours on end. A twenty-foot rod gave you approximately a forty-foot reach, which is more than most modern trout-fishing casts.

String Theory

Most fly lines before about 1800 made these big rods all the more necessary. As mentioned in chapter four, the lines often were assembled of

Prior to the development of modern lines and rods, fly fishers often used extremely long rods, like that used by this mid-nineteenth-century Atlantic salmon fisherman. From Colonel James Edward Alexander, Salmon Fishing in Canada, by a Resident *(1860).*

knotted segments of twisted horsehair. Segments were maybe a couple feet long, depending on the line maker's needs, and each segment was made with progressively fewer strands of hair, thus creating a nice taper that stepped down from twenty or so hairs at the butt to five or even fewer at the tip, thus allowing for the smooth transfer of energy necessary for a tidy, accurate cast.

Of course, the knots that connected the segments wouldn't have run smoothly through guides, so unless you had that one big loop at the end of the rod and were willing to risk the line getting hung up even on it, there wasn't much point in having any extra line to give to a fish so it could run. You fished the line you had, raising and lowering the rod depending on the distance you needed.

In the later 1700s and early 1800s, however, anglers began to discard the knotted horsehair fly lines in favor of a variety of smoother lines made possible by advances in line-making technology. Anglers built lines from combinations of silk, grass, and hair, then gradually settled on silk alone. After 1800, more and more rods appeared with guides along their whole length, reels became more popular, and fishermen discovered the joys of having extra "running line" for handling a big fish. By the mid-1800s, thanks to silk lines and good reels, most fly fishers could not only retrieve line, but even shoot a little of it. The traditional fly fisher now became, to a much greater and more ambitious extent, a fly caster.[5]

Angling historian John Betts has traced the growing popularity of the false cast to this great period of change in the early 1800s. The false cast didn't just enable the angler to redirect his cast better; it set him up to develop the trajectory and power needed for much longer casts.[6]

Thoroughly Modern Casting

Once the average fly fisher could cast, shoot, retrieve, and otherwise manipulate the line, practically no time at all passed until the competitive urge kicked in. Bypassing the obvious opportunities for Freudian commentary presented by a bunch of guys standing around waving really big sticks in the air, we notice that the first American fly-casting tournaments started around 1860 and soon became a big deal, much more widely publicized throughout the sporting press in the late 1800s than their counterparts are today.

As far as the origin of the double haul goes, here is what I think happened then. Almost as soon as these smart, well-coordinated, and energetic people had nice, smooth fly lines with equally smooth metal guides for them to slide through, they had to notice the advantages of increased line speed. As they whipped a big long silk line into a backcast, whether they were using a solid-wood rod or one of the new-fangled split bamboo models that became popular in the 1870s, they couldn't help feel the dynamics of the line's powerful motions.

I'm sure of this scenario because more than thirty years ago, when I first put a shooting head with a fine monofilament running line on my Fenwick ten-weight glass rod, even someone of my limited skills could feel those things; all the apparent gibberish I had been reading about the double haul suddenly became clear. I learned when to haul mostly by feeling the line tell me when it was time to haul. Once the tools existed, the talent had to follow. (In my own case, talent was in somewhat short supply, but I eventually did become moderately proficient at responding to what the line was telling me to do.)

Frank Moore (left) and Steve Rajeff, two modern masters of distance casting for steelhead and salmon, on the North Umpqua River near Steamboat, Oregon. Photograph by Dale Greenley.

Competitive caster R. B. Lawrence in the middle of a long cast in a tournament in the 1880s. From Edward Samuels, With Fly Rod and Camera *(1890).*

I am also sure of it because when you look at the earliest photographs of these tournament casters in the late 1800s, say in Edward Samuels's *With Fly Rod and Camera* (1890), it is unimaginable that these fellows couldn't feel the same dynamics in a long cast line that we do today. There's a wonderful photograph of R. B. Lawrence making an eighty-nine footer. Set aside his suit and fancy hat for a moment and just concentrate on that arm stretching behind him in a backcast worthy of Lefty Kreh. As the line drifts back, and the line hand keeps the tension tight, it would eventually be little more than reflex for Mr. Lawrence to feel the urge to give a little tug.[7]

That is why I believe that at least some of these people did just that. I think that the single and double haul were probably "discovered" many times over the years between 1850 and 1937, usually by anglers with no need or opportunity to share the trick. We invent and reinvent things all the time.

This description of events takes nothing away from Hedge and his colleagues in the 1930s. They had to discover the double haul for themselves and then incorporate it into the entire system of new rods, new lines, and new rivers that made up their fishing world. And when they did, they made the most of it.[8]

10 Grasshopper Country

On August 28, 1972, which seems both a long time ago and only yesterday, I caught my first bragging-size brown trout. "Bragging size" is a context-driven notion, of course, and the salient context that day included my then brief two-month career as a fly fisher and the modest size and reputation of the stream I was fishing. Under those circumstances, my fifteen-inch brown, caught on a Joe's Hopper, was worth the accolades it received when I took it back to the bunkhouse and showed it off to my fellow Yellowstone seasonals—most of whom probably hoped that by being nice and praising the fish, they'd get to eat it.

But there is even more context. Every fish we catch is a story reaching backward and forward in our experience and revealing more the harder we think about it. At the time I caught that fish, I owned about six flies. Seasonal ranger salaries were not only small, they were, well, seasonal. Lucky for me, I had seen so few fishermen's vests and fly boxes that I had no idea how many flies one was "supposed" to have to do this right. I needed only one at a time, right?

But I can say for certain that among that first little crew of flies, the Joe's Hopper that I caught the brown on was without question the star. According to the primitive fishing log I kept that first summer, I used the hopper more than all the others combined. I had been using it almost exclusively for a month when I caught the brown and would have seen no reason to change my ways after such a triumph.

I say using "it," although possibly not all my hopper fishing was done with the very same fly. For all I know now, I might have lost one

Open-meadow streams in sprawling western landscapes, in this case Flat Creek near Jackson, Wyoming, are home to grand populations of grasshoppers in season—and to equally grand fly fishing with hopper imitations. Photograph by the author.

hopper in a fish, bought a new one, eventually lost it, too, and bought yet another (I bought flies one at a time, with almost as much soul searching and deliberation as other people put into buying cars). But considering the chewed-back leaders I used those first couple years, on which the finer diameter tippet was quickly gone, I probably didn't break off many flies. The point is that from my start as a fly fisher, I was a hard-core hopper fisherman.

At the time, Joe's Hopper seemed to me the gold standard for grasshopper imitation, but then it was also the only standard I knew. Some said that a Muddler Minnow could be greased with flotant (Chap-Stick worked well in a pinch) and used for hopper fishing. Some even said it worked as well as Joe's Hopper (not for me). It was also known, at least among the literati I had not yet met, that other parts of the country had their own distinct answers to the grasshopper question. If you talked to well-traveled anglers, you might hear of the Letort Hopper, the Pontoon Hopper, the Whitlock Hopper, and others.

But if you dropped by your typical dusty little fly shop in Montana or Wyoming in those days, what you'd get if you asked for a hopper was Joe's. If they were out of Joe's Hopper, they'd probably suggest the Muddler or a Humpy. I eventually considered the Sofa Pillow—though formally intended to imitate a very large stonefly—a reasonable hopper alternative, but I always fished Joe's Hopper with more confidence.

Joe Who?

Nobody seemed to know for sure who Joe was. I later heard, informally, that Joe was in fact Joe Brooks, the great *Outdoor Life* fishing editor of the mid–twentieth century, but it appears that the creation of the pattern predated Joe Brooks's career. However, I have also heard, just as informally, that the fly was given his name because he was such a successful popularizer of the Michigan Hopper (more on this pattern later) that people began to call it Joe's Hopper. George Grant, one of the West's original fly historians, tried to pin down the source of the name and was never able to learn more than that as a western fly pattern, Joe's Hopper was "evidently first used with success by a 'guy named Joe.'"

Perhaps more important, Grant did discover that as you traveled around the West, you could "find this same pattern assuming the name of 'Jack's Hopper' or 'Jim's Hopper,'"[1] leading us to the conjecture that the name "Joe" was just the market's way of saying "some guy." After all, would you buy a fly called "Some Guy's Hopper"?

Not that the real Joe, if there were one, had any right to feel deprived of historical glory when we lost track of him. As Grant also points out, Joe didn't invent the fly anyway. And it wasn't even western. Grant explains the situation like this:

> It would be difficult for most Montana fly fishermen to concede that "Joe's Hopper" did not ride the riffles of the Madison or the Big Hole before it was used elsewhere, but the original of this fly was known as the 'Michigan Hopper' and was created by Art Winnie of Traverse City, Michigan.
>
> It is consoling to realize that we adopted another's child, gave it a new name, dressed it quite well, provided it with an exciting place to live, and proudly presented it as though it was our own.[2]

Though I imagine that Grant is right about all this, I still must inject a little more uncertainty here. It comes to us courtesy of another George, George Leonard Herter, whose writings constitute the foremost loose cannon in the study of American fly-fishing history. Herter's once-world-famous fishing-tackle catalog business prospered well into the 1970s as a sort of proto-Cabela's, and Herter himself wrote an outrageously entertaining series of books on the outdoors, cooking, and life.[3] His self-published *Professional Fly Tying, Spinning, and Tackle Making Manual and Manufacturers' Guide* first appeared in 1941 and was, according to the fine print in the front of my copy, in its revised nineteenth edition by 1971. Almost six hundred pages long by 1971, Herter's book was enormously detailed and helpful, was praised by some very prominent outdoorsman, and has been conspicuously ignored by the fly-fishing establishment's authorities, who are apparently offended by his lack of decorum and his broadside attacks on many of the sports other famous experts.

Like Herter's famous catalogs, the fly-tying book is notorious for his generous self-promotion and what amounts to an alternative American history in which Herter and his friends were the center of the universe (see his comments on streamers in chapter eleven for further evidence of this approach). Still, it's worth checking in with Herter now and then just to keep us from ever being too sure of ourselves. He certainly had a different view of the Joe's Hopper story: "JOE HOPPER: Invented in 1929 by George Leonard Herter and named for Joseph McLin. This hopper has proved itself to be one of the great stream trout and pan-fish killers. It is widely used throughout North America."[4] Joe McLin's name figured in several Herter patterns, so I assume he was a friend or possibly a guide whom Herter knew and respected.

Though it would be easy enough to simply ignore Herter—at least that's the approach taken by most popular writers on fly-fishing history—we would be wise to hear him out now and then, if only because mixed in with all the bluster and chaff there may well be some truth. The problem is that it is very hard to identify. Perhaps, as George Grant suggests, Herter's Joe was just one of the Joes invoked by the fly pattern's various popularizers over the years.

Lost in the happy provincialism that was still possible along a western trout stream in 1972, my universe was uncomplicated by any knowledge of this history. Joe's Hopper was the fly for me, whoever Joe was—or were.

Modern fly shops routinely feature dozens of hopper patterns, typically with foam bodies, rubber legs, and other elements far removed from earlier generations of grasshopper imitations. This photograph by the author shows a case at George Anderson's Yellowstone Angler in Livingston, Montana.

But over the next thirty or so years, hopper patterns would come into their own. Before sitting down to write this chapter, I stopped by one of Bozeman's 411 fly shops and looked through their generous bin bank of hoppers—herds of hair, acres of foam, miles of rubber legs, battalions of parachutes, rainbows of fluorescents. One or two patterns looked so good I wanted to eat them myself. The hopper has clearly arrived.

But why did it take so long to get here?

Pretty Much Our Fly

As I've pointed out a number of times, many of the things we American anglers have convinced ourselves we invented—streamers, for example, or saltwater fly fishing—were actually done earlier in England. The use of grasshopper imitations are, at first glance, a good example. Many of the earliest British fishing books mentioned this or that grasshopper pattern, just as they routinely mentioned using live grasshoppers for bait.

Naturalist John Taverner, writing in 1600, favored the grasshopper among his baits for several fish species.[5] In 1614, Gervase Markham, probably because he read Taverner, made the same recommendation.[6] In 1659, in a discussion of insects to imitate, Thomas Barker added: "The Graffe-hopper which is green, imitate that. The fmaller thefe flyes be made, and of indifferent fmall hooks, they are better." For the bait fishermen, he added "your graffe-hopper which is green is to be had in any meadow or grafs in June or July."[7] James Chetham, in 1689, recommended two hopper patterns, the "Green Grafhopper," which had "Dubbing of Green and Yellow Wooll mix'd, rib'd over with Green Silk, and a Red Capons Feather over all," and the "Dun Grafhopper," which had "the Body flender, made of Dun Camlet, and a Dun Hackle at top."[8] But when I checked Charles Cotton's great 1676 masterpiece essay on fly fishing, I was reminded that Chetham was often not original; he obviously lifted these two hopper patterns nearly verbatim from Cotton's fly list for June.[9] Walton himself recommended both artificial hoppers and live ones, and said the latter were especially good for dapping "behind a tree, or in any deep hole."[10]

And yet even with the enthusiasm for hoppers displayed by all these authorities, grasshoppers seem not to be a significant element of modern fly fishing in the United Kingdom. At least my British friend and fly-fishing historian Andrew Herd sees it that way:

> The one really, really sad thing about living in the UK is that there is no opportunity to use hopper patterns. We do have grasshoppers, but they are small, live in low densities and rarely seem to fall in rivers. No doubt they do once in a blue moon and fish will take them because they make a good meal, but never in my wildest dreams would I actually go fishing with a hopper in the expectation of catching a fish rising to them.
>
> It is possible that in the past, when farm chemicals were less ubiquitous and grasshopper counts were higher that these insects did form a greater part of trout diets, but the trouble is that terrestrials became deeply unfashionable from the mid 18th to the early 20th century and so the

> literature isn't very helpful on the subject. But I have my doubts that hopper-fests ever were that common.[11]

I have also wondered if some of the insects that the early authors described as "grasshoppers" belonged to other insect families that we might now call "leafhoppers" or by some other name. The United Kingdom has at least a couple dozen species of genuine grasshoppers, but as Herd notes, they have not played the role in U.K. fishing that their counterparts have played here in the United States. So it turns out that this area of fly development and theory, in fact, is one in which we Americans launched our own original and largely uninherited inquiry.

The Victorian Hopper

Before crossing the Atlantic, however, we need to consider the combination of whimsy and mystery that characterized grasshopper imitations in British fishing circles in the late 1800s because some of the same characteristics appeared in American hopper theory of that period.

For me, the imitations that most perfectly capture the odd charm of this era in hopper fishing appear in Hewett Wheatley's extraordinary book *The Rod and Line* (1849), which prescribed the creation of an "artificial bait" to be cast with a fly rod. He called it a grasshopper, but it was in shape a tapered worm, green with yellow ribbing, tied on a leaded, eyed hook. It had no wings or legs, just the steeply tapered body (an alternative version had a treble hook as an outrigger on a short leader, dangling alongside the body).[12]

The eminent British angling authority Francis Francis, writing in 1867, provided a description and illustration of Wheatley's grasshopper and then expressed both admiration and vexation at this oddly shaped and even more oddly named fly: "The most slaughtering way of fishing for grayling is with the grasshopper. The grasshopper, so-called, is not a grasshopper at all, though actually an artificial bait, in nowise resembles a grasshopper; why it should have been called a grasshopper any more than a gooseberry, which it much more resembles, I cannot conceive. No matter; this is the grasshopper."[13] The only theory I can offer about why a wingless, legless, green-and-yellow, tapered, wormlike thing should be called a grasshopper is that for at least two and a half centuries before Wheatley's time, angling writers had recommended that anglers using live grasshoppers as bait should cut off the wings and legs.[14] Wheatley's grasshopper wouldn't be that improbable if it had a grasshopper's wings and legs.

It remains a mystery to me, however, why all these authoritative earlier angling writers should have so strongly insisted on removing the wings and legs of grasshoppers when modern fly theorists have for many years puzzled over how to imitate the actions of swimming grasshoppers, whose frantically thrashing wings and legs are thought to provide the very motions that attract trout.

As British fishing historian Frederick Buller has pointed out, the Wheatley "grasshoppers" also shared a similarity of shape with the category of lures known as "Devil Baits," as illustrated in Thomas Salter's *The Angler's Guide* (6th ed., 1825) and other works of the period.[15] So the Wheatley grasshopper's actual category of definition remains unclear.

But I bet it would work great on the Madison.

The American Revelation

Whatever may have been the status of grasshoppers in England, we had lots of them in America. Especially on the Great Plains, appropriate habitats in the Intermountain West, and the Pacific Coast, the grasshopper was among the species that met ecologist Aldo Leopold's definition of a "biological storm." Like the bison, the passenger pigeon, several species of salmon, and any number of other now sadly reduced species, the grasshopper was not so much an animal as a spectacle.

A few miles east of my neighborhood in Montana, traveling along the Yellowstone River on July 16, 1806, Captain William Clark was among the very first commentators to try to comprehend the abundance of grasshoppers in the American West: "It may be proper to observe that the emence Sworms of Grass hoppers have destroyed every Sprig of Grass for maney miles on this Side of the river, and appear to be progressing upwards."[16]

Not coincidentally, it is thanks to Clark's expedition that we know that at least one American tackle shop was selling grasshopper imitations in his day. Attached to a receipt for various basic supplies (including lots of fish hooks) purchased by Clark from George Lawton's shop in Philadelphia was a one-page circular that described and promoted Lawton's full line of tackle, including "Grafshoppers," among many other artificial baits, lures, and flies.[17] Judging from his invoice, Clark appears not to have bought any grasshoppers, and as long as his supply of hooks held out he wouldn't have needed them anyway, considering how many live grasshoppers were handy for his use.

Awed mentions of grasshopper plagues recur regularly in nineteenth-century western narratives. In my studies of American wildlife history, I've read many hundreds of early travel accounts of the Rocky Mountain West and have frequently encountered these shocked outbursts. Early travelers alternated between complaining that they couldn't keep grasshoppers out of the cook pot, their shirts, and everywhere else, and bragging about how many fish they caught on them.

The most famous grasshopper episode in American history textbooks must be the saga of the "Mormon crickets" that threatened the early Mormon settlers' crops in Utah in 1848 and were destroyed by the timely and evidently divine intervention of seagulls.[18] Other similar visitations by the grasshoppers were not so successfully met, however. Environmental historian Richard White describes a much more widespread and economically disastrous grasshopper eruption a quarter-century later: "In a bad year, such as 1874, the grasshoppers swarmed into the northern prairies in such numbers that farmers mistook them for storm clouds massing on the horizon. When the insects alighted, they sounded like hail. They fell from the skies until they lay four to six inches deep on the ground. Their weight on trees snapped off limbs, and when trains tried to move over them on the tracks, their crushed bodies greased the tracks and left the engine's wheels spinning uselessly. Grasshoppers ate the crops; they fouled the water. Attracted by the salt left from human sweat, they even ate tool handles."[19]

Although the West established the greatest legends of grasshoppers, they were sufficiently abundant in many parts of the East to justify anglers' creation of a variety of imitations. Early-nineteenth-century fly-fishing tracts in America were heavily derivative of British works, and British works themselves were also available, but before long American anglers were taking a hard look at grasshoppers and developing their own imitations. How could they not, when many must have had experiences like that of Thaddeus Norris, who, writing of the trout's fondness for grasshoppers in 1864, said that "the grasshopper is a good big mouthful; sometimes as the angler grasps his prize, to disengage the hook, he feels them crush like rumpled paper, as if wings and legs were cracking beneath his fingers."[20]

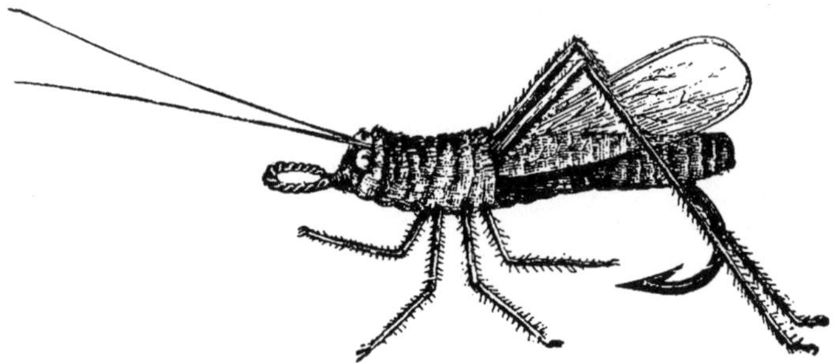

Vermont tackle manufacturer Thomas Chubb offered this reasonably realistic grasshopper pattern in his 1890 catalog. It featured fish-scale wings and came in both green and yellow. The body appears to be made of chenille or some similar material. Courtesy of the American Museum of Fly Fishing.

Robert Barnwell Roosevelt, one of American fly fishing's more critical yet open-minded thinkers in the mid–nineteenth century, expressed great skepticism about the flurry of exact-imitation bug replicas that were on the market in the 1860s. I don't know for sure because so little of the original assortment of commercial lures from that day has survived, but I suspect he was talking about things quite similar to what George Lawton claimed to be offering half a century earlier: "In addition to the imitations of the natural fly, efforts have been continually made to use artificial representations of the other food and baits for fish; exact and beautiful copies of grasshoppers and frogs have been constructed, and painted of the proper color, but either from the nature of the composition or some other cause, entirely in vain. Indeed it is doubtful whether any fish was ever captured with such delusions as grasshoppers, crickets, or frogs, and although they are still retained in the shops, they no longer find a place amid the angler's paraphernalia."[21]

Tackle historian and fly-rod lure authority Jim Brown has suggested a reason for the perceived and real shortcomings of these exact-model grasshoppers: "We may never know for sure, but I bet Roosevelt and others that took offense at molded rubber grasshoppers were at least in part expressing a taste for personal craft rather than manufactured product. Plus, I'm convinced that the old hard rubber bugs were easily damaged. I don't think the rubber that they used back then is like the soft kind that they use in rubber worms today."[22]

Whether anglers continued to buy them or not, the lures-baits-flies did continue to show up in both catalogs and books. A. B. Shipley and Son, a well-known Philadelphia tackle dealer, advertised and illustrated an apparently lifelike grasshopper in *Forest and Stream* in 1881, the year the same illustration was used in James Henshall's *Book of the Black Bass.*[23]

At the same time, in opposition to these lurelike flies, professional fly tiers were trying to develop more conventional patterns, which is to say flies made of furs and feathers. Orvis championed one such pattern, both in Charles Orvis and A. Nelson Cheney's 1883 fly-fishing classic *Fishing with the Fly* and in the much grander Mary Orvis Marbury book *Favorite Flies and Their Histories*, published in 1892.

Not everybody was impressed. Writing in the latter year, British fly theorist John Harrington Keene—who moved to the United States in the 1880s and tried his best to interest American anglers in modern imitative theory, Halford-style dry flies, and his own distinctive fly innovations—found nothing grasshopper-like in the Orvis pattern: "Why this is so called I do not know. Orvis & Co. (tackle-makers), figure it

Mary Orvis Marbury's preferred pattern for a grasshopper, as published in 1892, drew criticism from advocates of more precise imitations. Her grasshopper was just a large, colorful wet fly; neither its shape nor its colors were reminiscent of a grasshopper. Writer J. Harrington Keene complained that "it certainly resembles no grasshopper of this sublunary sphere." From Mary Orvis Marbury, Favorite Flies and Their Histories *(1892).*

in their elaborate catalogue, 'Fishing With the Fly,' but it certainly resembles no grasshopper of this sublunary sphere. All the same, it is a good Trout-fly, and with it I have taken some big fish. It is thus dressed: Tag, silver tinsel and green silk; tail, yellow swan and wood-duck (the black-and-white tipped feather); body, brown silk; hackle, cardinal; wing jungle-cock feather, with over-wing of red ibis and yellow swan (dyed); head, peacock herl."[24]

By contrast, Marbury defended the fly as the best in the large crop of grasshopper flies then being offered. Notice especially that she, like Roosevelt, rejected the more rigid, exact-imitation style of grasshoppers:

> Every one who attempts artificial insects sooner or later undertakes an imitation of the grasshopper. Some of these imitations bear close resemblance to the originals, and have been made with bodies of wood, cork, or quills, and covered with silk, wool, rubber, and silkworm gut; but they are apt to be clumsy, lacking as they do the spring and softness of the real insect. Any one who will invent a grasshopper with the natural "kick" in it has a fortune in his hands. That pictured in the plate [i.e., the pattern that Keene criticized as not looking at all like a grasshopper] can claim semblance only because of colors that in the water may suggest the red-legged grasshopper, so successful as bait. This pattern came to us ten or twelve years ago from Mr. Harry Pritchard, of New York, who for a time made the only flies sold of the combination; they were in great demand with his customers. Since then this fly has become generally known, and has proved excellent for large trout and bass, as well as small trout.[25]

Keene, who had lived in Manchester and worked with the Orvis family for a while but had a falling-out with them of unknown cause, probably disapproved of their grasshopper for several reasons: first, because he was right, and it didn't look much like a real grasshopper; second, because he was on the outs with them for whatever reason; and third, because he had his own much more realistic pattern, which was pictured in the 1892 book containing his criticism of the Orvis fly: "Red-legged

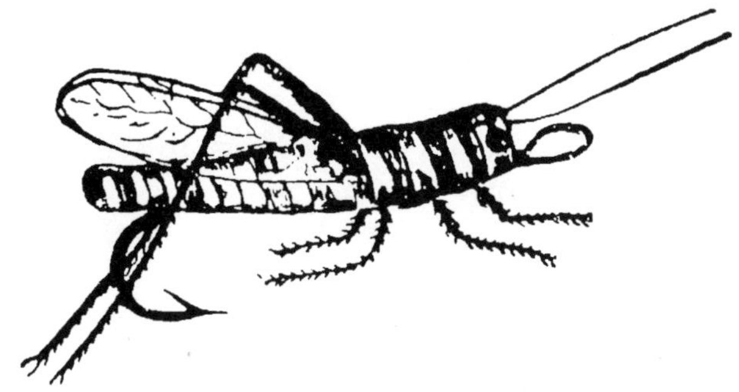

John Harrington Keene was one of many tiers to attempt an exact imitation of a grasshopper. His pattern featured fish-scale wings and, apparently, a cork body. From John Harrington Keene, Fly-Fishing and Fly-Making, *2d ed. (1891).*

GRASSHOPPER.—Body, yellowish green chenille; legs, mid-rib of hackle, fibers clipped close; wings, sparrow small quill-feathers; head, peacock heil [sp.]. As will be observed, this is an imitation of nature. I have tried all kinds of imitations, and this is the one with which to best fool Trout, in a clear stream, in the grasshopper season. Of course the natural insect is more killing, but this is very effectual, even in comparison."[26] Keene's grasshopper used trimmed hackle stems bent to create the leg joints, and it attempted to match the long, thick body of real grasshoppers with chenille. With such materials, it must have been a wet fly after the first couple casts.

American fly theorists continued to experiment. In the late 1800s and early 1900s, not only tackle companies as well known as William Mills and Thomas Chubb, but writers as prominent as Louis Rhead offered their own versions of the hopper, as did any number of lesser-known tiers and writers.[27] By contrast, the extensive writings of Catskill dry-fly advocate Theodore Gordon are almost devoid of mentions of grasshoppers, as are the writings of some of American dry-fly fishing's other pioneers.[28]

The Loyal Opposition

The reasons that some people ignored grasshoppers were complicated. As Andrew Herd suggests, the best-read anglers widely regarded aquatic insects, especially mayflies, as the true "flies" in fly fishing. A combination of fashionableness and a growing literature on mayfly imitation certainly would have inclined fishermen to focus on them. Vincent Marinaro, writing in the mid–twentieth century, suggested that grasshoppers were just too large and aesthetically inappropriate to appeal to many anglers in Frederic Halford's day and mood. In fact, Marinaro admits that even at the time his first book, *A Modern Dry Fly Code* (1950), was published, there were probably still many anglers, including himself, with serious doubts about hopper fishing. Marinaro's observations on grasshoppers are among the most important ever published about hopper fishing because they suggest the complexities of the fly-fishing aesthetics and ethics that prevailed by Halford's time—and that endured well past Marinaro's time among at least some anglers. Marinaro pointed out,

> It is with some diffidence that the grasshopper (Melanoplus Differentialis) is accorded a prominent position in formal dry-fly practice. The size of this creature and the attendant difficulty of using a comparable imitation on ordinary tackle ally its use more closely to the art of bass bugging than to that of dry-fly fishing. It must be admitted too that it lacks a great deal of the grace and refinement which accompanies the employment of dry flies in the 16, 18, and 20 sizes. Aesthetic values are rather low where the use of Melanoplus is concerned, and its ungracefulness is somewhat aggravated by its terrestrial origin and lineage. In all likelihood an imitation of this animal would have not have agreed with the fine sensibilities of a man like Frederic Halford, who would have complained, no doubt, that it was at variance with true dry-fly practice. His deprecation of so large an imitation as the Green Drake [a mayfly] is indicative of his philosophy on this subject. I am in complete sympathy with his views, and would gladly trade the opportunity to fish to the grasshopper for that of fishing to the pale wateries, for example. Then, too, there is always a jarring note, a lack of harmony, associated with the ungainly efforts of even the most proficient caster in his

> attempts to make a smooth delivery of this cumbersome artificial. There must be many people, acutely aware of these differences, to whom the prospect of such fishing would be offensive, particularly those who delight in the oblique approach to the art of fly-fishing—the flashing elegance of the slender rod, the graceful curving movement of the line, and the fall flying like thistledown.[29]

Two things make Marinaro's comments all the more interesting: his confession that the opportunity to raise and hook really large trout overrode his own prejudices and tastes and his own introduction of one of the most intriguing and visually convincing hopper imitations to come out of American angling history, Bill Bennett's Pontoon Hopper, whose body was made of a hollow and therefore buoyant goose or turkey quill.[30]

The First Great American Hoppers

Like almost all fly patterns, virtually none of these American hoppers endured. Many didn't outlive their originators or even the second or third season of their careers. For mysterious reasons of quality and charisma, however, if enough people take part in this sort of informal fly-making sweepstakes, a pattern will stick and eventually make its way into the greater, longer-lasting national fly box. That is what happened with the Michigan Hopper.

According to Michigan writer George Richey, Art Winnie apparently popularized the Michigan Hopper in the 1920s and sold it for many years thereafter.[31] Winnie, a popular Michigan fly tier who was also known for developing the Michigan Caddis (an imitation of the big and generally misnamed *Hexagenia* mayflies so famous on many midwestern streams) and other regionally successful patterns, came upon the right combination of simple materials and visual appeal in the Michigan Hopper.[32] One original specimen of the Michigan Hopper in the collection of the American Museum of Fly Fishing is tied on a conventionally proportioned dry-fly hook. The fly has the shorter proportions of a regular dry fly rather than the extended lines of a modern hopper pattern. Its yellow chenille body, mottled turkey-feather wings,

Art Winnie first popularized his Michigan Hopper in the 1920s; this version has the traditional dry-fly proportions that prevailed among almost all floating trout flies at that time. Courtesy of the American Museum of Fly Fishing, photograph by Sara Wilcox.

and brown dry-fly hackle were easy to duplicate and easy to rename; it became the Joe's (or Jack's or Jim's) Hopper in the West, and by 1950 even as thorough and authoritative a reference work as J. Edson Leonard's *Flies* listed Joe's Hopper, but seemed unaware of Winnie's original.[33] So soon we forget. The museum collection also contains a more elongated Michigan Hopper, also tied by Winnie, so he apparently experimented with his original design.

One of the highly praised hoppers at midcentury was the Western Grasshopper, an all-hair pattern tied by Paul Stroud, of Arlington Heights, Illinois.[34] I have not yet seen an example or a picture of this pattern, but the idea of a hopper made entirely of hair, presumably but not necessarily deer hair, is intriguing.

Just why Winnie's Michigan Hopper and its various regional counterparts should have taken hold when so many other patterns didn't is hard to say, but based on what we now know about subsequent successful

Like many fly tiers, Art Winnie apparently varied his patterns. This original interpretation of the Michigan Hopper features an elongated body and extended tail as well as a gold hook. Courtesy of the American Museum of Fly Fishing, photograph by Sara Wilcox.

patterns, I'd guess it had to do with the mottled turkey feather he used as a wing. Although he tied the fly on a conventional (rather than extra-long) hook, the rather caddis-shaped feather wing reached far back over the bend of the hook and created the necessarily longer silhouette of a real grasshopper. It captured both anglers' and, presumably, trouts' imaginations. It "worked" in every sense of the word—practically, aesthetically, and commercially—and most of the subsequent successful hoppers prior to the foam-and-rubber-band era employed the same feather.

While the first enduring American hopper imitation, the Michigan/Joe's pattern became best known for its use on freestone streams in the Midwest and West, a different style of hopper fishing developed in the East, especially along the limestone streams of Pennsylvania.

Again, there was some confusion over this eastern pattern and its origin for a while, although the involved parties seem to have settled

The Letort Hopper, developed for the "limestoner" trout streams of southeastern Pennsylvania, presented a different profile than the often heavily hackled grasshopper imitations that preceded it. This version was tied by noted spring creek authority Ed Koch in 1988. Photograph by the author.

the question amicably and with clarity. In the years following the publication of *Matching the Hatch* (1955), which said only a few words about grasshoppers, Ernest Schwiebert developed his Letort Hopper, a low-profile, unhackled, and proportionately long floating fly, which he designed in cooperation with Letort regular Ross Trimmer. This fly had a yellow nylon-wool body, a combination of turkey-feather and deer-hair wings, and a trimmed, vaguely Muddler-style head: "The absence of hackle permitted the bulk of the imitation grasshopper and its yellowish body to float flush in the surface film. The principal character of a natural grasshopper is rectilinear and slender, while the hackles of conventional imitations [i.e., the Michigan Hopper] are indistinct and caddislike in form. The flaring deer-hair filaments were trimmed away under the throat of the fly to make sure the yellowish dubbing of the body rode awash, just the way the trout would observe a live grasshopper."[35]

Well-known fly-fishing and fly-tying expert Gary Borger has described Schwiebert's Letort Hopper as "the first fly to effectively imitate the low-slung silhouette of these big insects," but if the illustrations that survive of prototypical hopper patterns from the late 1800s and early 1900s are even vaguely accurate, they all would precede Schwiebert's pattern.[36] The big difference, of course, is that the latter pattern took, whereas those others faded away. The Letort Hopper has no doubt influenced many hopper patterns since its invention.

In the matter of influence, Schwiebert shares equal credit with veteran limestoner Ed Shenk, who, recognizing the conflict and confusion to be caused by there being two competing Letort Hoppers, chose to name his the "Shenk Letort Hopper" even though it originated at roughly the same time as the Schwiebert version. Whereas Schwiebert's hopper had a yellow nylon yarn body with divided turkey wings, Shenk's had a dubbed spun-fur yellow body and "a mottled turkey wing with the feather folded, tied flat, and trimmed in a broad 'V.'"[37] Both had trimmed deer-hair heads, and both have proven very effective on many waters. I've carried a small and alarmingly dwindling stock of them all over the country, acquired from Ed Koch about twenty years ago, taking trout on them with no regard for the presence or absence of real grasshoppers.

Styles Established, Blended, and Enriched

I end this saga perhaps early, about thirty years ago, because after that there is a proliferation of grasshopper models that build on both of the older themes—the upright, bushy, indistinctly silhouetted Michigan Hopper style and the low, flush-riding Letort Hopper style—and I see no need to recite them all, even the ones I like best.

It does appear to me that the best aspects of the two styles were more or less combined in Dave Whitlock's great and enduring Dave's Hopper. Writing in 1972, Whitlock described and beautifully illustrated this fly as a "hybrid grasshopper imitation that I designed out of a dissatisfaction with the older standard hopper patterns."[38] It used the down-wing curled turkey wing, an underwing of pail yellow deer hair, and long untrimmed fibers from the head that extend to the sides for stability and to imitate legs. The same-named pattern is now usually offered with legs made from trimmed and knotted hackle stems. Alas,

Dave's Hopper, the durable and enduring pattern created by the great American angling artist and pattern innovator Dave Whitlock, was originally tied without legs, but grew them as the pattern evolved. Courtesy of George Anderson's Yellowstone Angler, Livingston, Montana, photograph by the author.

the light and beautifully mottled turkey feathers that made the original Michigan Hopper and its early successors so appealing have become hard to come by; most modern commercial versions use darker and less strikingly colored turkey feathers.

In the explosion of hopper patterns created since Dave's Hopper appeared are some wonderful patterns that, I suspect, are often more effective than anything in existence before 1970. We have fulfilled the dreams of the early hopper pioneers and created patterns that successfully emphasize behavior, the big splat, and the rubber-legged action of real grasshoppers. But the two basic styles, the high/loose and the low/constrained, are still the prevailing blueprints for most construction of hopper imitations.

The amazing profusion of modern commercial grasshopper patterns available today indicates the extent to which this element of the fly-fishing aesthetic has changed in only a few decades. For a long time, many hard-core fly fishers didn't want to use hopper imitations because hoppers were so different from mayflies. People now enjoy using grasshoppers precisely because they *are* different from mayflies. Grasshoppers broaden the variety of experience in the sport.

And yet I still admire the decision of those earlier anglers who chose to ignore the grasshopper. For them, a grasshopper was much like a bass bug, an artificial mouse, or some other perfectly acceptable lure that just fell outside the realm of their idea of fly fishing. Many of those anglers refused to use hoppers for reasons that gave their sport a definition and scope that suited the times and their personal preferences. Good for them for thinking that hard about what fly fishing meant to them and how they wanted to play the game. When it came to hoppers, they just said no.

Or perhaps it would be more accurate to say that many of those anglers refused to use grasshopper imitations until they got their first startled glimpse of the caliber of trout that these unorthodox fly patterns could coax to the surface. Then, as the splash echoed in each angler's ears and the waves washed against the bank, his or her real commitment to convention, tradition, and aesthetics was put to the test. Hopper fishing does that to us.

11 Real Dogs and Dreadful Scourges

Have You Invented the Streamer Yet?

The streamer is a very old idea. In *A History of Flyfishing* (1992), British fly-fishing historian Conrad Voss Bark writes that at the time of Homer, various Mediterranean sea fishers "were used to creating artificial lures such as plumes—we would call them streamer flies—and had fished them for thousands of years."[1] It's not likely that those ancient Mediterranean fishing lures would have been castable with what we would consider a normal fly rod. But then the flies used today for tarpon and billfish might be as large as those ancient Mediterranean plumes, and in any case Voss Bark was right that the basic idea of a streamer—a hook with a long feather wing, intended to imitate a fish—is among the most venerable of fishing devices.

And yet American anglers, perhaps because we have so successfully made streamers and bucktails our own and have used them to catch so many species of fish, have always tended to assume that we must also have invented them. In *Trout* (1978), the late Ernest Schwiebert confidently asserts that these imitations of small fish "are unquestionably a fly type and method that originated on this side of the Atlantic."[2] Any number of other respected commentators have agreed.

The late Joe Bates, in his beautiful and encyclopedic *Streamers and Bucktails: The Big Fish Flies* (1979), does a comprehensive job of chronicling the various worthy figures involved in the saga of American streamer development since the late 1800s. His grand book offers all the detail most of us need for understanding the American part of the streamer story as it has been traditionally told.

Once in a while, however, the intensity of the historical competition over who "invented" the streamer reminds me regretfully of Thomas McGuane's description of modern fly-fishing commerce as "an era when famous fishermen scramble to name flies and knots after themselves with a self-aggrandizing ardor unknown since the Borgia popes."[3]

American Candidates

There is no more entertaining place to go for a lively opinion on the contentious issue of streamer paternity than that most forthright and opinionated of twentieth-century American fishing tackle manufacturers George Leonard Herter. Herter, whose pungent views I introduced in chapter ten, is an especially appropriate person to hear from on this question because he was notorious for taking credit for things and was fiercely protective of his proclaimed primacy. In the 1971 edition of his book *Professional Fly Tying, Spinning, and Tackle Making Manual and Manufacturers' Guide*, he was in fine form on the subject of streamers. "Many years ago," he complained, "outdoor fishing writers, who fish mostly with a typewriter, had run out of their usual fakery so they wrote up a bunch of streamers" that—in Herter's eyes, anyway—were just junk.[4]

In fairness to the various pattern originators, I have to protest that most of the supposed inventors of this fly type were not especially concerned about getting famous. If you're looking for immortality, there are better ways to go about it than tying new flies.

That said, it is true that we have a glut of candidates for the honor of creating this terrific and versatile style of fly. Included on any such list of American anglers whom someone has credited with inventing the streamer (all between around 1880 and 1910) are the outdoor writers Emerson Hough (Chicago and elsewhere) and Theodore Gordon (New York); professional fly tiers such as William Scripture (New York) and Herbert Welch (Maine); and a variety of lesser-known anglers such as Alonzo Stickney Bacon (Maine).[5] I should probably also add John Harrington Keene—not because I want to propose him as the real inventor, but because he was developing fish imitations earlier than most of these other men, so he might as well be given a little credit here, too.

Landlocked salmon were among the most important fish in inspiring new eastern streamer patterns in the late nineteenth and early twentieth centuries. Photograph by the author.

Candidacy for the distinction of being the originator of streamers isn't an easy job, however, in part because you're liable to be badmouthed by the others or, more probably, by their latter-day promoters.

Again, George Herter provides a good example of the contention involved. Discussing L. L. Bean's "Bean Special" streamer, Herter said, "Everyone in Maine tried his best to get his name on any kind of streamer simply for publicity and this is just such an example—a real dog." Herter claimed that the popular Maine guide and fly tier Herb Welch "widely and loudly stated that he even invented the streamer fly in 1901. This of course, was not even close to being true and he knew it. As early as 1833 Dr. William Beaumont was catching lake trout on streamer flies from Mackinac Island, Michigan. He in turn did not claim to have invented them but learned how to use streamers made of feathers from the Michigan and Wisconsin trappers who had been using them for well over a century. The trappers in turn, learned how to use streamers from the Indians."[6]

Whatever we may think about Herter's historical accuracy (among many other things, he claims to have caught sailfish on flies as early

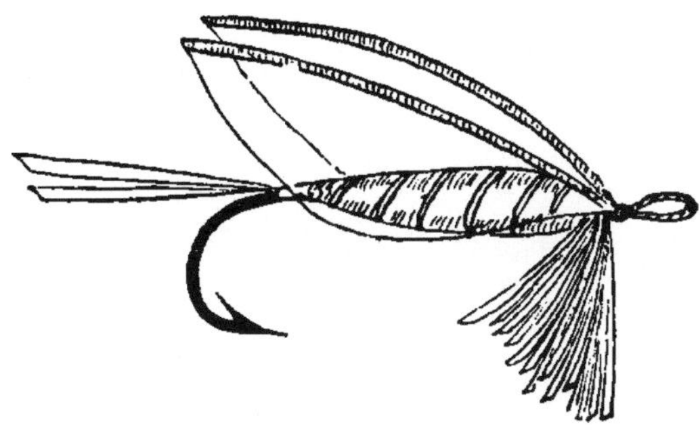

John Harrington Keene constructed his "Indestructible" fly on a very large hook with a twisted, multistrand, silkworm gut eye. The tail was scarlet-dyed, tarpon-scale membrane. The body was built-up wrapped silk covered with tarpon-scale membrane, and the wings were also made of the same membrane. Keene included with his description of the fly the account of a friend who caught thirty-five saltwater fish of various species on one fly without harm to it, but lost the fly in the thirty-sixth fish when the leader broke. From John Harrington Keene, Fly-Fishing and Fly-Making, *2d ed. (1891).*

as the 1920s), in this little rant he does describe one of the most plausible sources of information available to early American anglers: Native American fishing practices. But having established that there is no shortage of claimants in the contest for streamer paternity, we had better start by meeting some of the "inventors" who predated this American crowd.[7]

The British, as Usual

The first dead wood to be cleared away in this historical forest is the error of assuming that Americans invented the streamer in the first place. With all due respect to Ernest Schwiebert and the many others who claimed the fly as an American achievement, the streamer was repeatedly invented in England before Americans got into the act. As with almost every other idea that American fly fishers would like to take credit for, if you do a little homework, you will probably discover that the British had it first.[8] Considering that artificial minnows, made from a variety of materials, were mentioned in British books even in the seventeenth century, it shouldn't be any surprise that some anglers would experiment with imitations that could be cast with fly rods.

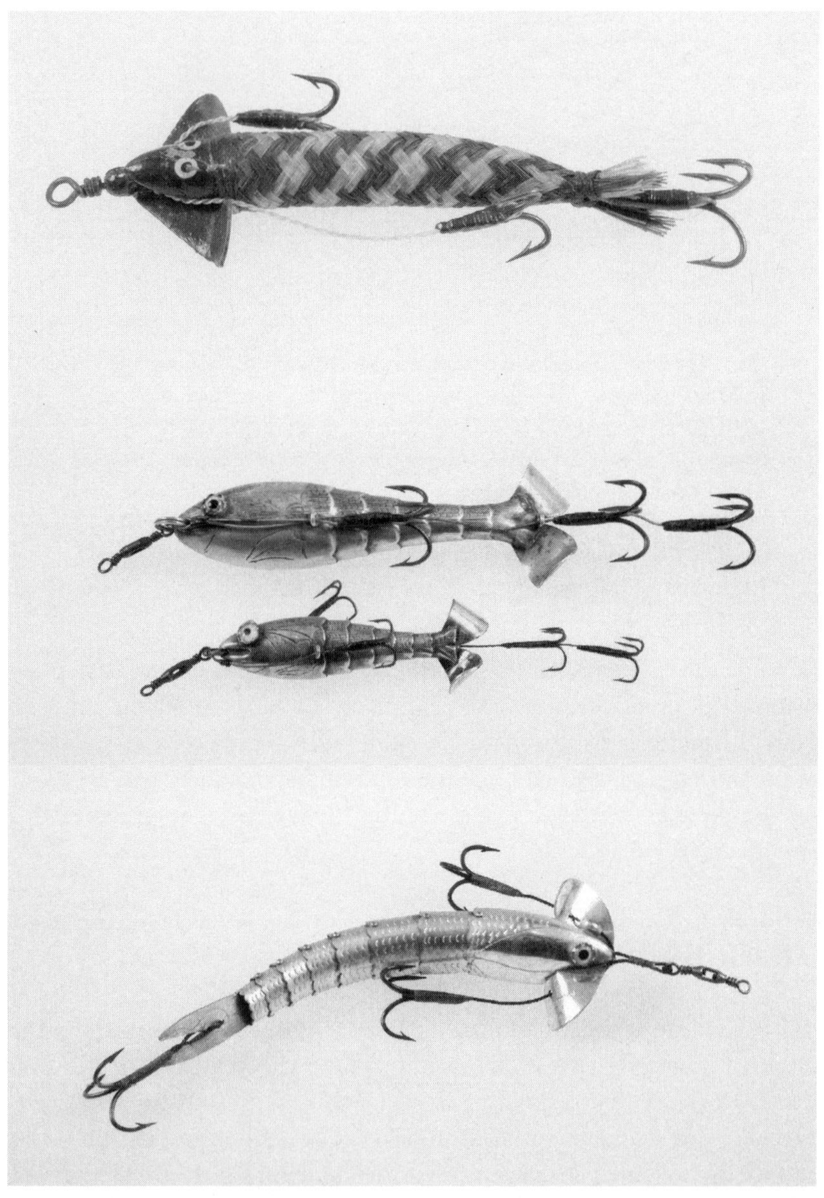

Fly fishers who experimented with small-fish imitations may have been inspired by the long history of artificial minnows and other lures, which were in use as early as the seventeenth century. By the late nineteenth century, when the lures pictured here were in fashion, the craft of lure making was both venerable and sophisticated. Courtesy of the Chris Sandford Collection, photographs by Andrew Herd.

In *The Fly Fisher's Text Book* (1841), the British writer Theophilus South (the pen name of Edward Chitty) quoted one Richard Hely, who said he had "fished a great deal in the tide-ways with the fly, and had admirable sport: mackeral [*sic*], whiting, pollock, and sand-eels, may be taken in great quantities. The fly is a white feather, projecting considerably over the hook, and it resembles the herring fry, of which both mackeral and pollock are very fond."[9]

In *The Rod and Gun* (1844), James Wilson stated that "a singularly successful fly for sea-trout, large or small, may be made with silver tinsel enwrapping the whole body from head to heel . . . the wings, of a narrow elongated form, composed either of pure white or pale gray or a mixture of both. It has a very glistening aspect in the water, looking somewhat like a small disabled fish, and sea-trout swallow it from a kindly fellow-feeling, believing it to be some relation of their own."[10] These two British anglers, Hely and Wilson, writing two or three generations before Gordon, Scripture, Welch, and the other American streamer pioneers, surely met any modern definition of streamer fishing in their descriptions.

In *The Rod and Line* (1849), Hewett Wheatley provided another example of an awareness of the value of imitating small fish. He said that he had "great sport with a sort of Minnowkin,—a minute Minnow, less than an inch long, and made of India Rubber or Gutta Percha, having only one small treble hook, hanging loose by the tail."[11] Wheatley fished this imitation with his fly rod, and although it sounds to me more like what we might call a lure than a fly, definitions of these terms are up for grabs today, anyway, because of the many synthetics we now employ. Rubber is certainly no less a legitimate fly-tying material than epoxy.

The best known of these early British descriptions of fish imitations is given in the rare and quite handsome book *Fly-Fishing in Salt and Fresh Water* (1851), which included several hand-colored plates of large, long saltwater flies used by the author to capture "whiting pollack" and other fish "off the coast of Connemara."[12] Although the author did not specifically state that the flies were intended to imitate small fish, little else is imaginable from the context.

The point of describing these earlier British examples of streamers and streamer-type flies is that it is hard to imagine that in any generation of fly fishers with access to piscivorous fish, it didn't occasionally occur to someone to try a fish imitation. Saying that someone "invented" this style of imitation seems as hopeless and naive as likewise trying to

Two large saltwater flies in use in coastal British waters in the mid-1800s. Although the author of the book these flies illustrated did not specifically state that they were intended to imitate small fish, no other likely alternative presents itself today; they almost certainly meet the modern definition of a streamer. From Richard Bowden-Smith, Fly-Fishing in Salt and Fresh Water *(1851).*

give someone credit for inventing the imitation of mayflies, frogs, or crayfish. Developing imitations to suit the demands of the local aquatic environment was and is an intuitive act.

My reading of the older fly-fishing books and tracts, however, does suggest to me that, at least as far as the written record reflects historical angling practice, if European fly fishers consciously imitated fish before the late 1700s, they didn't write about it. As I pointed out in chapter one, the well-rounded sport fisher of 1500, 1600, or 1700 might fish flies in the morning, minnows at midday, and a paste bait in the evening, and he would do it all with the same rod.[13] With that generalized an interest in fishing, if he was trying to catch fish that ate smaller fish, he probably just baited his hook with those small fish. It may not have been until fly fishers broke off from the general angling fraternity and began to perceive themselves exclusively as fly fishers that imitating small fish became an issue for them.

Once fly fishers began to identify themselves more and more as a subset of angling society—which is to say, once they decided to define their idea of the sport as involving only the use of fly-fishing tackle—it would take very little time for them to broaden their imitation array. Though it is impossible to pinpoint exactly when fly fishers began this process of separating themselves from other anglers, there certainly were such people in England by the early 1700s and perhaps earlier.[14]

I am intentionally saying little in this discussion about the most spectacular noninsect imitations to appear in numerous nineteenth-century British publications, the huge "pike flies" that were repeatedly illustrated and recommended. The most common prescription for pike flies involved the use of entire peacock eyes for the wings, with various other furs and feathers for the body and typically a set of large bead eyes for additional weight.

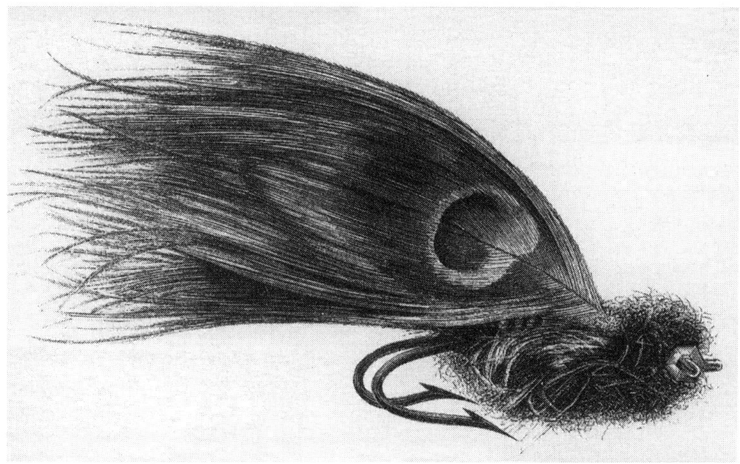

Through much of the nineteenth century, anglers used huge "flies" winged with entire peacock-eye feathers to fish for pike. It is difficult to call these flies "streamers" because they were rarely said to imitate fish; several authors believed that pike took them for small, low-flying birds. From H. Cholmondeley-Pennell, The Book of the Pike *(1865), courtesy of the American Museum of Fly Fishing.*

Even a century ago pike flies came in an assortment of patterns. The predominant characteristic seems to have been size and apparent bulk. Courtesy of the Chris Sandford Collection, photograph by Andrew Herd.

Pike flies occupy an unusual and fascinating position in the history of imitation because the writers who described and recommended them usually did not say what they were intended to imitate; they were simply known to be attractive to pike. In fact, when some specific life form was suggested as their inspiration, it was likely to be a small bird; more than one writer described seeing pike break the surface of the water to take low-flying swallows, so a "fly" the size of a small bird seemed appropriate to these anglers.[15] These flies were so spectacular, however, that I must include a couple of illustrations of them in this chapter despite their failing to be authentic streamers.

Americans at Last

I assume that from say, the early 1800s on, at least a few American fly fishers must have wondered now and then if they could imitate small fish. I think especially of the glory days of the brook trout and bass fishing so popular among American fly fishers in the nineteenth century. Many of the large, vividly colored "lake flies" sold by Orvis and other manufacturers, when retrieved vigorously across some lake anywhere

American anglers seem to have identified certain saltwater game fish, such as the striped bass, among their first quarry for flies imitating small fish. From Henry William Herbert, Frank Forester's Fish and Fishing of the United States and British Provinces of North America *(1849).*

from Maine to the Ohio Valley, could not have failed to trigger a predatory response in big fish that lived primarily on small fish. I realize that such fishing might not always qualify as "streamer fishing" in the formal sense of the term, if only because the angler may not have realized or cared what his fly was imitating.

But some of these fishermen knew exactly what their flies were imitating, and as in several earlier chapters, we need to hear from Robert Barnwell Roosevelt. Writing in *Game Fish of the Northern States of America and British Provinces* (1862), Roosevelt extolled the Scarlet Ibis fly as "a favorite with sea-going fish. A little tinsel wound round the body is supposed to improve its efficiency, as some fishermen suggest from a resemblance to the principal Winter food of the trout, the salt water minnow."[16]

During the next thirty years, there were numerous published mentions of fish taken on what were obviously fish imitations—most from relatively anonymous people who just saw the good sense of using them. British tourist-angler Alfred C. Harmsworth, writing about Florida saltwater fly fishing in *Forest and Stream* in 1895, stated that he easily caught spotted weakfish at Punta Gorda and that "my fly was a silver doctor, to which I had added a largish white feather."[17] No more complete prescription of a feather-wing streamer is necessary.

So not only did the British practice streamer fishing well before streamers were "invented" by various famous late-nineteenth-century anglers, a number of American fly fishers also fished streamer-type flies before the famous inventors came along. Even with this acknowledgment, however, we have neglected the real originators of fish imitations in the New World—the many native people who, as Herter pointed out, taught us to make and use bucktails of various kinds. It is common knowledge among angling historians that Native Americans were indeed an important source of much angling wisdom and method, and were especially important in the development of fish imitations.[18] It would be worth the trouble for some energetic fly-fishing researcher to seek out direct connections between native practice and the resultant development of known fly patterns.

In the meantime, it is worth considering the bucktail. A subset of the claims made for various American fly tiers as originators of the streamer involves similar claims for the originator of the bucktail. But the use of hair in the wings of flies and for related fishing lures is also a matter of longstanding practice. In a 1972 essay on hair-wing salmon flies, the late Ernest Schwiebert gave us some lore on the use of hair wings in Atlantic salmon flies in the late eighteenth century: "Charles DeFeo believes that the salmon hairwings have their roots in Newfoundland and patterns dressed from reddish calf tail, and his judgments are confirmed by Herbert Howard, another well-known American flytyer and fisherman. Howard tells of a Bible he examined on a backcountry Newfoundland farm that included a description of such a Hereford hairwing and its success in 1795."[19] Although this description is evidence neither of a modern bucktail (i.e., a hair-wing fly designed to imitate a small fish) nor of Native American influence on fly tying, it is noteworthy as evidence of a very early New World fly tied with animal hair as a prominent or dominant feature of the wing. It also fits with the received wisdom about the practicality of rural New World anglers, who adapted handy materials—as well as native practices—into their own angling. In 1972, the late Austin Hogan, the original curator of the Museum of American Fly Fishing, summarized our understanding of the early use of animal hair, especially bucktail, in the young United States:

A "bucktail"-style fly, tied with deer hair by Mary Orvis Marbury for display at the World's Columbian Exposition in Chicago in 1893. Courtesy of the American Museum of Fly Fishing, photograph by the author.

> Bartram fished the Florida "bob" of feathers and deer hair (1774), and white feathers on huge hooks were popular from Lake George to Lake Superior. . . . At the end of the 19th century, the feathered lure became a "flyminnow," "a worm fly," "a streamer fly" and eventually a "fly," to the confusion of everyone but an American. The bucktail was a survival tool popular with the early settlers around Lake Ontario.
>
> Reminiscing, W. T. (W— Thompson) recalled a youthful experience on Ontario's Skugog Lake when a chunk of deer hair he was trolling from a tiny dugout was gobbled by a 33 pound muzkelunge.[20]

Stories of big fish taken on such "chunks" of deer hair or on a calf tail or moose tail are a part of nineteenth-century angling lore to such an extent that the refinement involved in adapting such materials into a

A "Whitebait" fly used by British saltwater fly fishers to imitate herring. From the Duke of Beaufort and Alfred E. T. Watson, Sea Fishing *(1895), courtesy of the American Museum of Fly Fishing.*

named fly pattern hardly seems a historic distinction.[21] Again, as with feather-wing flies, the hair wings seem to have been a good idea for so long and for so many people that it's hard to see the sense in seeking a point of origin. I agree with historian Andrew Herd, who, after enumerating a number of nineteenth-century anglers who used hair-wing flies, reaches this same conclusion about the British experience with hair as a wing material:

> If I add that yet another early adapter of animal hair wrote in the *Fishing Gazette* in 1878 about tying saltwater flies using white hair from a goat's beard, you will see that you can take your pick as to who first thought of the method. My own view is that fishermen have probably experimented with hair wings for much longer than we think and that it is more than possible that the technique was copied from native North Americans. Perhaps the truth is that like so many discoveries, hair-winged flies were invented by many people at many different times, without any of them realising what an important step they had taken. Remember that in those days, people didn't place articles in fishing magazines the moment it occurred to them to make a minor variation to an existing pattern so that they could call it their own, so it can be tricky working out when exactly a thing was invented.[22]

Streamer Opposition

With so many people inventing and reinventing streamers and bucktails, we have to wonder why they didn't catch on faster than they did. What took so long, and why wasn't it until the generation of Keene, Gordon, Welch, Scripture, and their like came along that the streamer/bucktail idea flourished and was widely popularized?

There are probably several reasons for this delay, including the foot-dragging tendency among anglers that we have already witnessed, because of which silkworm gut, eyed hooks, and other ideas had to fight for angler acceptance and commercial endorsement.

Besides general stodginess, there is at least one especially interesting reason that streamers were a little slow off the line, and it has to do with how fly fishers defined themselves. For a sizeable segment of the fly-fishing crowd, it seems that fly fishing still meant *fly* fishing—that is, the imitation of actual flies. Those people would have agreed with James Chetham's pronouncement in *The Angler's Vade Mecum* (1689) that the "Palmer-fly and May-fly are the very ground or foundation of all Fly Angling."[23] If you wanted to fish with minnows, you used real minnows. The same thinking applied, for many people at least, to grasshoppers, frogs, and other nonfly creatures.

The Alexandra became controversial in the late 1800s among anglers who disapproved of its use as an imitation of a small fish; it was said to have been banned from exclusive British streams as unsporting. From Mary Orvis Marbury, Favorite Flies and Their Histories *(1892).*

Perhaps the most interesting example of an antistreamer bias dates from the 1880s and the controversial Alexandra wet fly. The Alexandra, with its long peacock-herl wing and silver body, was well known even in the 1880s as a small-fish imitation. Developed around midcentury, it was yet another British predecessor to America's first streamers. In 1892, Mary Orvis Marbury, the great American encyclopedist of the Victorian wet fly, wrote that the Alexandra "may not properly be called an artificial fly, being intended as a vague imitation of a minnow, and was originally recommended to be cast and played minnow fashion just below the surface of the water."[24]

In 1885, John Harrington Keene, the innovative British angler who developed many new fly patterns, including a fish imitation with a wing made of a tarpon scale, wrote that the Alexandra was "a grand killer of trout in Europe and is probably mistaken for a small minnow." As a testament both to the fly's effectiveness and to its controversial nature, Keene stated that "in many waters its use is looked on as unsportsmanlike and is forbidden."[25]

But the Alexandra infuriated Frederic Halford, the British "high priest" of dry-fly fishing, whose ranting against it in *Dry-Fly Fishing* (1886) was every bit the match for George Herter's most venomous outbursts. On the exclusive, carefully manicured chalk streams Halford and his crowd controlled, fly fishing was quite narrowly defined. One thing you certainly didn't do was go around dragging some infernal minnow imitation through the best pools and scaring the daylights out of all the upper-class trout in the neighborhood:

> What a profanation to bestow on this monstrosity the name of one of the most charming and amiable princesses of this century! It certainly is not the imitation of any indigenous insect known to entomologists; possibly the bright silver body moving through the river gives some idea of the gleam of a minnow. Long ere this its use should have been prohibited in every stream frequented by the *bona fide* fly-fisherman, as it is a dreadful scourge to any water, scratching and frightening an immense proportion of the trout which are tempted to follow it. It certainly would have been prohibited, too, but for the fact that experience shows that in any stream in which it has been

> much fished the trout soon become quite alive to its danger, and not only will not move an inch toward it, but when worked close to their noses will not so much as turn at it, but at times, on the contrary, even fly in terror from the dread apparition.[26]

Here was Halford at his most disapprovingly blustery. Not only did he not like the Alexandra and thought it wouldn't work, but he believed it would also ruin the fishing for everyone else. One wonders why, if the thing was doomed to such a miserable failure, he even bothered to talk about it.

Here also, incidentally, is an early case of a skilled angler announcing that trout can learn to recognize either a specific fly pattern or a specific fishing technique—it's not clear which one because Halford doesn't quite describe how the Alexandra was fished. The fishing technique was almost certainly part of what he objected to, though. Swinging a fly downstream through the water and retrieving it with lively jerks and other "unnatural" actions (unnatural in the sense that his favored mayflies never engaged in them) would have horrified him.

Like the rest of us, Halford was well within his rights to approve or disapprove of a particular fishing method. Nobody insisted he use the Alexandra. Besides, considering that he and his pals had paid good money for complete control over what was and wasn't allowed on their private streams, the Alexandra wasn't likely to get much stream time around him, anyway.

It's easy enough to fill in the rest of the story here to understand why Halford was so worked up. Whatever he admitted to his readers or to himself, he had to know, in some unhappy corner of his mind, that the Alexandra worked really well. For the Alexandra to be so effective was an embarrassment to anglers like Halford, who didn't like to think that their preciously husbanded trout could be gauche enough to fall for such a thing. The Alexandra was just bad form all around.

Invention Continues

I invented a streamer of my own recently. A fishing buddy has been enthusiastically promoting it among his friends. He even published the pattern and tying instructions in his club's newsletter, not in the least

The assortment of streamers enjoyed by modern fly fishers is the result of two centuries of experimentation by a host of talented fly tiers. Photograph by the author.

restrained by the hard truth that the pattern hasn't even caught a fish yet. George Herter would rise from the grave just for the satisfaction of being apoplectic over such blatantly promotional behavior. My pal is even trying to name it after me, but I have insisted that it have some nice bland, generic name of the sort that will no doubt guarantee its well-deserved obscurity.

But now I'm not so sure. Maybe I should call it the Dreadful Scourge. Or maybe I can cash in on a little historical melodrama and call it *Halford's* Dreadful Scourge. Or maybe, with a bow to George Leonard Herter, I should call it Halford's Typewriter.

PART FOUR

Fly-Fishing Secrets of the Ancients

A Brief Manual

Contents

Historic Smarts

I began this book with the supposition that besides being inherently interesting and fun to learn about, fly-fishing history can help make us better fishermen. With that in mind, and now that I've trolled through some of the sport's more obscure historical corners, perhaps it's worth considering the catch. In our modern rush for new tackle, ideas, and techniques, have we forgotten anything important or let some good ideas fall into neglect? And even if our ancestors didn't leave us any national treasure–grade secrets, such as miracle fly patterns, mysterious trick casts, or magical incantations, did they at least show us the way to wisdom that might give us a new slant on things we already know? Can we relearn some old lessons? It's worth a try.

I offer here a short manual—a treatise, if you will—of assembled lore, hints, and insights from earlier generations of fly fishers. Many are drawn from the previous chapters, but others I have rounded up from equally obscure historical literary territory that I've wandered into over the years.

Right off, I'd say that our ancestors often taught us more by example than by specific instructions. In fact, much of the time it's only by reading between the lines of their actual instructions that we find the larger lessons, which were often things they took for granted.

In constructing this manual, I generally use as my cutoff date the end of the nineteenth century, but I prefer that, whenever possible, we hear from people who are at least a couple centuries removed from us. I realize that nothing two hundred years old is authentically "ancient," but by angling standards it's profoundly remote, so I don't mind misusing the word.

Brevity being essential, I dispense with the quotations and citations that characterized the previous chapters. Instead of quoting all the early experts, I refer generically to one Old Guy or a few Old Guys who will stand for all of them. (For better or worse, and with regrettably few notable exceptions, almost everything we have in writing about fly fishing from before 1900 was in fact written by men.)

Please don't confuse what follows with a manual on how to fish using antique tackle and antique methods. I respect and even appreciate the gifted few who take on that challenge, and if that level of historical purity is what you're after, then the text you most need to read next is Darrel Martin's delightful and amazingly helpful book *The Fly-Fisher's*

Craft: The Art and History (Guilford, Conn.: Lyons Press, 2006). With that and anything written by Andrew Herd and John Betts, you're off to a good start.

What I do here instead is not so focused or narrow an enterprise as angling with historic tackle. It's more like angling with historic smarts. What did our predecessors do that we might have lost track of? How much of it can we incorporate into the sport today?

One other thing. I confess that I imagine myself to be the least likely person to write a manual on how to catch fish. In my previous books, I have often emphasized my own limitations as an angler. But I like to think that having such a harsh (and accurate) a view of my own skills makes me an especially sympathetic chronicler of the wisdom of people who were in fact nothing short of historic in their angling skills.

What follows, then, is only "mine" in the sense that I have compiled it. In these lessons, I recognize a few wise notions I have found my own way to as I fished, but I describe many more such insights I have noticed in the older angling literature, including some that I have yet to take adequate advantage of myself. Fly fishing remains a work in progress. We're all in this together.

2. Stream Savvy

Almost all of the fly-fishing literature we know of before about 1850 was European, and much of it involved fish that were hard to catch. Trout may have been uneducated on the Madison one hundred years ago or on the Beaverkill two hundred years ago, but our Old Guy fished Old World streams that had been fished hard by savvy and hungry fishermen for centuries. Realizing that many old-time trout were as spooky as today's trout is an important step in accepting that many of the Old Guy's skills might still apply today.

Now that I have read between the lines of many older fishing tracts, it seems to me that there were two underlying principles behind the Old Guy's fishing. These principles might better be called realities than rules; they weren't formal guidelines that he and his colleagues arbitrarily established because they wanted to bestow some preferred social tone on the sport. They were just how things worked at the time. These two realities were: (1) know your stream, and (2) get close to your fish.

Earlier generations of anglers traveled less often and less far; they tended to spend most of their time on a few local waters, which they came to know very well. From Henry William Herbert, Frank Forester's Fish and Fishing of the United States and British Provinces of North America *(1849).*

Living close has been a part of fishing close. Though some of us rightly pride ourselves on how well we know our streams, it's hard for us to comprehend the depth of our Old Guy's familiarity with his home water. For him, home water really meant *home*. Especially before about 1800, the odds were that his stream was within walking distance of his house and that he fished it his whole life. He probably started his fishing career in company with a father or uncle who had already fished that same water *his* whole life and who in his turn had learned the same way from some older and very experienced angler.

Few of us still live that close to our home stream, if we even have one. Few of us have a multigenerational connection to that water. We try to make up for these missing things by hiring guides, reading books and magazines, watching the Web sites, talking to each other, and employing other laudable methods that were generally unavailable to the Old Guy. But the truth is, when it comes to really knowing our home stream, most of us are still tourists compared to the Old Guy. Intense and frequent observation through a long life may not be the only way to learn a stream, but it will always be the best.

The question is, How does this "living close" principle help us today? Most of us can't afford to reshape our entire lives so that we live within strolling distance of our favorite river. Most of us probably wouldn't want to.

But I think that the Old Guy would say that we can actively engage in this very approach to fly fishing even if the water is far from home and we can get to it only a few times a year. Such engagement might mean relying less on received wisdom and doing more of the hard work of investigating the stream ourselves rather than delegating it to all those wonderful information sources we've come to rely upon. The Old Guy's experience seems to tell us that the point isn't getting to live on the water; it's making the most of our observational opportunities when we can. This almost certainly means casting less and watching more.

The philosophy of "hoarding the cast" prevailed among many an Old Guy for good reasons. It is not possible for most of us (myself included) to give our full attention to what the stream is telling us when we are frantically casting every second of the day.

I realize that this advice seems to contradict the equally wise old saying that you won't catch anything unless your fly is in the water, but many of our most valuable technical legacies were handed down to us by Old Guys who had the patience and fortitude to watch and otherwise explore the water for a long time before actually casting a fly—who knew that until they identified the *right* water, there was little point in putting their fly in it.

So they watched. Sometimes they watched the water. Sometimes they watched the fish. Sometimes they watched the other fishermen. Sometimes they just took in the whole scene until something attracted their attention. Observing nature is an acquired skill, not instantly easy. There is nothing idle or lazy in this apparent inaction, and I have often watched today's Old Guys practice this same alert patience to great effect.

3. Up-Close Angling

Second, for the Old Guy, fly fishing was about getting close to the fish. He walked or waded quietly and with a profound respect for both the water he displaced and the light he reflected. He dressed in his dullest, most sun- and wind-worn clothes. He took the shine off his fly rod. He kept his head down and his mouth shut.

The absolute necessity—in fact, the authentic sporting thrill—of all this hunkering and stalking and blending in is apparent at the first sight of our Old Guy's tackle. And here I must, just this once, quote someone, the ever-eloquent Charles Cotton, who, more than three hundred years ago, immortalized the admonition that we must fish "fine, and far off."

In a previous book, *The Rise*, I made the point that we have never really recovered from this magnificent exhortation. "Fine" did, indeed, sometimes mean as fine a leader as a single horsehair would make, and—trust me—that's mighty fine. Most of the time, however, most anglers would have used as coarse and strong a leader as the circumstances would allow. Through the century plus of silkworm gut's supremacy as the leader material of choice—say roughly 1830 to 1950—it was rarely fished as fine as we fish modern monofilaments. Much of the time, for most fishermen, 1X or 2X was about as fine as they'd go, and it worked well (I come back to this matter of leader diameter later).

It is in our celebration of "far off," however, that we've most gone astray from Cotton's reality. Cotton's admonition had nothing to do with double hauling across the Delaware. For our Old Guy, "far off" was typically no more than about thirty feet because that was the total stretched-out length of his rod and line. He might cast, or he might just let the wind carry the line out. Or he might reach out and dap his flies on a good spot.

There are extraordinary rewards in fishing really close. Yes, it is very demanding, but having watched some modern masters wade within a few yards of a spooky rising fish, then cast little more than a leader and take the fish, I have forever stopped thinking condescending thoughts about those "primitive" fly fishers of three hundred years ago. I've seen it done on the slickest, hardest-fished waters I know; I should surely be able to make it work on my nice splashy local freestone streams.

Unlike the life-disrupting changes most of us would have to go through in order to live next to our favorite water, learning to fish close seems entirely within our reach. It would be a shame to miss such exciting fishing just because we were too ignorant to know it's even possible.

There is a good reason that heron imagery is so prevalent in the early books. Some bait recipes even recommended heron fat in part because of its presumed mystical qualities of stealth. The heronlike patience the Old Guy exercised in studying his stream before casting

Like their hunting and fishing counterparts in other cultures, fly fishers took inspiration from the natural world; heron imagery was common in many early publications because herons were recognized as the consummate catchers of fish. From Stephen Oliver, Scenes and Recollections of Fly-Fishing, in Northumberland, Cumberland, and Westmorland *(1834).*

was simply extended into the act of fishing. Stalking skills were and are a matter of knowing which way the fish are looking and avoiding that field of view; of knowing how the currents go and moving through the water only in ways that don't telegraph your presence through those currents to the fish; of understanding the stream bottom well enough that you can wade along it without likewise alerting the fish by the clatter of rock or the clouding of silt and sand; and of doing all these things with the undisrupted smoothness and glacial pace of a crafty old heron. Trout have an amazing tolerance for an angler's presence if the angler respects what alarms them and what doesn't—or, as the heron would have it, when to stand and when to strike.

4. Fly Style

There have been big changes in almost everything about fly-fishing tackle since our Old Guy made his last cast two hundred years ago. It's hard to imagine the extent to which he was responsible for the manufacture of most of what he used. There were certainly a few shops, even three hundred years ago, where the well-off angler could buy a complete outfit, but I doubt that the average angler could afford to do that.

Practically every fishing book published before 1800 or so gave detailed instructions on how to build a rod; make and dye a line; make hooks; find, prepare, and dye fly-tying materials; and tie flies. Fishing itself may be neither art nor craft, but few other sports have employed as many arts and crafts to get the job done.

Few of us, and especially not me, would be interested in becoming proficient at many of these crafts. But they did inspire a sharp-eyed resourcefulness that most of us will never enjoy as long as we do most of our tackle gathering in modern fly shops. The Old Guy had to have an eye for just the right trees for rods, stallion's tails for lines, and fine needles for hooks. I don't mind not having those skills, but I kind of envy the finely trained eye it took to recognize the good stuff.

I especially admire the Old Guy's open-minded approach to fly tying. If he didn't pay attention to every little opportunity, he might miss great fly-tying materials thinly disguised as the outside or inside of fruits, hooves, horns, hats, ducks, carpets, dogs, shirts, cats, awnings, sheep, sails, pigs, cows, carpets, camels, or the tapestry on his well-heeled neighbor's wall. My impression is that many modern fly tiers are still just as attentive to these opportunities. The inspiration of the Old Guy's relentless foraging is good for us.

What I find more interesting than the Old Guy's adept cadging of unlikely fly-tying materials is what his flies looked like. They were usually quite simple, of course, and that has always been recognized as a strength when creating a new pattern. But what intrigues me most might best be categorized under the heading of "style." I'm not talking here so much about the age-old debate over whether flies should be very sparse or very thick, heavily dressed or lightly dressed, short or long. Those were worthy debates, and they indicate an admirable attentiveness to natural history. Rather, it's the Old Guy's general approach to the craft that seems most revealing of a different perspective than ours.

The examples of his flies that I've seen suggest to me that they were tied with a certain vagueness of silhouette and an apparent casualness of overall appearance that at first glance might now look crude or sloppy.

But they were tied that way on purpose. The Old Guy didn't have or especially need a ten-speed blender for his dubbing mixtures. He wanted each individual strand of fur and hair and thread to be long and intact and obvious enough to give its own special tint to the mix. At least some of the time, he also seemed to want those fibers a little more loosely wound than we would regard as seemly today.

The same goes for the wing: his fly's wing, undisciplined by modern varnishes, quickly eased itself into a smooth, imprecise form flowing over the back of the fly. Every time I see a fly tied with this wonderful looseness in a modern book or catalog (and I think I see more of them all the time), I am pleased to note that another fly stylist, knowingly or not, has found his way back to this earlier approach to fly tying.

As I have suggested, it's easy enough to come up with theoretical support for what the Old Guy was doing. The individual fibers on a looser fly body readily flexed in the current, maybe putting some extra life into a pattern. And the indistinct outline might, as the Old Guy thought, suggest the motion of gills, legs, a partially shed nymphal skin, or even a partially unfolded wing. Plenty of armchair hypotheses come to mind to justify the effects of such a tying style, but I don't claim to know precisely what the Old Guy had in mind. Whatever it was, his chosen style was important to him and accounted for many fish, so we shouldn't ignore it.

5. Home-Grown Flies

Lacking today's luxuriously mutated hackles, the Old Guy used many song-bird and game-bird feathers (having eaten their former owners). Those soft little secondaries, flank feathers, and minihackles, in many a diffuse and indeterminate shade, were a delicate complement to his dubbings.

I wouldn't want to have to say that all fly tiers long ago tied like this, but I have been fortunate enough to see quite a few nineteenth-century flies tied in this style, and every single one of them inspires instant covetousness and confidence in me. I believe many trout would feel the same way.

I'm very happy with today's wonderful fly-tying materials. I began tying back before genetic engineering brought us the marvel of the modern dry-fly neck. Thirty-five years ago I spent a great deal of time rooting through the nail keg of one-dollar hackle necks at the local fly shop in search of one with at least a few promising hackles, and I never found that kind of foraging in the least frustrating. It was part of the fly tier's endless treasure hunt. Besides, there was always the chance of the rare find of a much better neck that the shopkeeper had tossed into the keg by mistake. Nevertheless, I am grateful for the spectacular and enormously helpful new feathers—as I am for many other new materials that my favorite shops offer.

Just as the joys of casting have to a large extent displaced the joys of stalking, however, so has today's amazing array of terrific fly-tying conveniences, materials, and ideas largely displaced earlier notions of what made a good fly. There would seem no harm, but rather considerable potential advantage, in making a little more room in our repertoire for those older styles and the materials that seemed so wonderfully adapted to them—keeping in mind that we had better not emulate those earlier fly tiers in that aspect of their enthusiasms for certain fur and feathers that contributed to the demise of some beautiful species of wildlife.

Commerce conditions us to certain expectations. Here are a couple of examples to think about.

Effective marketing of the magnificent modern dry-fly necks can distract us from the reality that a couple of turns of starling hackle (and the feathers of other equally unglamorous birds) might keep a small dry fly afloat just as well.

Our passion for the stiffest possible dry-fly hackles—the result of the beautifully disciplined Halfordian and Catskill-style dry flies that dominated much of dry-fly theory in the twentieth century—can obscure the sport's cultural memory of all the other styles of flies that were effectively floated with a startling array of soft, webby hackles and other fibers.

6. Abandoned Directions

The obsession with imitation that arose among many fly fishers in the Halfordian revolution of the late 1800s led us away from most of the bright colors and combinations of colors that we should probably never have stopped experimenting with. When we replaced the vividly colored Victorian wet flies with more muted flies that seemed to us to suit the needs of the new imitative theories, we didn't so much improve on those older patterns as abandon them. The Victorian wet fly, with all its rich variety of married wings and other bright luxuries, was itself a work in progress when it was swept aside by other fashions. Who knows what we might eventually have made of it given time?

Some of today's new fly patterns that feature brighter colors—whether a fluorescent wing placed here for visibility or an iridescent strand of synthetic tinsel placed there for whatever mystical attraction we hope it will exercise—seem evidence enough that the Old Guys were on some interesting theoretical tracks with their development of all those gaudy flies in the 1800s. We tend to assume that those colorful old patterns worked merely because they were used mostly to catch undiscriminating brook trout and voracious bass, but we'll never know until we investigate the possibilities ourselves.

Another reason to think of fly-pattern development from the long historical perspective is that even the fly patterns that we tend to think of as relatively modern, ones that have so far survived changing fashions, have not always survived unscathed. I have made this point previously, most emphatically about what has become of the Adams dry fly since its creation in Michigan in the early 1900s, but it also applies to a number of our so-called classic patterns.

The biggest surprise for me when I first had the opportunity to examine original versions of the great American fly patterns some thirty years ago was that the patterns no longer look much like they did when the originals were created. Such widely recognized American standards as the Adams, Hendrickson, and Quill Gordon dry flies and the Muddler Minnow and Gray Ghost streamers have been remarkably revised from the form and intent of their originators.

It is difficult to overstate the magnitude of these changes, all of which have occurred in less than a century. Indeed, it only took a generation or so from the time Vincent Marinaro introduced his thorax-style dry fly in 1950 to the time his vital and novel approach to hackling the fly was replaced by the traditional hackling method on flies still sold as "thorax style." The changing tastes of each generation and the demands of commercial fly production have again and again overruled the intentions of some of our greatest fly-pattern creators.

Fortunately, thanks to the exhibits and publications of several fishing-oriented museums, the books and articles of many history-minded writers, and the ever-expanding attention of countless fly-fishing Web sites, it's now possible to track down sharp photographs of these flies tied as their originators' intended them to be tied. Take a look, compare and contrast, and give some thought to which version you'd rather cast on your local stream.

Maybe the changes we've made to these flies over the years have improved the patterns; maybe not. But with a little effort, you can get a good look at the originals now and decide for yourself. My own opinion is that most of the changes we've subjected these flies to were made for the wrong reason. The most common wrong reason was the need for the commercial standardization of fly style, which resulted in an intolerance of the quirky little abnormalities that the pattern may originally have featured. Because the originators were the only people in this process who displayed anything approaching creative genius, if I had my druthers, I would always fish the original pattern with more faith than any of its overrefined and homogenized descendants. There were usually very good reasons that those original flies were such successes in the first place.

7. Presentation

The Old Guy fished his flies on top, either literally floating or in the first few inches of depth. Fishing close to the surface like that gave him a more limited reach than the modern fly fisher has with fast-sinking lines and weighted flies. Our desire for access to the rest of the water column is one of the things that most clearly separates us from our ancestors, who happily switched to bait if they needed to fish deep. But even within that shallow realm, the Old Guy fished his flies differently than we do today.

He probably fished at least two flies, often as many as four, with a few extremists using as many as ten or twelve. The biggest, heaviest fly was the tail fly on the end of the line. The droppers were evenly distributed every foot or two up the line.

Many of us fish multiple flies today, but the Old Guy's example makes me wonder why we promote so few kinds of multiple-fly rigs. What gets publicized today are mostly either the two- and three-fly wet fly/nymph rigs or a two-fly combination with a nymph tail fly and a dry-fly dropper/strike detector. The Old Guy and at least a few of his immediate successors in the early 1800s seem to have been more broadminded than that, using long, involved casts of flies in many settings, including salt water. I hope that today there are some adventurous souls out there who, assuming they can find waters where such things are still legal, are still experimenting and following the Old Guys' example.

Willingness to study the stream carefully and patiently before casting seems to have been a hallmark of many of fly-fishing history's most proficient anglers. This photograph by the author shows midge-fishing expert Ed Koch on Pennsylvania's Letort Spring Run in 1988.

Two or more centuries ago, when fly fishers stopped fishing only "on top" and began to consider the entire water column their appropriate domain and to tie weighted flies to reach deeply into their favorite pools, they launched an internal philosophical tension within the sport that still survives today. There are still many disagreements over whether weight, especially masses of metal (in eyes, wrapped on the hook shank, attached to the line) disqualifies a technique from meeting the definition of fly fishing. That debate aside, the sport of fly fishing has been permanently changed by the development of deeply fished flies, whether the quarry is just a wary brown trout under a log, a lake trout on its spawning shoals, a salmon in a deep swift pool, or some otherwise unreachable saltwater fish. I suspect that relatively few people are offended by weighted flies anymore, but it wouldn't hurt any of us to understand why the Old Guy and his pals got so worked up about the question.

8. Control and Action

Once the Old Guy's flies hit the water, long drifts were pretty rare. Having gotten close, he finessed the flies into just the right place—but not for long. They might cover only a few inches of water before they were whisked away. With his much longer rod and shorter line, and with his stalking skills kept sharp by daily use, he did a lot of pinpoint work.

By the way, there was another advantage to his type of fly rod, especially before about 1860, when most fly rods were just continuously tapered sticks that ran from broomstick diameter at the butt to a tip not much thicker than a pencil lead. Today we have grown accustomed to using a small arsenal of fly rods as the local conditions demand. I can't begin to count the times I suddenly found myself under a low canopy of tree limbs, wishing I was using a seven-foot rod rather than a nine-footer, but being too far from the car to switch rods even if I'd remembered to put the shorter rod in the car.

This sort of thing might have been less of a problem once. In the late 1800s, when split bamboo rods came along, and we first shortened fly rods and lengthened our casts, we locked ourselves into certain

Our ancestors were much more comfortable than we are today with "shortening up" on the rod when overhead clearance required casting in tight quarters. Photograph by Marsha Karle.

preconceptions by giving the new rods distinctive handles. We soon knew no other way to manage a fishing rod than by gripping the handle.

But our predecessors' rods, with their slowly tapered pool-cue butt sections, invited the angler to slide his hand to whatever location best suited the moment. Many of these same Old Guys also had reels mounted not on a stationery reel seat built into the rod, but on a sliding ring so that they could just as easily move the reel up and down the butt section to whatever position seemed most helpful. If need be, the whole butt section was the handle of the rod.

The point is, we can still fish that way. As inelegant as it may seem, and as odd as it may feel the first time you try it, give yourself permission to abandon the official authorized handle and choke up a couple feet on the butt section the next time you find yourself needing a rod that is two feet shorter. You can cast just fine like that.

With close-up line control, the Old Guy could work the fly to great advantage. He could swing it into a tiny eddy behind a rock and just let it jive around for a little while. He could make it rise almost to the surface and then sink back a little, like a mayfly nymph that was not quite ready to break through the surface film. If he had two or three flies on, he could pitch the tail fly a couple feet beyond the feeding lane of a visible fish as an "anchor" and entice the fish up with a few little hops from the droppers that were still dangling in the air. We forfeit much of this kind of maneuvering flexibility on a sixty-foot cast with an eight-foot rod, but, again, with some adjustment in our habits and especially with a closer approach to the fish, we can reactivate many of these techniques without abandoning any of our comforting high-tech gear.

Perhaps an even more significant change since the Old Guy's day is our modern obsession with dead drift. We're all conditioned from birth to abhor drag, but the Old Guy preferred it. Some of the Old Guy's pals regarded it as a fatal mistake *ever* to allow a fly to drift unmanipulated. A little motion, just the slightest shiver down the line, might be the trick. Or maybe they'd give the fly a few good jerks just to attract attention. Some of them even made such motions with flies on the surface (imitating actual adult mayflies floating along on top), but many of them did so constantly with flies submerged somewhere in the first few inches of the water column.

Again, such delicate manipulation was much more precisely possible up close. With that long rod and short line, the Old Guy was in the enviable position of having his flies within sight almost all the time.

He could get very good at small, subtle redirections, jumps, and shakes of his flies.

With respect to leader size, some of our best instructional writers today have pointed out the advantage of very short leaders, a foot or two, in certain extreme situations. Keeping in mind the century or so during which even our fine and far-off expert Old Guy was using very supple gut leaders of 1X or 2X to take selective trout, we probably should be experimenting more often with heavier tippets today.

In the mid- to late 1900s, the idea prevailed that the most sporting method of taking a fish was the method that used the lightest tackle to give the fish the most advantage. Then, as scientific research indicated that playing a fish to exhaustion on such tackle might kill the fish, we began to draw back from that definition of good sport. Now, historical evidence and some modern commentators have shown that, especially with a fly that is kept in motion, fish will often tolerate a remarkably heavy tippet. The Old Guy had little choice but to use a fairly heavy tippet, and he made it work; that sounds like a pretty tidy metaphor for "good sport."

9. Choosing Our Way: The Baited Fly

One of the most entertaining and persistent minor tactics in the literature and lore of fly fishing is the baited fly. Every now and then as I read through the sport's seemingly endless number of books and shorter works, I find yet another mention of it. The reference is usually casual and slight, maybe just as an aside in a fishing story that has nothing to do with fishing methods. The technique never seemed to rise to the level of a formal "method" with its own rationales and tactical subtleties. It just happened. The Old Guy was out there, the fishing was slow, some big sturdy insect or worm was available, and he baited the fly and pitched it out there. It seemed to work really well.

If the Old Guy was of a mind to worry about the technicalities of the sport's definition (and I doubt he was), he might still have insisted that he was fly fishing. In his day, bait fishing with mayflies and other aquatic insects was common. It was widely recognized as a type of fly fishing, and it involved the same tackle and techniques as fishing with artificial flies. There were no fussy regulations to consult and no fly-fishing subculture to apply peer pressure against such behavior. The Old Guy was inclined to take every advantage he could, and the baited fly must have seemed like a very good one. Who could doubt its promise?

Today, virtually all serious fly fishers would agree that using bait (or even using scents, which have periodically enjoyed popularity among fly fishers) falls outside of the fly-fishing realm. Even our fish- and wildlife-management agencies define fly fishing as a method of angling that is absolutely exclusive of baited hooks (though they say little about chumming up fish with some kind of organic bait and then offering them a genuine inorganic fly while they're busy feeding on the meat).

Short of actually putting meat on the hook, however, practically everything else has at some time or other, in some angler's mind, qualified as fly fishing. Among the other curious aspects of fly-fishing history is the persistence of confidence; the champions of a hundred different approaches have all been convinced they had it figured out better than anyone else ever had before.

We abandoned many of the Old Guy's methods for reasons that seemed good at the time. Modern transportation allows us to live hundreds of miles from our favorite streams. Huge technological advances in rod and line construction over the past 150 years have led us into a romance with the happy athleticism and frequent advantages of distance casting. When I began fly fishing in the early 1970s, I could still expect to hear skeptics say that distance casting was very pretty to watch, but was otherwise pointless because even if a fish took your fly it was impossible to hook them at those distances. Nobody believes that anymore.

The rise in popularity of dry-fly fishing in the nineteenth century doomed many methods—and fly patterns—that suddenly seemed old-timey or unexciting. The countless people who chose to stay behind and keep fishing the older way became irrelevant to later historians of the sport, who tended to stick to the innovative side of the story and portray fly fishing as a sport with a simple, single evolutionary process. For the writers who saw the sport that way, it was a short step from ignoring all those anglers who still favored older methods to believing that the older methods had never worked very well anyway. We're still that way. Fashions change, and on we go.

But when it came to pure fishing wits and practical streamcraft, our predecessors centuries ago were our equals—and maybe sometimes our superiors. I have no intention of abandoning modern fly fishing's technological luxuries, but I'd be foolish not to pay attention to what the Old Guy accomplished without them.

10. The Better Fly Fisher

If there is one most important fly-fishing secret we should learn from the Old Guy, it's what his experiences taught us about how to *fish* in the broadest sense of that term. It's about what it takes to operate a society of anglers successfully. Even if there were no chance at all that the Old Guy could teach us something that would help us to catch fish, his books, articles, and journals would be worth reading just for what he can teach us about being good fishermen in the higher sense I described in the introduction to this book.

Most of us have at one time or another—and, I hope, much more often than that—been exposed to the standard broadsides and lectures on the importance of good sportsmanship. We are just as regularly bombarded with the urgency of being good stewards of the natural resources that enable us to enjoy fishing. Whenever those lessons grow stale or seem boring or even seem not to apply to us, we owe it to ourselves and to the sport to go back to the Old Guy's adventures and teachings, not because he always did such a great job of articulating these particular lessons, but because his experiences were the raw material from which we have inherited our own convictions about sportsmanship and conservation today.

The Old Guy lacked our grounding in aquatic ecology and our technological luxuries. He was a few centuries short of us in opportunities to grasp the historic picture of how to keep the sport on the ethical high road and how to keep the fish populations thriving. But he wasn't stupid about these things, either. Considering his times, his often very different values, and the urgency of many of his other priorities, it is remarkable how often he still intuited his way to the workable fundamentals of both good sportsmanship and good conservation. He didn't always manage to do so, and his failure rate in these essential enterprises may have been even higher than ours is today, but there is still no better way to illuminate our own successes and shortcomings than by spending some fishing time with the Old Guy from whom we inherited them.

Acknowledgments

My wife and hero, Marsha Karle, has always provided essential encouragement and patiently participated in some stupendously obscure conversations about everything from the wool of extinct pigs to the social construction of sporting ethics.

Books grow from earlier books. *Fly-Fishing Secrets of the Ancients* is the latest in a series of books I have written exploring the history, culture, and wonderful complications of fly fishing. I should acknowledge and emphasize the impetus provided by previous books, most especially *American Fly Fishing: A History* (1987). Readers of the current book will notice that most chapters here had their start in—and sometimes necessarily restate—earlier discussions in that book.

But this book also owes a lesser debt to some of my other previous books, especially *Royal Coachman* (1999), *The Rise* (2006), *Cowboy Trout* (2006), and *If Fish Could Scream* (2008). In all of these works, to one extent or another, I have pursued the overlapping tangles of this or that part of fly-fishing history. *Fly-Fishing Secrets of the Ancients* continues that pursuit, and the endnotes invite you to my previous considerations of related topics in other books.

As I suggest in the introduction, *Fly-Fishing Secrets of the Ancients* was made possible by the study and research I did for my column in *American Angler*. But those columns were rather like abstracts—the briefest of overviews—for the stories I tell here. That said, I'm grateful beyond saying for *American Angler* editor Phil Monahan's continued enthusiasm for this column and for his frequent suggestions along the way. The present longer forms of these articles have in some cases also appeared in *The American Fly Fisher*, the journal of the American Museum of Fly Fishing, so I thank Kathleen Achor, editor of *The American Fly Fisher*, for her interest in and help with this material.

Much of the acknowledging I must do for a book like this is handled in the endnotes, where I try very hard to recognize all the significant sources of information and ideas gathered here. But I would also like to thank many other people.

At the American Museum of Fly Fishing, Gary Tanner and Yoshi Akiyama were unfailingly helpful. As soon as you finish reading this book, you should think seriously about joining the museum; it's doing fly fishers a world of good, and far too many of them don't even know it's there. Find out more about it at http://www.amff.com.

At Montana State University, former dean of libraries Bruce Morton, present dean Tamara Miller, Special Collections librarian Kim Scott, and their staff have helped not only by running such an exemplary and exciting research facility, but also by their championing of the university's outstanding trout and salmonid collection, which deserves the generous support of thinking anglers everywhere. For more information about this perfectly intentioned project, go to http://www.lib.montana.edu/trout.

At York University, historian Richard Hoffmann has helped by his friendship, good counsel, and stellar example of how historical scholarship should be practiced. His many writings on the early history of sport fishing, especially fly fishing, constitute a dramatic illumination of what was previously a fairly murky scene for most of us.

Ken Cameron, long-time commentator on fly fishing's cloudy values and quirky history, has been a patient and always stimulating correspondent for more than thirty years now, alerting me to information and ideas from his own research and experience.

Others who have helped me sort through all this theory and intention for myself over the past thirty-five years or so—by taking me fishing, explaining their ideas, sending me exciting material and references, doubting my opinions and interpretations, listening to me ramble on about this or that, or otherwise helping me keep these inquiries going—include Bob Behnke, Jim Brown, John Betts, Gordon Brittan, Bill Cass, Ted Comstock, David Detweiler, Bob DeMott, Brian Dippie, the late George Grant, Dale Greenley, John Harder, the late Jack Heddon, Andrew Herd, Wes Hill, the late Austin Hogan, Alec Jackson,

Martin Keane, the late Hermann Kessler, Ed Koch, Richard Kress, David Ledlie, Bud Lilly, Esther Lilly, Nick Lyons, E. J. Malone, Leon Martuch, John Merwin, Leigh Perkins, Perk Perkins, John Randolph, Tom Rosenbauer, Dianne Russell, Judith Schnell, Steve Schullery, the late Helen Shaw, Reverend Robert Spaight, John Varley, Mark Webster, the late Bob Wethern, Lee Whittlesey, and the late Craig Woods.

A special thanks to Clark Whitehorn at the University of New Mexico Press for his interest in this topic. The press's anonymous reviewer of the manuscript made dozens of suggestions and corrections that substantially improved the final version. Copy editor Annie Barva's refinements of the text were beyond counting.

I should note that the spelling in the three opening epigraphs has been modernized—without, I hope, any harm to their spirit or meaning. The lovely little Samuel statement is in fact only part of a longer sentence.

Fly-Fishing Secrets of the Ancients is dedicated to two life-long angling friends, Bill Cass and John Harder. In 1977, when I moved to Vermont to become director of the American Museum of Fly Fishing, they were working for Orvis and generously and patiently introduced me to many of the finer points of the world of fly fishing. I still can't believe they put up with me. They have also moved on from Vermont, Bill to Maine and John to Idaho. We have never lost touch and in recent years have even managed to fish together again. It has been my privilege.

Notes

Chapter One

1. Alfred Ronalds, *The Fly-Fisher's Entomology* (London: Longmans, 1836; reprint, Secaucus, N.J.: Wellfleet Press, 1990); William C. Stewart, *The Practical Angler* (Edinburgh: Black, 1857).
2. I stand by my comments on the dame in *Royal Coachman: The Lore and Legends of Fly Fishing* (New York: Simon and Schuster, 1999), 33–41, which summarize the long scholarship on the *Treatyse* and its rumored author.
3. Frederick Buller and Hugh Falkus, *Dame Juliana: The Angling Treatyse and Its Mysteries* (Moretonhampstead, U.K.: Fly Fisher's Classic Library, 2001). Though I happily disagree with a number of their points, or at least with the extent to which those points are either persuasive or conclusive, anybody at all interested in the *Treatyse* as a fishing manual must read this handsome and thoughtful book.
4. As is so often the case in matters of fly-fishing history, Andrew Herd's *The Fly* (Shropshire, U.K.: Medlar Press, 2003) is a handy source on the newer views. Chapter 2 covers fly-fishing techniques in the seventeenth century.
5. Ernest Schwiebert's *Trout*, vol. 2 (New York: E. P. Dutton, 1978), covers wet flies on pages 1347–66 and nymph fishing on pages 1417–49.
6. Jack Heddon, "An Attempt to Reproduce Early Nineteenth Century Fly Dressings," *American Fly Fisher* 2 (2) (Spring 1975), 12. I also celebrate, rather briefly, the work of Heddon and others as well as some of the high points of Heddon's theorizing in *Royal Coachman*, 101–5.
7. Conrad Voss Bark, "Dry Fly Dogma in Dispute," *The Field*, April 3, 1981, page number unavailable.
8. Herd, *The Fly*, 89.
9. It's also worth pointing out that Heddon, although the most outspoken of the dry-fly revisionists, was not the first. In the United States, A. I.

Alexander published the thoughtful and well-documented article "Exploring Dry Fly Origins," *Trout* 15 (2) (Spring 1974): 12–13, 32–33, which outlines many of the same points and cites a variety of pre-1800 fishing books that plainly described fishing floating flies. Another very important contribution to this dialogue is David Ledlie, "Dry Flies on the Ondawa: The Tragic Tale of John Harrington Keene, Part II," *The American Fly Fisher* 13 (2) (Spring 1986): 9–17. The special strength of Ledlie's article for our purposes is that it remains the most thorough summary of publications about the formal, Halfordian style of dry-fly fishing in America in the late 1800s. Specifically, it lists numerous books and lengthy series of articles published in America that exposed angling readers to the dry fly in great detail in the years prior to 1890, in contrast to the popular and erroneous myth that maintains that Theodore Gordon received in a letter from Frederick Halford the first British dry flies ever to reach America. In 1986, I published "Dry Fly History Is All Wet," *The Flyfisher* 19 (1) (Winter 1986): 14–15, 20–21, which lists many nineteenth-century accounts of fishing floating flies. I repeat much of this argument in my book *American Fly Fishing: A History* (New York: Nick Lyons Books, 1987), 100–110.

10. Paul Schullery, *The Rise: Streamside Observations on Trout, Flies, and Fly Fishing* (Mechanicsburg, Penn.: Stackpole Books, 2006), 162–64.

11. It surprises many of us to learn that even in the nineteenth century—and even on the famous chalk streams of southern England—the term *fly fishing* also meant fishing with large, live mayflies or other insects impaled on a hook. Blow-line fishing with such a dainty bait remained popular well into the late 1800s. In the fascinating book *River Keeper: The Life of William James Lunn* (London: Geoffrey Bles, 1934), John Waller Hills offers this wonderful description of the practice on the famous River Test as of 1887:

> The rod was eighteen to twenty feet long, usually of bamboo, the line undressed silk, with a gut casting line of three yards. With this, a good blower could get out thirty or forty yards of line, working it out gradually and, of course, keeping the fly and the line off the water all the time. Indeed, it was considered bad fishing to let any of your reel line touch the surface, even when you put the fly before a fish: for it was believed that undressed silk was toted by wetting. But this practice had one great disadvantage. With thirty yards of line in the air, on one of those wild May days common in the Test valley, it was difficult to keep your fly from being blown off the water. Lunn discovered that by laying a few yards of reel line on the surface, your bait was steadied and more fish killed. And for other reasons, blow-line fishing was not the easy amateurish business which we are apt to assume. It required considerable skill to work out

> thirty yards of line. At thirty yards, your hooked mayfly was hard to pick out amid the cloud of natural insects, and it was still harder to place in front of a rising trout. (15)

12. Herd cites Pulman and gives the same quote in *The Fly*, 90.
13. Thomas Barker, *Barker's Delight: Or, The Art of Angling* (London: Humphrey Moseley, 1659), 11. I use the second edition, reprinted in facsimile by J. Milton French, *Three Books on Fishing (1599–1659) Associated with* The Complete Angler *(1653) by Izaak Walton* (Gainesville, Fla.: Scholars' Facsimiles and Reprints, 1962).
14. G. P. R. Pulman, *The Vade-Mecum of Fly-Fishing for Trout* (London: Longman, Brown, Green, & Longmans, 1851), 159.
15. Robert Venables, *The Experienced Angler: Or Angling Improved* (London: Richard Marriot, 1662), 17.
16. John Betts, "Fly Lines and Lineage," *The American Fly Fisher* 26 (4) (Fall 2000), 18. This article is a splendid overview of how fly-line construction may have affected casting styles.
17. Schullery, *The Rise*, 113–15.
18. See Richard C. Hoffmann, *Fisher's Craft and Lettered Art: Tracts on Fishing from the End of the Middle Ages* (Toronto: University of Toronto Press, 1997), 147.
19. The quotes from Venables are given in Herd, *The Fly*, 102.
20. For me, the most startling realization involved in understanding early terminology related to the top, middle, and bottom has been that the "middle" as early writers defined it was surprisingly shallow. For Cotton, the middle was "half a foot or a foot within the superficies of the water" where he fished minnows. It wasn't, as might be supposed from the term, halfway between the surface and the bottom. See Charles Cotton, "Directions How to Angle for Trout or Grayling in a Clear Stream," part II of *The Compleat Angler* by Izaak Walton (London: John Lane, 1897), 353.
21. Hewett Wheatley, *The Rod and Line* (London: Longman, Brown, Green & Longmans, 1849), 65. I work from the beautiful facsimile edition from the Flyfisher's Classic Library (Moretonhampstead, U.K., 2002), the first new edition of this book since the original.
22. John Younger, *River Angling for Salmon and Trout* (Kelso, Scotland: Rutherfurd, 1864), 63–64. Again, I am working from a fine facsimile reprint by the Flyfisher's Classic Library (Moretonhampstead, U.K., 1995).
23. In Younger, *River Angling*, 65.
24. James E. Leisenring and Vernon S. Hidy, *The Art of Tying the Wet Fly & Fishing the Flymph* (New York: Crown, 1971), 123. This edition is heavily augmented by Vernon S. (Pete) Hidy, who added the material on the *flymph*, his term for a wet fly of the Leisenring style fished near the surface (123, 18).
25. Taverner quoted in James Robb, *Notable Angling Literature* (London: Herbert Jenkins, 1947), 90–91.

26. Sara McBride, "Entomology for Fly Fishers," edited by Ken Cameron, *The American Fly Fisher* 5 (2) (Spring 1978): 11–14.
27. Kenneth Cameron, "Sara McBride: Pioneer Angling Entomologist," *The American Fly Fisher* 5 (2) (Spring 1978), 10–11. Although McBride stands out as a sharp observer of stream entomology in the late 1800s, she was hardly alone. My favorite earlier example of emerger imitation was reported by William Harris, prominent American angling editor and author, from a trip to the Yellowstone River in Montana in 1885: "I was somewhat surprised at the fly-fishing methods of the resident anglers of Livingston. Casting the fly is not the practice, albeit every fisher uses a cast of from three to six flies weighted with a split shot, with which they plumb the depths, bringing the flies by successive short, quick jerks to the top of the water, and then allowing them to sink; then repeating the operation, which is very similar, hence successful, to the rise of the caddis and other ephemera from their watery home to assume the butterfly form." William C. Harris ("W. C. H."), "Editorial Notes on the 'Cut-Throat Trout,'" *The American Angler*, August 8, 1885, 24. I quote this description in my book *American Fly Fishing*, 86. These Montana fly fishers may have been unschooled in the finer points of entomology, but like many generations of European anglers before them, they knew what was happening in their rivers and what to do about it.
28. Examples from the spectrum of opinions abound. On one side of the issue, in England George Bainbridge said that the metal beads sometimes used as eyes for dragonfly imitations were "reprehensible," and he didn't even approve of the extra weight added to a fly by a heavy wrapping of gold or silver wire. Any such weight, Bainbridge said, would sink the fly too deeply (*The Fly Fisher's Guide*, 1816 ed. [reprint, [N.p. given]: Flyfisher's Classic Library, 1992], 100). On the other side of the issue, by happenstance in the United States, J. Whyte recommended that the fly tier "form the head of your fly with a No. 1, 2, or 3 shot as you please: it makes an excellent head, and enables you to throw five or six yards further against the wind, nor does it sink your fly one jot too much" ("A Wrinkle for Anglers," *The Spirit of the Times*, May 9, 1857, 150).
29. Robert Barnwell Roosevelt, *Superior Fishing* (New York: Carleton, 1865), 270.
30. Francis Francis, *A Book on Angling*, 6th ed. (London: Longmans, Green & Company, 1885), 161. Francis, however, provides us with an example of how confused and complicated the issues of defining fly fishing could be even back then. He was quite willing to cast a fly downstream "and work the fly up against it," but, as he said, that was "not *fly*-fishing." When fishing downstream like that, one apparently was violating the idea of fly fishing because one was no longer imitating adult insects, but a "larva, spider, or some other water insect." Francis also recommended that when fish are "only on larva don't worry them with fly or you spoil them." He said that when fishing

downstream like this to imitate larvae, you would do best to let the fly and line sink, and then work the fly up and down "by gently rising and falling the top of the road." Whether knowing it or not, he was, like others long before Leisenring, imitating emergers. Oddly enough, he seemed to use the same fly *pattern* for all these purposes, even though some did not meet his definition of fly fishing (all quotes on p. 163).

31. Henry P. Wells, *Fly-Rods and Fly-Tackle* (New York: Harper Brothers, 1885), 292.
32. Doug Swisher and Carl Richards, *Emergers* (New York: Lyons Press, 1991).
33. For a nice recent consideration of the changing wet-fly universe, see Gordon Wickstrom, "Where Are the Flies of Yesteryear? An Essay with Interlinear Commentary," *The American Fly Fisher* 30 (1) (Winter 2004): 14–19. And anyone interested in the subject of evolving flies must not miss the milestone essay on fly-tying theory by Ken Cameron, "Fly Styles," *The American Fly Fisher* 8 (1) (Winter 1981): 2–7.

Chapter Two

1. Ed Van Put, "Ed Van Put, Technician," *Fish & Fly* (Spring 2003), 76.
2. I am most indebted to my friend Ken Cameron for insights on this development. I cite Ken's articles here and there throughout this book, and all demonstrate one of modern angling's most critical and penetrating perspectives at work.
3. Easily the best review I have seen of the early literature of fly tying appears in Darrel Martin's wonderful new book *The Fly-Fisher's Craft: The Art and History* (Guilford, Conn.: Lyons Press, 2006), especially the generously long chapter "Antique Tying," 5–68. This documentary history traces the known development of the early techniques.
4. For some excellent photographs of flies from the late 1700s and early 1800s, with equally helpful commentary, see *The American Fly Fisher* 26 (4) (Fall 2000), 14–16. The photographs include Sara Wilcox, "Gallery," 14–15, and Ken Cameron, "First Impressions of the Harris Flies," 16. For a variety of pre-1800 illustrations of flies, many of which are variants on the same original illustration, see Ken Cameron and Andrew Herd, "Standing on the Shoulders of Giants," *The American Fly Fisher* 27 (3) (Summer 2001): 12–19. This article, which traces the complex lineage of certain important eighteenth-century illustrations, is a model of the kind of historical detective work that makes the study of fly-fishing history so engaging.
5. F. Fernie, *Dry-Fly Fishing in Border Waters* (London: Adam and Charles Black, 1912), 58.
6. Polly Rosborough, *Tying and Fishing the Fuzzy Nymphs* (Caldwell, Idaho: Caxton, 1965, and later editions), and John Atherton, *The Fly and the Fish* (New York: Macmillan, 1951). I do not understand why a book as excellent and significant as Atherton's has been out of print for so long.

7. Doug Swisher and Carl Richards, *Emergers* (New York: Lyons Press, 1991), and Ted Fauceglia, *Mayflies* (Mechanicsburg, Penn.: Stackpole Books, 2005).
8. Gary Borger, *Nymphing* (Harrisburg, Penn.: Stackpole Books, 1979), 72.
9. G. E. M. Skues, *Side-Lines, Side-Lights, and Reflections* (London: Seeley, Service, 1932), 419–20. The material quoted first appeared in *Salmon and Trout Magazine* (October 1925).
10. Peter O'Reilly, *Trout & Salmon Flies of Ireland* (Shropshire, U.K.: Merlin Unwin Books, 1995).
11. Vernon Edgar, "Having a Dabble," *Trout Fisherman* (June 1990), 18–19, and E. J. Malone, *Irish Trout and Salmon Flies* (Machynlleth, U.K.: Coch-Y-Bonddu Books, 1998), 103.
12. Malone, *Irish Trout and Salmon Flies*, 103.
13. E. J. Malone to the author, March 24, 2003.
14. Brian Clarke and John Goddard, *The Trout and the Fly* (New York: Nick Lyons Books, 1980), 72. (This work is not easy to cite. On the cover, the authors are listed as Clarke and Goddard, but on the title page they are listed as Goddard and Clarke. I assume the difference was their little joke at the time and have tried to stick with Clarke and Goddard.)
15. Roderick Haig-Brown, *Fisherman's Spring* (New York: Morrow, 1951), 130.

Chapter Three

1. James Chetham, *The Angler's Vade Mecum, or a Compendius, Yet Full, Discourse of Angling*, 2d ed. (London: T. Basset and W. Brown, 1689), 69, 73.
2. Ibid., 140, 217. This information was plainly cribbed from Charles Cotton's pioneering essay, first published in 1676 as a second part of the fifth edition of Izaak Walton's *Compleat Angler*. There are several hundred editions of Walton's book to choose from, so I refer you to the handsome edition edited by Richard Le Gallienne (London: John Lane, the Bodley Head, 1897; paperback reprint, London: Senate, 1994), 327. In *A Book on Angling* (London: Longmans, Green, & Company, 1867), the British writer Francis Francis, however, traced the name of the fly to a specific insect rather than to the cow pies themselves. He wrote that "wherever there be meads and cows, there the angler may be sure, particularly in the spring, to find the cow-dung fly, and a large number may always be observed, thanks to the wind's agency, upon the water, where, maugre their savory origin, they afford much delectation to the hungry trout" (189). Whether the fly's name and characteristics came from the cow, the dung, or the bug apparently depended on the tier's observations and imagination. It does little for the trout's now refined and high-society reputation that it was ever known to enjoy such an earthy snack as fresh feces.
3. John Hawkins, footnote commentary in Izaak Walton, *The Complete Angler* (London: Thomas Hope, 1797), 100. The Hawkins editions generally but not always used *complete* rather than *compleat* in the title. Although the

historical record leaves little room for doubt that the animal that these fly tiers were discussing actually was a pig, and although current efforts to increase populations of these rare pigs may bode well for increased use of this type of wool, there is an interesting uncertainty in this story, too. According to Thomas Wright, the compiler of *Dictionary of Obsolete and Provincial English. Containing words from the English writers previous to the nineteenth century which are not longer in use, or are not used in the same sense. And words which are now used only in the provincial dialects*, vol. 2 (London: Henry G. Bohn, 1856), there was a time when the term *hog wool* also meant the first fleece of new lambs (573). So it could be that some of our pre-1800 prescriptions for the use of hog wool in fly tying referred not to actual pigs, but to sheep.

4. Hawkins, notes to Walton, *The Complete Angler*, 98.
5. Ibid.
6. Quoted in Harold Smedley, *Fly Patterns and Their Origins* (Muskegon, Mich.: Westshore, 1946), 55.
7. Art Flick, *Art Flick's New Streamside Guide to Naturals and Their Imitations* (New York: Crown, 1969), 69. This edition is somewhat enlarged and improved, containing a number of excellent color photographs of the insects and their imitations taken by Doug Swisher and Carl Richards. Thus, besides its own grand contribution to the literature of fly tying and fly-fishing entomology, Flick's book served as one of the early previews of the immensely influential book Swisher and Richards themselves would publish only two years later, *Selective Trout* (New York: Crown, 1971).

   To my knowledge, the two most thorough treatments of the history of the Hendrickson fly patterns and their use are Ernest Schwiebert, *Remembrances of Rivers Past* (New York: Macmillan, 1972), 144–51, and Paul Schullery, *Royal Coachman: The Lore and Legends of Fly Fishing* (New York: Simon and Schuster, 1999), 139–56.
8. W. H. Lawrie, *English Trout Flies* (New York: A. S. Barnes, 1969), 186.
9. George Leonard Herter, *Professional Fly Tying, Spinning, and Tackle Making Manual and Manufacturers' Guide*, rev. 19th ed. (Waseca, Minn.: Herter's, 1971), 448–49.
10. Charles Bowlker, *The Art of Angling* (Ludlow, U.K.: Richard Jones, 1839), 128. Note that Bowlker (and many others, as it happened) often did use the term *warp* where we would now use *wrap*. The latex product known as "gutta percha," from a southeastern Asian or Australasian tree by the same name, was another rubber-type variant that fly tiers occasionally employed.

    A number of modern writers have emphasized that the Bowlker book is very important historically, and I certainly agree, but it is a difficult book to cite comfortably because new editions of it appeared after its authors, father and son Richard and Charles Bowlker, were long dead. The first edition probably appeared sometime between 1746 and 1758; authorities are congenial in admitting their uncertainty about the publication date.

The first edition was apparently solely the work of Richard, but by the third edition, in about 1785, the books were attributed to Charles. However, even the son was dead by 1779, so although we would like to presume that an 1839 edition of the book preserves the words of at least one or possibly both Bowlkers, it really speaks, as it were, from the grave. Convention among angling historians has been simply to quote "Bowlker" without reference to the complications of there being two of them or of their being long gone by the time the book's later editions appeared. Among the writers who have summarized this bibliographical genealogy is John Waller Hills, *A History of Fly Fishing for Trout* (London: Allan, 1921), especially 88–90. See also, of course, the magnificent bibliography by Thomas Westwood and Thomas Satchell, *Bibliotheca Piscatoria: A Catalogue of Books on Angling, the Fisheries, and Fish Culture* (London: W. Satchell, 1883), 39–40.

What's worse, when reading Bowlker, one is not always sure that one is reading Bowlker. Although a number of the early angling writers notoriously cribbed extended passages of instruction from earlier books, and although Bowlker is actually given some credit for discarding or at least tidying up generations of previous cribbing by earlier authors, reading the later editions of the book is still a trying experience. Editors working with the text long after the death of both Bowlkers felt free to borrow extensively from other, later authors who might also be dead, so reading the 1839 edition is an adventure in second-guessing the narrative as you try to discern who is speaking from which grave.

11. James Rennie, *Alphabet of Scientific Angling* (London: Orr and Smith, 1836), 82.
12. Francis, *A Book on Angling*, 211.
13. For Hall's experiments, see Tony Hayter, *F. M. Halford and the Dry-Fly Revolution* (London: Robert Hale, 2002), 80.
14. Mary Orvis Marbury, *Favorite Flies and Their Histories* (Boston: Houghton Mifflin, 1892), 382. I suspect that one of Marbury's sources of information on the use of scale wings was John Harrington Keene, mentioned next, who worked with the Orvises in this period. For an outstanding summary of Keene's remarkable career, see David B. Ledlie, "Dry Flies on the Ondawa: The Tragic Tale of John Harrington Keene," *The American Fly Fisher* 13 (1) (Winter 1986): 8–17.

As early as 1973, well before the later debates over Theodore Gordon's supposed paternity of the American dry fly arose, angling historian Austin Hogan declared unequivocally that Keene "introduced the first dry fly pattern to America," referring to an article Keene contributed to *American Angler* on August 18, 1885. See Austin Hogan, *American Sporting Periodicals of Angling Interest* (Manchester, Vt.: Museum of American Fly Fishing, 1973), 99. It now is clear that Keene, who wrote many articles on fly fishing, imitation, and dry flies, was only one of several writers in the American press who, along with several fishing-tackle companies, introduced American anglers to dry flies in the 1880s. He was, however, undoubtedly one of the most fully descriptive of these early dry-fly experts, basing his articles and books on his long personal experience on British waters.

15. John Harrington Keene, *Fly-Fishing and Fly-Making*, 2d ed. (New York: Forest and Stream Publishing, 1891), 125–26.
16. Ibid., 125–32.
17. Theodore Gordon, *Theodore Gordon on Trout: Talks and Tales from a Great American Angler*, edited by Paul Schullery (Mechanicsburg, Penn.: Stackpole Books, 2007), 100.
18. George Edward Mackenzie Skues, *Silk, Fur, and Feather: The Trout-Fly Dresser's Year* (Moretonhampstead, U.K.: Flyfisher's Classic Library, 1993), 12. This book was first posthumously published in 1950 by the *Fishing Gazette*, from a series of articles it had published. The Flyfisher's Classic Library edition is, as usual, a beautiful production.
19. Theodore Rogowski, "Crackerbarrel Discourses," in *The Gordon Garland*, edited by Arnold Gingrich (New York: Theodore Gordon Flyfishers, 1965), 127. This isn't to say that nylon didn't receive the attention of fly tiers before the 1960s. In *Fly-Fishing Pioneers & Legends of the Northwest* (Seattle: Northwest Fly Fishing, 2006), Jack Berryman reports that in 1941 Seattle-based fly fishers Ken (father) and George (son) McLeod developed what they called their "Nylon Nymph" (180).

Chapter Four

1. A splendid modern overview of the horsehair line and parallel developments in other lines in recent centuries is Darrel Martin's elegantly illustrated chapter "The Line," in *The Fly-Fisher's Craft: The Art and History*, 217–39 (Guilford, Conn.: Lyons Press, 2006), which also contains much about how you make your own.

   For more on the history of fishing lines and fly lines, see William Radcliffe, *Fishing from the Earliest Times* (London: Murray, 1921), which contains many brief discussions of various kinds of lines; John Waller Hills, *A History of Fly Fishing for Trout* (London: Allan, 1921), 20, 21, 48, 68, and 87; Paul Schullery, *American Fly Fishing: A History* (New York: Nick Lyons Books, 1987), 72–73, 205–6, 209–11, and 252; and Andrew Herd, *The Fly* (Shropshire, U.K.: Medlar Press, 2003), throughout. Among older works, Henry P. Wells's *Fly-Rods and Fly-Tackle* (New York: Harper Brothers, 1885), 40–89, offers a good summary of the state of lines and leaders in the late nineteenth century. Just for fun, to get a modern, practical perspective on how a horsehair line is made, see Charles Brooks, "Making and Fishing the Horsehair Fly Line," *The American Fly Fisher* 3 (4) (Fall 1976), 28–29.
2. Martin, *The Fly-Fisher's Craft*, 222.
3. According to Radcliffe, *Fishing from the Earliest Times*, this avoidance of urine-weakened mare's tail hair dates back at least as far as Plutarch

(237). Gervase Markham, *The Pleasures of Princes, or Good Mens Recreation* (London: John Browne, 1614), typified the preferences of many later writers in selecting the best horsehair. He specified not only that it must be hair from a large, healthy male horse tail (not from the mane), but also that it be "that which growest from the middle and inmost part of his back" (7).

4. Robert Venables, *The Experienc'd Angler, or Angling Improv'd* (London: Richard Marriot, 1662), 5.
5. Ibid.
6. For one strong opinion among many regarding the relative merits of hair and silk fly lines in the mid–nineteenth century, here's G. P. R. Pulman, writing in *The Vade-Mecum of Fly-Fishing for Trout* (London: Longman, Brown, Green, & Longmans, 1851): "The silk line is totally useless; it imbibes the water too readily, and thus becomes over heavy. The silk-and-hair lines are generally considered best, and when they contain only a very small proportion of silk, they certainly have very considerable claims to that distinction; especially the London patent lines, which are very evenly and beautifully spun. But for the style of rod which we recommend—namely, a light and stiff one—there is perhaps nothing better adapted than a hair line, if its extreme fine end be rejected, and the tapering, for a yard or so, before joining the collar, be continued with a substitution of twisted gut, forming what is called a 'point' or 'bottom'" (76–77).
7. Radcliffe offers a fascinating summary of fishing tackle and techniques, with numerous mentions of silk or gut, in *Fishing from the Earliest Times*, 449–68. In *Trout*, vol. 1 (New York: E. P. Dutton, 1978), Ernest Schwiebert adds additional notes on more recent scholarly findings relating to early Chinese angling (11–14, 762). As helpful is John Orelle's "Evolution of the Fishing Reel," *The Flyfisher* 9 (1) (1976): 3–6. But the real historical mother lode of background on silkworm production as it relates to fly fishing is found in a series of articles in *The American Fly Fisher:* Lothar H. H. Martin, "The History of Silkworm Gut," *The American Fly Fisher* 17 (3) (Fall 1991): 3–7; John Mundt, "Silk Fly Line Manufacturing: A Brief History," *The American Fly Fisher* 17 (3) (Fall 1991): 8–13; and Richard C. Hoffmann, "The Oldest Silk in Fly Fishing," *The American Fly Fisher* 19 (1) (Winter 1993): 16–19. The Hoffmann article is a fine summary of early mentions of silk in European (including British) writings from the fifteenth century and later, especially as the thread of choice for fly tying.
8. Stanley Sadie, ed., *The New Grove Dictionary of Music and Musicians*, 2d ed. (New York: Macmillan, 2002), 580–82. This book is the primary source for my discussion of animal sinew and "gut."
9. Pepys is quoted in Alfred M. Mayer, *Sport with Gun and Rod* (New York: Century, 1883), 605.
10. Venables, *The Experienc'd Angler*, 5.
11. In *The Fly Fisher's Craft*, Martin provides additional early citations to the use of animal gut line used by eighteenth-century anglers and offers

additional insights on the confusion between catgut and silkworm gut (19, 218–19). In *The Vade-Mecum of Fly-Fishing for Trout*, Pulman mentioned that "an inferior kind of gut is manufactured from the sinews of herons and other birds" (87).

I should at least go into a little more detail here about yet another confusing term in the historical tangle that is the history of gut, *gutta percha*, which I mentioned in chapter 3(note 10). The gutta percha is a tree native to Southeast Asia and the islands between there and Australia, and the same name is used for the latex produced by that tree. This substance, which came to the attention of the British in the 1840s, had many uses; it was a tough and easily worked material that sometimes found its way into fly-tying practice. Some have even described it as an early plastic.

12. Thaddeus Norris, *The American Angler's Book*, 2d ed. (Philadelphia: E. H. Butler, 1865), 68–69.
13. Wells, *Fly-Rods and Fly-Tackle*, 56.
14. Saunders is quoted in both Mayer, *Sport with Gun and Rod*, 605, and Herd, *The Fly*, 184.
15. Mayer, *Sport with Gun and Rod*, 605.
16. Hills, *A History of Fly Fishing for Trout*, 95.
17. David Webster, *The Angler and the Loop Rod* (Edinburgh: William Blackwood, 1885). Webster's line and "gut-line" were attached, or looped, directly to the end of the fly rod. He did not use a reel. He did, however, use a cast of nine flies.
18. Herd, *The Fly*, 183–88.
19. John Brown, *The American Angler's Guide* (New York: Burgess, Stringer, 1845), 31.
20. In *Fly-Rods and Fly-Tackle*, Wells gives a very detailed discussion of the leaders of the day (1885), with digressions into various Americans' then hopeful but eventually unsuccessful attempts to produce gut domestically from native insects (55–89). The quote is from the 1901 edition of Wells's book (New York: Harper Brothers), portions of which were reprinted in facsimile without original pagination in Cliff Netherton, *History of the Sport of Casting: People, Events, Records, Tackle, and Literature, Early Times* (Lakeland, Fla.: American Casting Educational Foundation, 1981), 192.
21. Leon L. Martuch, "Fly Leader," in *McClane's New Standard Fishing Encyclopedia and International Angling Guide*, edited by A. J. McClane (New York: Holt, Rinehart and Winston, 1974), 382. The name designations did not signify precise diameter. For example, according to the *Hardy Brothers Catalog* (Alnwick, U.K., 1914), Refina varied from 0.007- to 0.009-inch diameter, and Fina varied from 0.011- to 0.013-inch diameter (111). Note that the Refina measured by Martuch (manufacturer unspecified) was 0.011. Cynical observers of these numbers pointed out that for all the advertised precision, the reality was much less consistent, and the advertised diameters were usually less than the real diameters.

22. Wells, *Fly-Rods and Fly-Tackle* (1901 ed.), as reproduced in Netherton, *History of the Sport of Casting*, 192.
23. J. C. Mottram, *Fly Fishing: Some New Arts and Mysteries* (London: Field & Queen, Horace Cox, 1915), 223.
24. I have tried a few times to graduate to the new fluorocarbons and their ilk, but always with disappointing results. Perhaps I'll stick with regular old mono for another generation or so and try again.
25. Ray Bergman, *Trout*, reprint with revisions by Edward C. Janes (New York: Knopf, 1976), 157–58.
26. Roderick Haig-Brown, *A Primer of Fly-Fishing* (New York: Morrow, 1964), 41.
27. Leigh Perkins, "Notes and Comment," *The American Fly Fisher* 31 (2) (Spring 2005), 24.
28. Samuel Camp, *Fishing with Floating Flies* (New York: Outing, 1913), 44.
29. Herd, *The Fly*, 327.

Chapter Five

1. Joe Brooks, *Trout Fishing* (New York: Harper and Row, 1972), 167.
2. Richard C. Hoffmann, *Fisher's Craft and Lettered Art: Tracts on Fishing from the End of the Middle Ages* (Toronto: University of Toronto Press, 1997), 125.
3. Thomas Evan Pritt, *The Book of the Grayling* (Dumfriesshire, Scotland: Signet, 1992; reprint of the 1888 edition), 38.
4. Theodore Gordon, *Theodore Gordon on Trout: Talks and Tales from a Great American Angler*, edited by Paul Schullery (Mechanicsburg, Penn.: Stackpole Books, 2007), 71.
5. Ibid., 92.
6. H. C. Cutcliffe, *Trout Fishing on Rapid Streams* (South Moulton, U.K.: Tucker Printer Square, 1863), 84. I review at some length the history and variety of actions we have imparted to surface flies and above-surface flies in the chapter "Skippers, Skaters, Dappers, and Dancers" in *The Rise: Streamside Observations on Trout, Flies, and Fly Fishing* (Mechanicsburg, Penn.: Stackpole Books, 2006), 159–73.
7. George Bainbridge, *The Fly Fisher's Guide* (Liverpool: n.p., 1816; reprint, [N.p. given]: Flyfisher's Classic Library, 1992), 52.
8. Cutcliffe, *Trout Fishing on Rapid Streams*, 85.
9. David Webster, *The Angler and the Loop Rod* (Edinburgh: William Blackwood, 1885), 123–24.
10. Alfred Ronalds, *The Fly-Fisher's Entomology* (London: Longman, 1836; reprint, Secaucus, N.J.: Wellfleet Press, 1990), 46–47. The Wellfleet Press edition is an inexpensive one that is perhaps the only edition many of us can readily find or afford, so I offer here some possibly helpful background on it. For some reason, Wellfleet Press (rather discourteously, in my opinion) obscured all references to the edition date in the book's front matter. For

those readers who are interested, I will say that I suspect that the Wellfleet edition comes from the fourth edition of the book, published in London in 1849 by Longman. According to the author's preface in the Wellfleet edition, "The present edition of the 'Fly-Fisher's Entomology' has the full sanction of the Author, for whose approval the chief alterations were sent to him in Australia" (viii). According to Hugh Sheringham's "Editor's Introduction" to a later edition of the book, published in 1921 by Herbert Jenkins Limited of London, Ronalds moved from North Wales to Australia in 1848. According to Thomas Westwood and Thomas Satchell, the third edition of Ronalds's book was published in 1844, and the fourth edition was published in 1849 (*Bibliotheca Piscatoria: A Catalogue of Books on Angling, the Fisheries, and Fish Culture* [London: W. Satchell, 1883], 178). Thus, 1849 is the year of the first edition of the book to be published after Ronalds left for Australia. Thus, I assume that the Wellfleet edition reprints no earlier edition than the fourth. The preface in the fifth edition, the one reprinted by Jenkins in 1921, is much shorter than the preface in the Wellfleet edition, so the Wellfleet edition is evidently not a reprint of the fifth. The sixth and later editions have longer prefaces, according to Westwood and Satchell, so for the moment I will stick with my best guess that the Wellfleet edition reprints the fourth edition. I suspect that the quotation I have given is essentially unchanged from the first edition to the fourth.

11. Francis Francis, *A Book on Angling* (London: Longmans, Green & Company, 1867), 138.
12. Charles Bowlker, *The Art of Angling* (Ludlow, U.K.: Richard Jones, 1839), 112.
13. Thomas Tod Stoddart, *The Angler's Companion to the Rivers & Lochs of Scotland* (London: Herbert Jenkins, 1923; reprint of the 1853 edition), 69.
14. John Younger, *River Angling for Salmon and Trout* (Kelso, U.K.: Rutherford, 1864); I quote from a recent facsimile reprint: Moretonhampstead, U.K: Flyfisher's Classic Library, 1995), 80–81.
15. Henry William Herbert, *Frank Forester's Fish and Fishing of the United States and British Provinces of North America* (New York: Stringer and Townsend, 1851), 62, in the supplement to the third edition of the book, which was originally published in 1849.
16. I describe cross-lining in Schullery, *The Rise*, 172–73. Webster called it "double-rod" fishing; see *The Angler and the Loop Rod*, 24.

    Another nineteenth-century (and perhaps earlier) variation involved what was known as an "otter" or "otter board," a wooden device that an angler could release from his boat, with a line (or "cross-line") suspended between the boat and the board, and many droppers extending from the line so that the boater could move through the water with many, many flies at play between himself and the otter. See O'Gorman, *The Practice of Angling, Particularly as Regards Ireland* (Dublin: William Curry, 1855), 2:56–58. O'Gorman (whose first name is unknown) disapproved of the method as unsporting and said only that it was common in Switzerland. His description of the actual device is difficult to follow, but I wonder if any still survive or are put to use.

17. Stoddart, *The Angler's Companion*, 70–71.
18. Edwin Beard Hendrie, "My Trip Through the Yellowstone in 1870," unpublished manuscript typescript, dated December 28, 1931, Yellowstone National Park Research Library manuscript files, 1. I have retained Hendrie's spelling and punctuation in this quotation.
19. Richard Bowden-Smith described one of the most surprising and impressive of these many-fly rigs in *Fly-Fishing in Salt and Fresh Water* (London: John Van Voorst, 1851). He used as many as seven flies at once, apparently trolling for "whiting pollack," and claimed to have caught eight fish on the seven flies on one occasion, one fly having a fish by the mouth and another by the tail. The most accessible version of this very rare book (I have seen it only once) is a reprint of much of the saltwater fishing text: "Sea Fly Fishing: British Saltwater Sport 130 Years Ago," *The American Fly Fisher* 8 (4) (Fall 1981): 15–19. This reprint features color reproductions of the original hand-colored illustrations of these grandly colorful fly patterns.

    I am especially grateful to Judith Bowman, bookseller, of Bedford, New York, who, in her catalog 54 (Spring–Summer 2007), finally provides angling book enthusiasts with the information that Bowden-Smith was the author of this fascinating, rare, and important book (on page 4 of the catalog).
20. Webster, *The Angler and the Loop Rod*, 84–85. In *The Fly-Fisher's Craft: The Art and History* (Guilford, Conn.: Lyons Press, 2006), a wonderful new study of historic fly-fishing techniques and tools, Darrel Martin tells all about the loop rod in such an entertaining narrative that you may be tempted to build one of your own.
21. Cutcliffe, *Trout Fishing on Rapid Streams*, 85.
22. Quoted in Ewen Tod, *Wet-Fly Fishing Treated Methodically* (London: Sampson Low, Marston, 1903), 9.

Chapter Six

1. Frederic Halford, *Floating Flies and How to Dress Them*, 2d. ed. (London: Sampson Low, Marston, Searle, & Rivington, 1886), 1.
2. Any discussion of the history of fly hooks is enhanced by Darrel Martin's *The Fly-Fisher's Craft: The Art and History* (Guilford, Conn.: Lyons Press, 2006), especially the chapter entitled "The Hook," 197–215. Whether you ever decide to make your own hooks or not, reading this chapter will give you an infinitely improved idea of what was involved in the process for countless generations of anglers who made their own. I, for one, am really glad I don't have to.
3. In the posthumously published *Silk, Fur, and Feather* (Beckenham, U.K.: Fishing Gazette, 1950), G. E. M. Skues resisted using eyed hooks for wet

flies because the eyed hooks "have a tendency to skirt or make a wake on the water, and, moreover, take down bubbles" (46–47). This book was based on articles written much earlier in the twentieth century, perhaps between 1915 and 1919. Skues apparently made the adjustment to eyed hooks not long after the articles were published, but it is still significant that as late as the early 1900s, a writer and angler as perceptive as Skues still had serious doubts about eyed hooks.

4. The easiest reading and still among the most helpful popularly written books on hooks is Hans Jorgen Hurum's charming and thoroughly illustrated little book *A History of the Fish Hook, and the Story of Mustad, the Hook Maker* (London: A. & C. Black, 1977). That this book is dominated by the story of one distinguished hook-making firm doesn't detract much from the greater story. Fishing writers have for many years also taken a special interest in this same history. See, for example, Barnet Phillips, "The Primitive Fish-Hook," in *Sport with Gun and Rod in American Woods and Waters*, edited by Alfred M. Mayer, 337–50 (New York: Century, 1883). Phillips illustrates a number of early eyed hooks and equivalents. The handiest modern historical fly-fishing-related commentary on hooks appears here and there throughout Andrew Herd, *The Fly* (Ellesmere, U.K.: Medlar Press, 2003). For a short but very full account of the development of the manufacture of fly hooks, see Charles Brooks, "From Drawing Room to Dry Fly," *The Flyfisher* 7 (4) (1974): 10–11. And for a penetrating and intriguing consideration of just about everything interesting to do with seventeenth-century hooks, flies, and the lines that connected them to the fisherman, see John Betts, "Robert Venables's Experience as an Angler," *The American Fly Fisher* 29 (4) (Fall 2003): 12–24.
5. John Waller Hills, *A History of Fly Fishing for Trout* (London: Alan, 1921), 53.
6. Hurum, *A History of the Fish Hook*, 73.
7. Leonard Mascall, *A Booke of Fishing with Hooke & Line* (London: John Wolfe, 1590; facsimile, New York: Da Capo Press, 1973), 22.
8. Izaak Walton, *The Complete Angler*, edited by John Hawkins (London: Thomas Hope, 1760). The foremost source on the amazing postpublication life of the beautiful engravings in this edition of Walton's book is Ken Cameron and Andrew Herd's article "Standing on the Shoulders of Giants," *The American Fly Fisher* 27 (3) (Summer 2001): 12–17. It is also my primary source for this discussion.
9. Cameron and Herd, "Standing on the Shoulders of Giants," 13.
10. The easiest place to see these engravings, considering the age and rareness of the many editions of Hawkins's edition of Walton that were published in the 1700s and 1800s, is in the Cameron and Herd article "Standing on the Shoulders of Giants," 13–14. The article also shows several examples of later versions of the flies in the books of authors who copied them from the Hawkins edition.

I am curious about the engraving of the Great Dun because of the way the line is depicted. It seems that although the line is shown passing through the eye of the hook, the engraving can also be interpreted as showing the line (I call it a *line* for want of a better term; it is the *tippet* of modern terminology) emerging from the "head" of the fly and then looping up to pass through the eye. Perhaps this depiction was meant to suggest that the fly was still tied snelled when new, and then the eye was available for attaching a new line when the original line began to fray, so that the fly would still be useful.

11. Hewett Wheatley, *The Rod and Line* (London: Longman, Brown, Green & Longmans, 1849).
12. Robert Barnwell Roosevelt, *Game Fish of the Northern States of America, and British Provinces* (New York: Carleton, 1862), 270.
13. Herd, *The Fly*, 188–89.
14. Herd also suggests that the reason gut-loop eyes were more popular for use on salmon flies than on trout flies was that such eyes, made of twisted multiple strands of gut, were "impractical to construct" on smaller hooks (ibid., 189). But it still seems to me that a sturdy single strand of gut could have been easily employed to provide a fair variety of trout hooks with a usable eye. For that matter, so could a variety of softer wires and other materials.
15. Tony Hayter, *F. M. Halford and the Dry-Fly Revolution* (London: Robert Hale, 2002), 59.
16. Ibid., 58. Aside from the firsthand accounts written by Halford himself and by a few of this contemporaries and adversaries, especially G. E. M. Skues, Hayter's book is the best source on the historical complications of the Halford legacy.
17. Ibid., 59, quoting an unnamed correspondent in *The Field* in 1900.
18. Theodore Gordon, *The Complete Fly Fisherman: The Notes and Letters of Theodore Gordon*, edited by John McDonald (New York: Nick Lyons Books, 1989), 50.
19. Ibid., 99. Gordon is pretty clearly talking about his own fishing here rather than about the flies he tied for his customers. That the man now most closely identified with the popularization of the dry fly in the United States (though that identification is simplistic and partly erroneous) should have still been using snelled hooks half of the time after nearly fifteen years of serious dry-fly fishing suggests how deeply ingrained the snelled-fly habit was. We can apparently assume that any number of other dry-fly fishermen probably still used snelled dry flies.
20. Albert C. Orvis to Dr. Arthur Holbrook, Milwaukee, Wisconsin, March 7, 1910, Orvis Collection, American Museum of Fly Fishing, Manchester, Vermont.
21. Herd makes this point, but also adds that the eyed hook "saga is probably the best example I know of why it is dangerous to assume that just because a thing has been invented, it would be widely used" (*The Fly*, 147).

22. Ewen Tod, *The Wet-Fly Treated Methodically* (London: Sampson Low, Marston, 1903); James Henshall, *Favorite Fish and Fishing* (New York: Outing, 1908).

Chapter Seven

1. Mick Lunn with Clive Graham-Ranger, *A Particular Lunn: One Hundred Glorious Years on the Test* (London: A. & C. Black, 1991), 69.
2. Stephen Oliver, *Scenes and Recollections of Fly-Fishing, in Northumberland, Cumberland, and Westmorland* (London: Chapman and Hall, 1834), 75.
3. William Stewart, *The Practical Angler* (Edinburgh: Black, 1857), 60, 65. Another example of the same skepticism comes from G. P. R. Pulman, who in *The Vade-Mecum of Fly-Fishing for Trout* (London: Longman, Brown, Green, & Longmans, 1851) launched his discussion of the occasional need for imitation with a wonderful rant on why it didn't matter most of the time:

> At the outset, then, we unhesitatingly say that much of the exact imitation system appears to us very much like *quackery*. We have been for twenty years mixed up with anglers of different grades of intelligence and skill, and have invariably found that what is commonly called *imitation*—namely, an old-womanish fastidiousness about the minutest colours, the most daguerreotype copy of some fancied fac-simile of nature, selected as a "pattern fly,"—is by no means a proof of the existence of a commensurate amount of practical skill and consequent success. As a general rule, and for ordinary circumstances, we believe that a very few sorts of flies (say the red palmer and the duns) are sufficient for every useful purpose. But there are peculiar circumstances, arising from the natural fastidiousness of trout in the waters of *England*, at all events, and also from the variations in the state of the water and the atmosphere, which occasionally render necessary a greater variety. (125–26, emphasis in original)

4. For a thorough overview of the early days of imitation and floating fly fishing in the United States, see Paul Schullery, *American Fly Fishing: A History* (New York: Nick Lyons Books, 1987), 83–121. For a fine back-and-forth nineteenth-century American discussion on the need to have a large variety of flies, see George Dawson, *Pleasures of Angling with Rod and Reel for Trout and Salmon* (New York: Sheldon, 1876), 246–48.
5. George M. L. LaBranche, *The Dry Fly and Fast Water* (New York: Scribner's, 1914), 119. It's interesting that imitation's supposed father figure in the United States, Theodore Gordon, also recognized how most fly fishers actually operated out on the water when he said, "The bulk of our captures

will be made with a few favorite flies in which we have confidence, but do not despise a large assortment." See Theodore Gordon, *Theodore Gordon on Trout: Talks and Tales from a Great American Angler*, edited by Paul Schullery (Mechanicsburg, Penn.: Stackpole Books, 2007), 100.

6. LaBranche, *The Dry Fly and Fast Water*, 156.
7. Arnold Gingrich made the claim that LaBranche had used the Pink Lady through entire seasons. See Arnold Gingrich, "LaBranche, George Michel Lucien," in *McClane's New Standard Fishing Encyclopedia and International Angling Guide*, edited by A. J. McClane (New York: Holt, Rinehart and Winston, 1974), 526. However, John Betts disputes this argument, saying, "There were occasions, but not entire seasons, when LaBranche used the Pink Lady to the exclusion of other flies, but in those instances it was to prove his point that presentation matters more than the pattern being presented. Given the kind of water LaBranche fished, this is probably true." See John Betts, "George LaBranche: 'A Very Beautiful Fisherman,'" *The American Fly Fisher* 28 (4) (Fall 2002), 17.
8. E. W. Harding, *The Flyfisher & the Trout's Point of View* (London: Seeley, Service, 1931), 24.
9. Quoted in Schullery, *American Fly Fishing*, 201.
10. It's important to point out that very few of these hatch-matchers, and certainly not Schwiebert himself, claimed that they were precisely imitating the insects; they were instead presenting reasonably accurate impressions of the many species of insects involved.
11. Andrew Herd, *The Fly* (Ellesmere, U.K.: Medlar Press, 2003), 358.
12. LaBranche, *The Dry Fly and Fast Water*, 157.

Chapter Eight

1. An English Sportsman, "Salmon Fishing and Deer Stalking in California," *The Spirit of the Times*, June 22, 1850, 209.
2. Ibid.
3. Chinook, "The 'Genus Salmo' and Other Fish Taken in the Rivers of the Pacific," *The Spirit of the Times*, July 17, 1852, 254. I suspect that the story probably gained its widest currency among nineteenth-century angling readers from being told by Thaddeus Norris in *The American Angler's Book* (Philadelphia: E. H. Butler, 1865), 33. Norris was, however, one of the early hopefuls, noting that "they are never known to take a fly. This may be for the want of the proper kinds of pools that make a fly-cast; there is no doubt, however, that it will yet be found, that there are casts on some of those rivers where a proper combination of fur and feathers will entice them" (208). Genio Scott, author of the likewise well-read *Fishing in American Waters* (New York: Orange Judd, 1875), also included a brief rendition of the story (483). Between Norris and Scott, a great many American anglers must have been assured of being exposed to the story, even discounting all the later accounts.

4. L. A. Beardslee, "The Salmon and Trout of Alaska," in *Fishing with the Fly*, edited by Charles F. Orvis and A. Nelson Cheney, 20–21 (Boston: Houghton Mifflin, 1886). I continue to accumulate later renditions of the story but see no need to cite them here.
5. Beardslee actually broadened his claim and his stupendous inaccuracy by asserting that "no Alaska trout will take a fly" ("The Salmon and Trout of Alaska," 41).
6. Paul Schullery, *Real Alaska: Finding Our Way in the Wild Country* (Mechanicsburg, Penn.: Stackpole Books, 2001).
7. I'm sure there has been some improvement in public understanding of fish species since the late 1800s, but I nevertheless encountered a number of confusing terminological informalisms among fishermen when I first visited and fished in the Pacific Northwest in 1974.
8. See Paul Schullery, *Lewis and Clark among the Grizzlies: Legend and Legacy in the American West* (Guilford, Conn.: Falcon Press, 2002), 54–57.
9. A most important general reference on early attempts to catch Pacific salmon on flies is Trey Combs's pioneering book *The Steelhead Trout, Life History—Early Angling, Contemporary Steelheading* (Portland, Ore.: Northwest Salmon Trout Steelheader, 1971). Combs traces some of the naming history in his discussion "2. A Problem of Nomenclature," 64–68. A prevailing source on the history of the definition of these species of fish is Robert Behnke, *Trout and Salmon of North America* (New York: Simon and Schuster, 2002).
10. For a good introduction to many aspects of Grinnell's amazing career, see John Reiger, *American Sportsmen and the Origins of Conservation*, 3rd rev. ed. (Corvallis: Oregon State University Press, 2001).
11. Editorial note (probably written by George Bird Grinnell or Charles Hallock), "Fly Fishing for Salmon on the Pacific," *Forest and Stream*, August 5, 1875, 411.
12. I cite a number of these problematic salmon-on-a-fly accounts from the 1870s in *American Fly Fishing: A History* (New York: Nick Lyons Books, 1987), 54–55, 169–71. Among the ones worth considering because they bear on the question of salmon and steelhead and fly fishing, are Monmouth, "Humboldt Bay Salmon Fishing," *Forest and Stream*, February 12, 1874, 1–2; "In the *Overland Monthly* for February 3d.," *Forest and Stream*, February 19, 1874, 29; "Salmon Fishing on the Noyo River, on the Northern Pacific Coast of California," *Forest and Stream*, December 2, 1875, 267; "Salmon Fishing in the Novarro River, California," *The Country*, January 26, 1878, 187, reprinted from the *San Francisco Chronicle;* David Starr Jordan, "Rainbow Trout and Steelhead," *Forest and Stream*, June 12, 1884, 386; "Clackamas River Salmon Angling," *Forest and Stream*, November 28, 1889, 369; and W. F. B., "Oregon Salmon Angling," *Forest and Stream*, January 30, 1890, 29. See also Charles Hallock, *The Sportsman's Gazeteer and General Guide* (New York: Forest and Stream Publishing, 1887), 364–65, and C. H.

Townsend and H. M. Smith, "The Pacific Salmons," in *Salmon and Trout*, by Dean Sage, Charles H. Townsend, Hugh M. Smith, and William C. Harris (New York: MacMillan, 1904), 178. Both of these sources give specific occasions when Pacific salmon may be taken on the fly. I have not made a systematic effort to gather these early salmon-fishing accounts given either in the numerous sporting periodicals of the time or in the period's books. The sources listed here are just a few that have come my way in the process of reading generally in the periodicals. I assume there are many more.

A most important general reference on early attempts to catch Pacific salmon on flies is Combs, *The Steelhead Trout*, 71–78. Combs describes noted American fishing writer Henry P. Wells's efforts to catch "steelhead-salmon" on the Clackamas River not far from Portland, Oregon, in 1889. He also relates other salmon-steelhead fishing episodes and emphasizes American attempts to develop their own distinct fly-fishing practices, dissimilar from traditional British fishing techniques, as an important part of the regional angling scene of the day.

Combs also addresses a long-standing uncertainty among readers of salmon-fishing literature—the question of whether Rudyard Kipling, on his historic visit to the United States in 1889, also caught salmon on a fly from the Clackamas River. He makes a good case that, based in part on local information from Kipling's American contemporaries who fished the Clackamas regularly, Kipling caught steelhead, not salmon. But Combs closes the case by invoking Kipling himself, quoting a letter that Kipling wrote to R. B. Marston, editor of the British *Fishing Gazette* in 1899. Kipling's published account of the experience had apparently raised enthusiasm for such fishing. When Marston heard of it, he asked Kipling for the details of his reported fly fishing for Pacific salmon. Kipling objected strongly that he did not catch the fish on a fly and that the confusion had resulted from some kind of mistaken use of the word *fly* in his original account. According to Combs, Kipling wrote to Marston that "in the language of the immortal Jorrocks, Spoon! Spoon! Spoon! 'Fly' is a slip of the rod. Those brutes won't rise to it" (74). A full recounting of Kipling's experience, with the quotation of his one use of the word *fly* in reference to these fish, is found in Paul Schullery, "Rudyard Kipling and American Fly Fishing," *The American Fly Fisher* 4 (2) (Spring 1977): 2–5. See also Carole Steen, "Salmon on a Fly? Not Rudyard Kipling," *Flyfishing* (January–February 1987): 65.

13. Bruce Ferguson, Les Johnson, and Pat Trotter, *Fly Fishing for Pacific Salmon* (Portland, Ore.: Frank Amato, 1985), 16.
14. C. R. (Cleveland Rockwell), "Salmon Fishing on the Pacific," *Forest and Stream*, October 30, 1879, 769.
15. A. Bryan Williams, *Rod & Creel in British Columbia* (Vancouver: Progress, 1919), 19.
16. Letcher Lambuth, "Salt Water Fly Fishing," *The American Fly Fisher* 2 (2)

(Spring 1975), 15. There is no better introduction to many of the most important early- and mid-twentieth-century fly fishers of the West Coast than Jack Berryman, *Fly-Fishing Pioneers & Legends of the Northwest* (Seattle: Northwest Fly Fishing, 2006). This book gives an excellent profile of Lambuth (152–59), including information about his coho flies. Although Berryman concentrates primarily on steelhead fly fishing in discussing the West Coast fishermen, he necessarily details the development of the rods, lines, and flies for steelhead that were also eventually of great use for salmon.

17. Charles Hallock, *The Sportsman's Gazetteer and General Guide* (New York: Forest and Stream Publishing, 1878), 366.
18. Quoted in Schullery, *American Fly Fishing*, 162.
19. Lee Spenser, personal communication to the author and draft manuscripts, September–November 2003.
20. Williams, *Rod & Creel in British Columbia*, 20.
21. For a good overview of the different life histories of the fish, see Ferguson, Johnson, and Trotter, *Fly Fishing for Pacific Salmon*, 19–24.
22. Ibid., 12–18.
23. The term *flossing* also describes using an actual fly-type lure, often a salmon egg imitation, attached up the leader some inches from a bare hook. When the salmon (or trout, for which such lures are also used) takes the imitation, the current similarly drags the line through its mouth until the hook is caught on the outside hinge of the jaw.
24. Someone wanting to compile a history of the development of fly fishing in Alaska would have a great deal to work with because of all the memoirs written by outfitters and other twentieth-century adventurers in that glorious wilderness country. For one great example, over its many years of publication, *Alaska* magazine has been the mother lode of biographical material about pioneering guides, lodges, and notable anglers.

    But what about the beginnings of Alaskan fly fishing? Who were the first, what did they catch, and how did they catch it? Imagine carrying the first fly rod into the Kenai or the Southeast or any of a hundred other fabulous fishing regions. Imagine swinging the first fly through those huge runs of salmon and steelhead. Someone should track down the stories of those lucky fly-fishing pioneers.

    It isn't at all uncommon to find mentions of fly fishing in the most formal scientific reports of early western survey parties as far back as the 1850s. After all, a fly rod was an efficient way to collect specimens. But I have had much less luck at finding similar details on fly fishers in the early Alaska literature. Both L. M. Turner, *Contributions to the Natural History of Alaska* (Washington, D.C.: U.S. Government Printing Office, 1886), 105, and Edward W. Nelson, *Report upon Natural History Collections Made in Alaska Between the Years 1877 and 1881* (Washington, D.C.: U.S. Government Printing Office, 1887), 317, mention fly-caught fish in Alaska. Both men apparently either fly-fished themselves while there or observed others fly fishing. My reading of Alaskan exploration and early travel literature is sizeable but hardly comprehensive enough to have exhausted the possibilities for early accounts of fly fishing in the region. It would be both rewarding and fun for someone with access to the earliest Alaskan literature (scientific and travel literature, local newspapers, and so on) to track down this story.

25. Russell Chatham, *The Angler's Coast* (Garden City, N.Y.: Doubleday, 1976; reprint, Livingston, Mont.: Clarke City Press, 1990).
26. Ibid. (1990 ed.), xvii. See also Berryman, *Fly-Fishing Pioneers & Legends*, 62–69, for another profile of Bill Schaadt.
27. Roderick L. Haig-Brown, *The Master and His Fish* (Seattle: University of Washington Press, 1981), 57.
28. Ibid, 58. A somewhat different transcription, though essentially similar in the important points, is provided in Leigh Burpee Robinson, *Esquimalt: "Place of Shoaling Waters"* (Victoria, Canada: Quality Press, 1948), 30. It seems that even writers conscientious enough to have found their way to the Finlayson journal can't agree on the exact language of the quote. The Finlayson journal seems not to have been published until much later, so in its unpublished form it seems unlikely to have been the source of such a widespread public knowledge of the quotation. See Barry M. Gough, *The Royal Navy and the Northwest Coast of North America, 1810–1914: A Study of British Maritime Ascendancy* (Vancouver: University of British Columbia Press, 1971), 73, especially notes 43–45. It seems possible from the context of Gough's discussion that perhaps Finlayson retold the story and quoted Gordon's comment on salmon in a letter or report to his superior in the Hudson's Bay Company, yet another avenue for future research.

    I don't mean to understate my own efforts to settle this point. My check of many issues of the *London Times* for the period surrounding the dates of the Finlayson account revealed a number of interesting and detailed reports on the boundary controversy, but not a word about this salmon anecdote. But I did not check numerous other possible outlets in the British press of the day, to say nothing of the American press, so there is a wealth of additional material to explore. The several regional Canadian historical scholars whom I asked about it were willing to help and directed me to a number of possible sources, but none was productive. I continue to suspect that some specialist researcher has already traced this quotation to its published source.
29. Captain John T. Walbran, *British Columbia Coast Names, 1592–1906* (Seattle: University of Washington Press, 1972, a reprint of the 1909 edition), 210.
30. Reverend Spaight has referred me to James Morris, *Heaven's Command: An Imperial Progress* (London: Penguin, 1979), where Morris states: "No, in 1837 England seemed to need no empire, and the British people as a whole were not much interested in their colonies. How could one be expected to show an interest in a country like Canada, demanded Lord Melbourne

the Prime Minister, where a salmon would not rise to a fly?" (30). If Lord Melbourne made this statement in 1837, as Morris implies, then we do indeed have a whole new search on our hands.

Chapter Nine

1. The best overview of Marvin Hedge's exploits I've read is in Jack Berryman's excellent new book *Fly-Fishing Pioneers & Legends of the Northwest* (Seattle: Northwest Fly Fishing, 2006), 134–41. My account of Hedge is based primarily on Berryman's chapter, with additional material from V. S. Hidy, "The Champion from Oregon," *The Creel* 3 (1) (July 1964): 6–12.
2. Hidy, "The Champion from Oregon," 10.
3. Berryman also credits Maurice Abraham, a fly fisher from Portland, Oregon, with developing the double haul in 1931 and teaching it to Marvin Hedge and others (*Fly-Fishing Pioneers & Legends*, 111).
4. Darrel Martin, *The Fly-Fisher's Craft: The Art and History* (Guilford, Conn.: Lyons Press, 2006), 217–64.
5. See Paul Schullery, *If Fish Could Scream: An Angler's Search for the Future of Fly Fishing* (Mechanicsburg, Penn.: Stackpole Books, 2008), 51–74, for a discussion of how these changing technologies allowed for the increase in popularity in angling competitions, which no doubt in turn led to an increased interest in improving the technology.
6. John Betts, "Fly Lines and Lineage," *The American Fly Fisher* 26 (4) (Fall 2000): 17–21. This essay is extraordinary, ranging into a number of important historical matters, including the origins and development of wet- and dry-fly practice.
7. Edward A. Samuels, *With Fly-Rod and Camera* (New York: Forest and Stream Publishing, 1890).
8. A short history of modern fly casting appears in Paul Schullery, *American Fly Fishing: A History* (New York: Nick Lyons Books, 1987), 133–41. It includes a remarkable series of drawings by the New York–based angler and artist Louis Rhead, published in *Forest and Stream* in 1923, which seem to illustrate the forward-cast haul. Although the present chapter does take a different look at the subject of the origin of the double haul by using mostly different source material, it is supplemental to a more heavily documentary discussion of the early double haul in *American Fly Fishing*, 136–41.

Chapter Ten

1. George Grant, *Montana Trout Flies* (Portland, Ore.: Champoeg Press, 1981), 123.
2. Ibid.
3. The most recent notable portrayal of George Leonard Herter is Paul Collins, "The Oddball Know-It-All," *New York Times Book Review*,

December 7, 2008, 71, an informative and entertaining consideration of Herter as a literary figure.

4. George Leonard Herter, *Professional Fly Tying, Spinning, and Tackle Making Manual and Manufacturers' Guide*, rev. 19th ed. (Waseca, Minn.: Herter's, 1971), 466.
5. John Taverner, *Certaine Experiments Concerning Fish and Fruite* (London: William Ponsonby, 1600), 21.
6. Gervase Markham, *The Pleasure of Princes* (London: John Browne, 1614), 30.
7. Thomas Barker, *Barker's Delight: or, The Art of Angling* (London: Humphrey Moseley, 1659), 9, 10.
8. James Chetham, *The Angler's Vade Mecum*, 2d ed. (London: T. Bassett, 1689), 220.
9. Charles Cotton, "Directions How to Angle for Trout or Grayling in a Clear Stream," part II of *The Compleat Angler*, by Izaak Walton (London: John Lane, 1897), 338.
10. Walton, *The Compleat Angler*, 122.
11. Andrew Herd, e-mail message to the author, July 16, 2006.
12. Hewett Wheatley, *The Rod and Line* (London: Longman, Brown, Green & Longmans, 1849), 60–61.
13. Francis Francis, *A Book on Angling* (London: Longmans, Green & Company, 1867), 281. Both Wheatley and Francis illustrate this wormlike "bait."
14. Paul Schullery, *If Fish Could Scream: An Angler's Search for the Future of Fly Fishing* (Mechanicsburg, Penn.: Stackpole Books, 2008), 137, 184.
15. Frederick Buller, "A Hoard of Mysterious Salmon Flies," *The American Fly Fisher* 30 (4) (Fall 2004): 13–15; see Thomas Salter's *The Angler's Guide*, 6th ed. (London: Sherwood and Company, 1825). John Betts, exercising his uncanny eye for the curious detail in historical literature, has pointed out that an 1856 catalog of the British tackle firm Milward's contained a drawing of a remarkably modern, gut-loop-eyed grasshopper-like lure or fly, and that among the flies that Buller illustrated in his article is very likely an example of this very grasshopper imitation. See John Betts, "Some Notes and Comment," *The American Fly Fisher* 30 (4) (Fall 2004): 16. Betts, I suspect, has identified the earliest known attempt at a precise imitation of a grasshopper in the United Kingdom.
16. Gary F. Moulton, ed., *The Journals of the Lewis & Clark Expedition, June 10–September 26, 1806* (Lincoln: University of Nebraska Press, 1993), 205.
17. The circular was reprinted in Paul Schullery, *American Fly Fishing: A History* (New York: Nick Lyons Books, 1987), 38. The invoice to which it was attached was from an 1803 shopping trip Clark made while provisioning the expedition.
18. Utah State University Extension information paper, "Fishing Grasshoppers and Mormon Crickets for nearly 100 Years," available at http;//www.sidney.ars.usda.gov/Research/gh_crweb.pdf, consulted August 4, 2006. Although the title of this very informative paper makes a distinction between two

insects, it and other sources indicate that the species in question, *Anabrus simplex*, is not a cricket, but a grasshopper.

19. Richard White, *"It's Your Misfortune and None of My Own": A New History of the American West* (Norman: University of Oklahoma Press, 1991), 229. My research in early travel accounts of the greater Yellowstone area has turned up many accounts of tremendous flights of grasshoppers that disturbed, inconvenienced, or shocked writers of nineteenth-century narratives.

    Mentions of grasshoppers as bait are also common among early western travel and adventure writers.

    For example, in 1860 J. G. Cooper, while near Fort Benton, Montana, described fishing for cutthroats on the Missouri River. "They bite readily at almost any artificial fly; also at insects, meat, pork, and even leaves and flowers, after they had been tempted with grasshoppers." J. G. Cooper, "The Fauna of Montana Territory," *American Naturalist* 3 (3) (May 1869), 125.

    Lieutenant Colonel R. I. Dodge stated that "the Western trout takes the fly well, but not so greedily as the Eastern fish. The reason is, that they are from early spring gorged with food in the myriads of young grasshoppers that fall into the streams before getting their wings. The best months for trout fishing in the Rocky Mountains are August and September, although good sport may be had in July and October." Quoted in Charles Orvis and A. Nelson Cheney, eds., *Fishing with the Fly* (Manchester, Vt.: Orvis, 1883), 157.

    In *Cutthroat & Campfire Tales* (Boulder, Colo.: Pruett, 1988), John Monnett has a nice summary of some of the historical details of western hopper fishing, with both artificial and live grasshoppers (62–66).

20. Thaddeus Norris, *The American Angler's Book* (New York: E. H. Butler, 1864), 201.
21. Robert Barnwell Roosevelt, *Superior Fishing* (New York: Carleton, 1865), 272–73.
22. Jim Brown, e-mail message to the author, August 11, 2006.
23. The Shipley advertisement appeared on January 13, 1881, and possibly on other dates even earlier, in *Forest and Stream* and in James Henshall, *Book of the Black Bass* (Cincinnati: Robert Clarke, 1881), 316. The Shipley grasshopper was made on a rather loosely loop-eyed hook. According to Henshall's text, it was an artificial bait rather than a fly.
24. John Harrington Keene, "Fishing Tackle and How to Make It," in *American Game Fishes*, edited by George Oliver Shields (Chicago: Rand, McNally, 1892), 479.
25. Mary Orvis Marbury, *Favorite Flies and Their Histories* (New York: Houghton Mifflin, 1892), 118. The fly is pictured on plate F, number 47. Its predominant coloring is brownish red and, indeed, does not have anything particular to recommend it as a grasshopper imitation. It seems safe to presume, though, that in many waters that were still inhabited solely by native brook trout, if grasshoppers were prevalent, this fly would work as well as many other imitations.

26. Keene, "Fishing Tackle and How to Make It," 481.
27. A sampling of grasshopper patterns, illustrations, and ideas from the 1880s into the early 1900s includes the following. Thomas Chubb lists "green grasshopper, yellow grasshopper," and several other nonaquatic insects including beetle, bee, cricket, and hornet (*Angling Papers, Accompanying Catalogue, Angler's Supplies* [Post Mills, Vt. (?), 1888], 71). The hopper on page 45 of *William Mills Catalog* (New York, 1894) looks like a grasshopper imitation with the turkey wing, but page 43 shows another variation on the Shipley grasshopper theme.

    Louis Rhead's *American Trout Stream Insects* (New York: Frederick Stokes, 1916) included a photograph of a grasshopper (opposite page 144) in Rhead's "Nature Lure" series that was an attempt at precise imitation of a grasshopper. He said that "the June green grasshopper, [is] made of solid cork wound in vivid green raffia. It floats upright, and the quivering back wings of red cock's hackle make it a choice irresistible lure" (149). For fishing this hopper, Rhead recommended "playing the rod-tip so that the bait skips along in short jumps, to imitate the natural insect when by accident it falls on the water. Strike instantly the bait is taken; for the fish can immediately tell the difference between the artificial and live bait" (147).

    Much later, George Leonard Herter would offer a drawing of a hopper in this same spirit, but said to be made of deer hair. In *Professional Fly Tying, Spinning, and Tackle Making*, he illustrated a deer-hair hopper drawn to appear very realistic (345).

    In the often very helpful little book *Fly Patterns and Their Origins* (Muskegon, Mich.: Westshore, 1940), Harold Smedley listed a Palmer Grasshopper and said that "this cork-bodied, floating imitation grasshopper was the idea of and made by Mr. M. Palmer of Pasadena, California. It dates about 1915" (88).

    In the department entitled "Nessmuk's Camp Fire," *Forest and Stream* of February 1921 featured "Further Notes on the Grasshopper Fly," written by R. L. Montagu of California. This feature showed a variety of patterns and discussed experiences with several, following up on an earlier article from August 1917. Montagu fished both wet and dry for hoppers. Speaking of the 1918 season, when Montagu saw more hoppers than usual and noted that they had reduced crops in his area, he said, "It is not much good putting one's fly into a mass of grasshoppers where possibly none are [*sic*] more than eight or nine inches away from each other. About the only thing to do when conditions are so bad, is to watch out upstream for an open space in the floating insects and then put one's fly in this place as it comes over the feeding fish. Fortunately, however, it was not quite so bad as this all the time; if it had been, very few trout would have been caught" (74).

    Montagu gave the following pattern for his successful fly:

    "Body—Quill dyed naples yellow (No. 29, shade 3).

    Body Hackle—Same color but a shade lighter.

Tail—Mallad (barred feather).

Wings—Pheasant.

Cheeks—Primrose yellow pale (No. 19, shade 1).

Neck Hackle—A few turns of ginger.

For hooks he used "Nos. 8, 9 and 10 Pennell limerick eyed hooks."

The drawing accompanying his discussion shows a down-wing, palmer-bodied fly, with a wing seeming almost like a tent over the body. The article included several other drawings that he said showed stages in the fly's construction, but they don't look like it. The editors apparently somehow fouled up the series of illustrations, which seem to have nothing to do with the final fly pattern.

28. Theodore Gordon, George LaBranche, Emlyn Gill, Samuel Camp, and other early dry-fly writers in the United States had little or nothing to say about grasshopper imitations, although some without question fished waters where hoppers might have been useful. Perhaps hopper season came after the mayfly hatches were over and was not noticed.

29. Vincent Marinaro, *A Modern Dry-Fly Code* (New York: G. P. Putnam's, 1950), 195–96. In the foreword to the 1970 edition of this book (New York: Crown), Marinaro softened his earlier hesitation even further, saying, "The unreasonable scorn for anything but mayfly imitations never made any sense to me. The established ethics for dry-fly fishing have not been changed by the used of terrestrial imitations. You must still find a surface-feeding trout; you must use an imitation of an insect that he is taking from the surface. You must cast accurately and delicately, and you must continue to dry your fly in the approved fashion" (ix).

30. Marinaro and Bennett credited Pennsylvania angler Charlie Craighead with originating the pontoon-style body.

31. George Richey, "Arthur Garfield Winnie: Northern Michigan Fly Tyer," *The American Fly Fisher* 19 (3) (Summer 1993): 16–18.

32. Smedley, *Fly Patterns and Their Origins*, 78; for the pattern for Michigan Hopper, see William Blades, *Fishing Flies and Fly Tying* (Harrisburg, Penn.: Stackpole & Heck, 1951), 126. For a photograph of the fly and additional discussion, see Paul Schullery, "Michigan Originals," *The American Fly Fisher* 7 (3) (Summer 1980): 12–13.

I am not sure where Cooper's Hopper, a Michigan pattern mentioned by Ray Bergman, fits into this genealogy, but with its turkey-feather wing it is quite similar to Winnie's Michigan Hopper. See Ray Bergman, *Trout* (New York: Knopf, 1952), 195–96.

One of the most famous of all American fishing stories, Ernest Hemingway's "Big Two-Hearted River," is a tale of grasshopper fishing, using live grasshoppers cast gently on a fly rod. Between that story and a less lengthy description of how to capture live grasshoppers in another Nick Adams story, "A Way You'll Never Be," Ernest Hemingway provided the live-grasshopper fisherman and to a lesser extent the fly fisher with the essentials for this sport. Both stories are included in Ernest Hemingway, *The Nick Adams Stories* (New York: Scribner's, 1972).

33. J. Edson Leonard, *Flies* (New York: A. S. Barnes, 1950), 197.
34. Smedley said of the Western Grasshopper, "This all hair fly is the product of Mr. Paul D. Stroud, of Arlington Heights, Illinois. It is an excellent floater and very realistic. It is easy to cast, durable—a good point for fishermen—and effective—a good point for fish. As Mr. Stroud is an expert fisherman, and a naturalist, he is an adept fly-tier" (*Fly Patterns and Their Origins*, 128).

    Bill Blades also mentioned Paul Stroud's deer-hair hopper (*Fishing Flies and Fly Tying*, 128). The Blades' Hopper (p. 240) had a shaped-cork body.
35. Ernest Schwiebert, *Trout* (New York: Dutton, 1978), 2:1467. Schwiebert told this story in different form but with the same essentials in Arnold Gingrich, ed., *The Gordon Garland* (New York: Knopf, 1966), 137–38. Schwiebert mentioned the Michigan Hopper, Joe's Hopper, Fore-and-Aft Hopper, and Muddler Minnow as influences.

    Ed Koch gives a nice history of the Letort Hopper variations in *Terrestrials* (Harrisburg, Penn.: Stackpole Books, 1990), 83–96.

    In *What the Trout Said* (New York: Knopf, 1982), Datus Proper offers a nice variation on the low style—a simple yellow, deer-hair body tied lengthwise and doubled back on itself, with a hair wing. "In my experience," Proper states, "trout have not been very selective when feeding on grasshoppers" (226).
36. In *Naturals* (Harrisburg, Penn.: Stackpole Books, 1980), Gary Borger states that Schwiebert's Letort Hopper was "the first fly to effectively imitate the low-slung silhouette of these big insects," but that he prefers the wing of Dave's Hopper (162–63). I especially thank Bud Lilly for his insights on the divergent development of the two styles of grasshopper imitation. His views on grasshopper patterns and grasshopper fishing are most thoroughly presented at several points in Bud Lilly and Paul Schullery, *Bud Lilly's Guide to Fly Fishing the New West* (Portland, Ore.: Frank Amato, 2000).
37. Ed Shenk, *Ed Shenk's Fly Rod Trouting* (Harrisburg, Penn.: Stackpole Books, 1989), 127.
38. Dave Whitlock, "Western Fly Patterns," in *Art Flick's Master Fly-Tying Guide*, edited by Art Flick (New York: Crown, 1972), 115.

Chapter Eleven

1. Conrad Voss Bark, *A History of Fly Fishing* (Shropshire, U.K.: Merlin Unwin Books, 1992), 1. This chapter represents one of the clearest cases in which I am pleased to have the opportunity to amplify discussions in *American Fly Fishing: A History* (New York: Nick Lyons Books, 1987). That earlier book contains a summary of the known origins of streamers (147–51). The much longer version here necessarily reviews that material and even quotes a few

of the same sources, but I am grateful for the chance to expand the story in order to capture so many more of its details and so much more of its flavor.

For a consideration of the historic rationales behind wing construction, including a brief consideration of the origin of the term *streamer* as applied to flies, see Paul Schullery, *The Rise: Streamside Observations on Trout, Flies, and Fly Fishing* (Mechanicsburg, Penn.: Stackpole Books, 2006), 147–58. In that chapter, I also consider the shape and wing length of nineteenth-century wet flies that we have always assumed were just traditional trout patterns, but that, at least in the versions illustrated in some of the books from that era, are essentially streamer-style tyings. They appear to have both elongated hooks and elongated wings, and whatever the anglers thought they imitated, to the trout such flies may have looked much like little fish.

2. Ernest Schwiebert, *Trout* (New York: Dutton, 1978), 2:1395.
3. Thomas McGuane, *The Longest Silence: A Life in Fishing* (New York: Knopf, 2000), 245.
4. George Leonard Herter, *Professional Fly Tying, Spinning, and Tackle Making Manual and Manufacturers' Guide*, rev. 19th ed. (Waseca, Minn.: Herter's, 1971), 428.
5. Schwiebert lists many of the names that became most closely associated with the American streamer and bucktail developments of the late 1800s and early 1900s, including most of the ones mentioned here (*Trout*, 2:1395–96). The big book and standard work on the subject is Joseph D. Bates, *Streamers and Bucktails: The Big Fish Flies* (New York: Knopf, 1979).
6. Herter, *Professional Fly Tying, Spinning, and Tackle Making Manual*, 429, 430. My inquiries to the historical specialists at Mackinac Island have so far led to no documentary evidence to support Herter's statements. I have checked those of the famous Dr. Beaumont's publications that I could find, and experts at Mackinac Island are unaware of any writings by Beaumont to support Herter's claim. Beaumont's stay at the island did not even occur in the year Herter gave. I suspect that Herter's information was perhaps casually given him by a guide at the island in the early to mid-1900s and was part of local folklore. If it turns out to be true, and I kind of hope it does, it will be a nice addition to early American angling folklore to have such a distinguished medical figure added to the sport's history.
7. I purposely do not refer to the streamer as a "streamer fly." For a discussion of the terminology of the word *fly*, see my *American Fly Fishing*, 83–84.
8. In *The Fly* (Ellesmere, U.K.: Medlar Press, 2001), Andrew Herd has reproduced two startling engravings from a Spanish book by Sañez Reguart, *Diccionario histórico de las artes de pesca nacionales*, published in 1795 (Herd does not give a publisher or place of publication), which show long, feathered, multihooked lures that Herd deems, in some cases, to be streamers. I agree.
9. Quoted in Schullery, *American Fly Fishing*, 147.
10. Quoted in ibid., 148.

11. Hewett Wheatley, *The Rod and Line* (London: Longman, Brown, Green, & Longmans, 1849), 41.
12. Richard Bowden-Smith, *Fly-Fishing in Salt and Fresh Water* (London: John Van Voorst, 1851). For the saltwater fishing text, reprinted as "Sea Fly Fishing: British Saltwater Sport 130 Years Ago," see *The American Fly Fisher* 8 (4) (Fall 1981): 15–19. A special thanks to dealer of antiquarian sporting books Judith Bowman for publishing a very helpful note on this rare book in her spring–summer 2007 catalog 54 (4), in which she explains the discovery of the true author of this important and intriguing book.
13. See chapters one and two on these anglers' early wet-fly techniques.
14. Paul Schullery, *If Fish Could Scream: An Angler's Search for the Future of Fly Fishing* (Mechanicsburg, Penn.: Stackpole Books, 2008), 140–47.
15. The most thorough review of these nineteenth-century pike flies is a paper by Andrew Herd, "Pike Fishing with a Fly," now in preparation, which Herd shared with me in manuscript. An interesting early American instance of recommending this type of fly appeared in Dinks, "A Treatise on Fly-Fishing," an appendix to *Frank Forester's Fish and Fishing of the United States and British Provinces of North America* (New York: W. A. Townsend, 1859), 485. Dinks also noted, "I have not the least doubt, however, that a fly tied to represent a young duck or gosling (if so be it can be called a fly) would be just as effective, to say nothing of one like a mouse or a small water-rat." This statement indicates that in the United States, as in England, at least some anglers took a very broad view of the opportunities provided by fly fishing for imitation of life forms far removed from the traditional mayflies and other insects. At the same time, it's worth noting that some British and American anglers just went ahead and used real birds, casting them out and dragging them back across the surface to great effect.
16. Robert Barnwell Roosevelt, *Game Fish of the Northern States of America and British Provinces* (New York: Carleton, 1862), 259.
17. Alfred C. Harmsworth, "An Englishman's Experience of Florida Fishing—I," *Forest and Stream*, January 5, 1895, 3.
18. I must include one account of a native fly pattern from Joe Brooks: "In 1953, when I visited his Estancia Maria-Behety on remote Tierra del Fuego, in Argentina, Carlos Menendez-Behety gave me a 'fly' that he said had been used by the Ona Indians, now almost extinct, which he estimated to be some hundred-odd years old. It was a piece of skin and fur from the *juanaco*, impaled on a hook, and tied in behind the eye. The fur of this beautiful, romantic and most graceful runner of all the deer species in the world looks alive in the water and makes a truly effective bucktail fly" (*Trout Fishing* [New York: Harper and Row, 1972], 239). Brooks gave the following caption with the illustration: "The fly made by the Ona Indians of Argentina, over a century ago, from the hide and fur of the juanaco, a member of the deer family" (240). The fly pictured had a modern eyed hook, so it was evidently a replica rather than a fly from one hundred years earlier. But if

Menendez-Behety's estimate is reasonably close to accurate, then here was a South American bucktail pattern in use in the 1850s.

19. Ernest Schwiebert, "Salmon Flies," in *Art Flick's Master Fly-Tying Guide*, edited by Art Flick (New York: Crown, 1972), 154.
20. Austin S. Hogan, "An Introduction to the History of Fly Fishing in America," in *The Museum of American Fly Fishing, Acquisitions Catalogue 1969–1973*, by Austin S. Hogan and G. Dick Finlay (Manchester, Vt.: Museum of American Fly Fishing, 1973), unpaginated. I have done some minor editing—correcting comma placement and deleting endnote numbers—to make this passage readable, but I have retained the author's sometimes unusual spelling.
21. E. T. D. Chambers described the use of the "moose-tail" fly, a hair-wing fly trolled behind a boat, on Lake Batiscan, Canada. The fish caught were large brook trout. See E. T. D. Chambers, "Big Trout of the Nepigon, Lake Edward, Lake Batiscan, Etc.," in *The Speckled Brook Trout*, edited by Louis Rhead (New York: R. H. Russell, 1902), 37.
22. Herd, *The Fly*, 342.
23. James Chetham, *The Angler's Vade Mecum, or a Compendius, Yet Full, Discourse of Angling*, 2d ed. (London: T. Basset and W. Brown, 1689), 35.
24. Mary Orvis Marbury, *Favorite Flies and Their Histories* (Boston: Houghton Mifflin, 1892), 95.
25. John Harrington Keene, "How to Make Trout Flies, Third Installment," *American Angler*, August 1, 1885, 65. Thanks to David Ledlie for providing me with this series of articles.
26. Frederic Halford, *Dry-Fly Fishing in Theory and Practice* (London: Sampson Low, 1889), 128–29.

Index

Page numbers in italicized text indicate illustrations.